MASTURBATION AND ADULT SEXUALITY

MASTURBATION AND ADULT SEXUALITY

PREVIOUSLY PUBLISHED AS "SEXUAL EXCITEMENT/SEXUAL PEACE"

BY SUZANNE SARNOFF AND IRVING SARNOFF, Ph.D.

M. EVANS AND COMPANY, INC.
New York

Library of Congress Cataloging in Publication Data

Sarnoff, Suzanne.
　Sexual excitement/sexual peace.

　Bibliography: p.
　Includes index.
　1. Masturbation.　2. Masturbation—Psychological aspects.　I. Sarnoff, Irving, 1922-　joint author. II. Title.
HQ447.S27　　155.3　　78-23755

ISBN 0-87131-281-6　HARDCOVER

ISBN 0-87131-469-X　PAPERBOUND

Copyright © 1979 by Suzanne Sarnoff and Irving Sarnoff

All rights reserved. No part of this book may be reproduced or transmitted in any form or by any means without the written permission of the publisher.

M. Evans and Company, Inc.
216 East 49 Street
New York, New York 10017

Design by Ginger Giles

Manufactured in the United States of America

9 8 7 6 5 4 3 2 1

To our parents
and our children

Contents

Preface	ix
Introduction: The Problematic Pleasure	1
Part I: The Experience of Masturbation	19
1. Orgasm	21
2. Fantasy	42
Part II: Masturbation and Child Development	67
3. Infants and Toddlers	69
4. Early Childhood	91
5. Middle Childhood	126
6. Adolescence	159
Part III: Masturbation and Adult Fulfillment	199
7. Couples	201
8. Singles	242
Epilogue: From Confusion to Understanding	287
Index	315

PREFACE

As college teachers with a common research interest in the psychology of love, we first approached this book as an opportunity to formulate a general conception of how masturbation fits into the growth and expression of a person's capacity for sexual love. In the process of articulating our ideas, we also began to see how masturbation may affect a person's ability to fulfill his unique talents and potentials. Thus, our book developed into a systematic and comprehensive formulation of the implications of masturbation for two basic sources of human realization: love and creativity, considered within the realities of contemporary society.

However, our motivation for doing this book was not entirely academic. We also wanted very much to understand the effects of our own masturbatory urges, inhibitions, and conflicts on our individual lives and on our marriage. By openly discussing the skeletons in our sexual closets, we succeeded in confronting and overcoming our separate fears and hang-ups about masturbation. At the same time, we increased our self-acceptance, the effectiveness and gratifications of our work, and the joys we could share in the sexual expressions of our love for each other.

Of course, we cannot claim that our individual cases and our marriage fully represent the ways in which other people experience and are affected by masturbation. But honest communication about the contents of one's inner life is the core of intimacy—whether between close friends, lovers, spouses, or parents and their children. In an atmosphere of love and trust, we believe people can help each other to understand the personal and interpersonal meanings of their masturbation. Informed by such an understanding, people can succeed, as we did, in making desirable changes in their personalities and in their loving relationships.

In the course of our dialogues about masturbation, we gradually distilled the essences of our theoretical position and wrote them into this book. We also present vignettes from our personal histories to illustrate our various ideas, realizing that we could not expect to find any more authentic and true-to-life examples than the ones we were willing to disclose publicly about ourselves. Contemplating our own histories in detail gave us a deep appreciation of the fact that both men and women are sexual beings, equally motivated by the human need for sexual love and equally involved in masturbation. Of course, we have sought to give appropriate attention to the ways in which the anatomical and physiological differences between males and females affect their masturbatory experiences. In discussing either men or women, we identify them separately. In referring to generalizations about people of both sexes, we rely on the conventional literary use of the pronouns "he," "his," and "him." However, our usage implies neither a sexual bias on our part nor a tendency to view masturbation from the standpoint of the male sex.

The structure of our book expresses our theoretical integration of the experiential, developmental, and interpersonal aspects of masturbation. In the Introduction, we deal with the inherent pleasures and problems of masturbation, explaining their origin in the basic needs and mental functioning of human beings.

In Part I, we focus on the actual experience of masturbation—how people arouse themselves, coordinate their arousal with the fantasies they create, and bring themselves to a solitary orgasm. We also explain mental masturbation and the potentially beneficial uses of both the orgasm and masturbatory fantasy.

In Part II, we trace the evolving role of masturbation through each stage of child development—infancy, early and middle childhood, and adolescence. We seek to provide an understanding of the impact of a child's approach to masturbation—and his parents' reactions to it—on his ability to develop the personality characteristics of a loving and productive adult.

In Part III, we discuss the implications of masturbation for the lives of both married and unmarried adults. We show how it is possible for people to approach their masturbation in ways that permit them to continue the development of their personalities and to find increasing fulfillment through sexual love and work from young adulthood through old age.

In the Epilogue, we summarize and evaluate the history of change in expert opinion about masturbation. We also examine the economic, social, and political significance of the relationship between masturbation and current trends in pornography and sex education.

Having scholarly backgrounds, we were naturally inclined, from the outset of our collaboration, to place our own observations and conceptions within a perspective of the relevant scientific and professional literature. Thus, we reviewed those writings, drawing on them to highlight and document our points of focus.

Going beyond what we could learn from publications, we sought to increase our knowledge by speaking directly with others about issues we felt needed clarification. Thus, we interviewed many people of both sexes, who differed widely in age, occupation, and marital status. They generously shared with us their thoughts and feelings about their involvements in masturbation. We cannot mention the names of the people who confided in us, having assured them that we would take care to disguise their identities. However, we want all of them to know that we are very grateful for their anonymous contributions.

Similarly, we are most appreciative of the assistance of those experts who kindly permitted us to interview them and to draw on their wide variety of professional experiences pertinent to masturbation. Specifically, we would like to thank Dr. Lowell Anderson, Dr. Charles DeBrovner, Dr. Helaine Gold, Dr. Helen Singer Kaplan, Betsy Jacobs, Judith Kuriansky, Peggy Marvel, Dr. Margaret McHugh, Dr. Raul Schiavi, Prof. Robert Sollod, Dr. Ava Siegler, Sandra Stark, Prof. Peter Stein, Dr. Barbara Waxenberg, and Dr. Ann Welbourne.

Finally, we are indebted to those who helped us to transform our long-held fantasy of this book into a reality. First, we want to thank our literary agent, Julia Coopersmith, for her initial and unflagging enthusiasm for our work. Her wise opinions often led us to bring our ideas into clear focus and to articulate their significance. Herb Katz, our general editor, validated our own perceptions of the importance of the subject and of the way we chose to deal with it. He also offered us valuable suggestions about how to present our work to the widest possible audience of readers. David Frederickson, our project editor, reviewed our manuscript with respect, concern, and sensitivity, helping us to tighten its structure and to improve the flow of its exposition.

MASTURBATION AND ADULT SEXUALITY

Introduction
THE PROBLEMATIC PLEASURE

Masturbation is something everyone does in one way or another. It may be limited to a fleeting, almost absentminded brush of fingertips on genitals. It may be done only under the cover of darkness and dreams. It may be confined to a passing fantasy of self-glorification. It may be heartily enjoyed as an exquisite delight; or it may be a bittersweet experience, its pleasures accompanied by anxiety, guilt, and despair. But no matter how it is done and how it is experienced, masturbation is practiced by both sexes everywhere.

Infants learn to masturbate naturally, as they explore ways of expressing their innate capacity to love. While growing up, children rely on masturbation as the main outlet for their budding sexuality; they also use it to siphon off some of the nonsexual tensions they inevitably experience in the process of adapting to their parents and society. Many adults, both single and married, continue to derive erotic pleasure and emotional relief from sexual self-stimulation. And all people, including those who completely avoid touching their own genitals, indulge in what we call mental masturbation, by "stroking" themselves with fantasies. In such daydreams, people try to compensate for feelings of frustration and inadequacy, give themselves solace for disappointments and failures, prepare for fear-arousing challenges, or enliven their existence.

Thus, everyone is involved in masturbation—physically or mentally—throughout life. Masturbation is not merely the earliest expression of human sexuality; it is also the most pervasive and enduring. In fact, people acquire their basic sexual attitudes toward themselves and others largely as a result of their developmental histories of masturbation. And those crucial attitudes have a profound and lasting influence on the quality of all their other sexual experiences, their intimate relationships, and their ability to fulfill their unique potentials.

Thus, we view masturbation from the perspective of its relevance for two of the most basic human yearnings: the desire for loving sexual relationships and the desire for self-expression and personal achievement. Throughout our book, we discuss the ways in which a person's approach to masturbation may either help or hinder his developing ability to fulfill those two needs. Because masturbation has such vital and lifelong significance for all human beings, we aim to bring to public awareness an appreciation of the full extent of its personal consequences and interpersonal implications.

I can't remember the first time I ever masturbated. But I can't remember a time when I didn't. One of my earliest recollections goes back to when I was a very small girl—two and a half, maybe three. I was in my little green bed in the room I shared with my thirteen-year old sister. I can still see the cane insets on the headboard. I was on my stomach. I always "did it" lying on my stomach. I thought I was covered so nobody could see me. Somehow, I had the feeling that what I was doing was wrong. My sister and my cousin from Pittsburgh were standing in the doorway. They were watching me, laughing and giving each other funny looks.

Did they really see me? Did they know for sure, or was it my imagination? But they were laughing, and I could feel their staring. I can still hear that laughing. Oh, the ecstasy! Even the fear of being caught didn't make me stop.

It was the same later on, after my mother found out that I did it. I knew she felt it was wrong. Still, I wouldn't stop. But the guilt! And those pains in my legs. Those slow, drawing sensations that pulled at the back of my calves whenever I felt I was doing something bad or secretive. Those pains used to haunt me. How terrified I was that all my mother's warnings about becoming crippled were true!

And yet, I never stopped. Not for the next twenty years. Despite the threats, despite the anxiety, despite the feeling of being crazy. From the first time I felt that certain "juicy" feeling oozing out of my immature flesh, I knew that I'd discovered something really good. And no matter what anyone else thought, I wouldn't let it go.

But what a mixture of emotions! What terror, what joy! That deep secret hiding place; how it separated me from all the others! Did *they* know what it was like? Did my sister have any idea what I was feeling as I rubbed myself into a frenzy, my head under the blankets to muffle my breathing? Who could possibly understand me? How could I explain it to anyone, or even *dare* to try? That's why I felt so different, so alone, so isolated. Yet, somehow, I also felt a little special—maybe even a bit superior to others.

Masturbating always felt both good and bad. I can clearly remember how the ecstasies of my self-indulgence were always dampened by the uneasy feeling that what I was experiencing couldn't possibly be connected to the rest of my daily life. It was like being two different people at the same time: one, the carefree child, cute, full of fun and games, and irresponsible; the other, a premature adult, full of seriousness and feigned innocence, having to bear the weight of my duplicity, old before my time.

Over the years, I pushed whatever small sense I had of myself further and further into a private fantasy world, where anything could be achieved and anything I wished could come true. My secret masturbation created a privileged and protected place where I turned all of my shortcomings into assets, where I built a flawless image of perfection for myself. It became a sanctuary that no one else could enter or share, where I never had to put my actual strengths and abilities on the line.

In my secret refuge, I could pass any test with flying colors. Every stumbling block to the solution of any problem was magically overcome. When I was little, every page I filled in my coloring book, even when I went outside the lines, became a masterpiece in my own eyes. Later, when I was an adolescent in art school, every painting that I feared I couldn't finish was completed in fantasy with a masturbatory flourish of my hands. And my illusory creation would be greeted with great acclaim and applause from my imagined audience—those in authority, my teachers, my parents, all the people whose regard I tended to worry about so much. Everything could be made perfect even when—or especially when—I was most terrified and unsure of myself.

During my childhood, I gradually came to realize that I was not the only one who masturbated. I had checked the meaning of "masturbation" in the dictionary. And whenever I came upon that emotionally loaded word in print, I devoured whatever information was given about it. But I could never find very much. There were never enough details, and it was never discussed in a way that seemed relevant to me. No one described just the way that I did it. And nobody ever mentioned the kinds of thoughts and fantasies that filled my orgiastic moments.

As long as I can remember, I was in a continual emotional turmoil about my masturbation. And I was unable to communicate with anyone about it. Even though my mother had caught me at it—I don't remember exactly how or when—I could never openly reveal to her the dirty nature I felt I was hiding behind my wholesome, smiling face. There was never a time when I didn't sense her rejection of what I'd been doing. But she never offered any advice that might have helped me deal with the problem. There was only a constant undercurrent of negative insinuation. And those overwhelming threats about becoming paralyzed, telling our family doctor, or what "nice" people would say if they knew.

In the 1930s, when I was growing up, the subject was too terrifying to talk about even with one's closest friends. However, there was one girl who lived on my block when I was about seven years old. I didn't really care for her, and I can't recall exactly what prompted our exchange. But I do remember how we cautiously tiptoed past her mother into the bedroom. In a hushed tone, she volunteered her techniques with relish, told how she put pencils and bobby pins up "there." She provided new fuel for my fantasy, and in return I told her exactly how I used my fingers, how I slowly stroked the outside lips of my vagina, teasing and tantalizing myself, touching and withdrawing my touch until I couldn't stand it anymore, how I worked my way down and back until my finger slid slowly into that warm, moist opening—gently at first, going as deep as I could, then gaining momentum, thrusting back and forth, faster and faster, in and out, in and out, until I reached the last bearable peak of pleasure.

Our relationship didn't last long. That fleeting confidence had been far too threatening. Many years later, when I noticed her walking on a main shopping street, I quickly crossed over, studiously avoiding her. But she was the first living soul to confirm for me that I was not the only one. From that time on, until I married Irv and finally had the trust and security I needed to confide in him, I never discussed such behavior with anyone, no matter how intimate we had been.

Ambivalence

Although masturbation is no longer widely regarded as a moral or medical evil, as it was in Sue's childhood days, its important functions and potential benefits for human development and intimate relationships have barely been explored. While most people may now intellectually accept the normalcy of masturbation, they continue to feel confused and ambivalent about the meaning of their own involvement in it.

The same kind of ambivalence that Sue felt as a young child many years ago was dramatically expressed to us recently by a seventeen-year-old boy who heard that we were going to write this book. His conflicting attitudes toward masturbation came out as he kept exclaiming, "Wow! Call it *The Evil Touch*, that would be a great title! Oh, no, but it's fabulous! How about *The Fabulous Touch?* No . . . it's evil . . . it's fantastic . . . Oh, God . . . I guess I just don't know . . ." This kind of reaction fits in with the conclusions that Robert Sorensen reached in his recent survey on adolescent sexuality in America: "Among the sex practices we discussed, there seems to be none about which young people feel more defensive or private than their masturbation."[1]

Adults of various ages tend to feel similar misgivings, as Morton Hunt observed from the results of his survey of adult sexual behavior in the 1970s. Although most of the respondents, in both the younger and older age groups, said they do not think masturbation is morally wrong, Hunt states that a majority of the people continue to feel ambivalent about their own desires to masturbate.[2]

It is not surprising, therefore, to find this ambivalence reflected in the ways that parents react to their children's masturbation. One clinical psychologist told us that she was very annoyed with her mother, who made negative comments to her two-year-old daughter when she masturbated. But this sensitive and sophisticated young woman later admitted that she herself had decided to put underpants on her little girl at bedtime, to keep her child from doing it too much.

Our own ambivalence toward masturbation showed up in our initial reluctance to admit to others—even to our closest friends—that we were working on this book. When we did begin to tell people about it, we found that they usually burst out laughing or lapsed into a period of embarrassed silence. Often they tried to dilute the emotional impact of the conversation, making witty comments or off-color jokes in an attempt to show us and themselves how free they were of any anxiety or conflicts about the issue.

These contradictory and excessive reactions to masturbation —avoidance and denial, or inappropriate humor and obscenity— are further indications that masturbation remains a problem for people even in this era of sexual permissiveness. Undoubtedly, the long history of social prohibitions against masturbation is still having some adverse effects on people's attitudes toward it. But even if people were entirely free of socially learned guilt or anxiety, they would experience an inescapable ambivalence that arises from the intrinsic mental processes involved in masturbation.

INHERENT PLEASURES

We believe that masturbation is *inherently* both a pleasure and a problem. Its inherent pleasures stem from the gratification of sexual impulses and sensual capacities that humans share with other animals. Great delight can be experienced in creating and savoring the sensations of one's own body. And the pleasure involved in masturbation gives many infants, children, and adults a passing respite from life's unavoidable frustrations.

A baby's desire to fondle his body is an expression of his innate need to be touched. Babies come into the world as very dependent and sensitive creatures, who need to be held and stroked to ensure their physical well-being and their emotional security.[3] Parents and others who take care of infants are the major source of this vital love and contact, of course; but the baby is also capable of taking the initiative to satisfy some of these needs himself, by sucking, rocking, and stroking his own body. This kind of self-stimulation often leads to sexual arousal, and masturbation includes the process of self-stimulation that produces such genital reactions.

Viewed in this light, it can be seen that masturbation grows out of a baby's need for comforting bodily contact. It is also an outgrowth of an infant's attempts to satisfy another basic human need: the need to explore and to learn about his own body. A baby's self-exploration serves as an important means of building an image of his body and a sense of himself as separate from other human beings. As part of this self-exploration, masturbation may help a growing child to develop a positive image of his own body, a distinct awareness of being an autonomous individual, and a sense of being able to provide himself with pleasure.[4]

Masturbation is, then, an integral part of the maturation of human sexual and emotional capacities. A child who learns to feel good about his body, his gender, and his sexual functioning is likely to grow up with positive expectations about sexual contact with others. In this way, masturbation may assist in the development of a child's potential to form loving and sensually expressive relationships in adulthood.

Inherent Problems

Although masturbation can make a positive contribution to psychological growth, the development of the human mind gives masturbation its problematic character. The mind and body function as a whole; no one who has attained self-awareness can masturbate without thinking about it on some level.

Instinctive sexual urges are present from birth until death. Yet sex is the only biological drive that a person does not need to gratify in order to exist. Other biological drives, such as hunger, must be satisfied if an individual is to survive. But a person can go through life without ever having given in to his sexual drive, either through masturbation or relations with others. Such a person may suffer badly because of his abstinence, but he can go on living without sexual gratification.

People usually have the freedom to choose whether, when, and how to express their sexual impulses. Even though fulfilling one's sexual needs can be the greatest of pleasures, the responsibility for choosing to appease an "optional" appetite can be a heavy burden to bear. And that responsibility is particularly salient in solitary masturbation, since the individual cannot attribute his choice of behavior to anyone else or share it with a sexual partner. Is it any wonder, then, that masturbation is so often a source of tension, ambiguity, and puzzlement?

The dilemmas posed by sex become increasingly apparent and inescapable during an individual's psychological growth. Naturally, a baby is not aware that he has decided to stimulate himself. But once a child is old enough to develop a clear sense of himself as a separate being, he is also old enough to be aware that he alone is choosing the way he deals with the promptings of his sexual drive. Masturbation is no longer primarily an instinctive groping for pleasure or bodily exploration; instead, it reflects the child's psychological complexity. Masturbation becomes a deliberate means of expressing many different thoughts and impulses, and it may, in turn, arouse a host of conflicting emotional reactions.

The key to understanding the problematic nature of masturbation lies partly in the use to which people put their minds when they seek solitary sexual gratification. To engage in solitary sex, a person has to split his consciousness deliberately, regarding his body as an object to be used for the attainment of both physical and emotional pleasure. To accomplish this, an individual has to imagine that he is both himself and another person. Mentally, he has to stand apart from the wholeness of his being, acting upon his own body as he would upon someone else, or as someone else would act upon him.[5]

Having given himself over to his own fantasies, a person may masturbate freely. The solitude allows him to become totally immersed in his own bodily sensations, emotional reactions, and mental reflections. The social controls he ordinarily imposes on himself to accommodate to the expectations of others are lifted; he does not have to modulate the expression of his sensual preferences or his fantasies for anyone else—he can be as completely self-centered and voluptuously idiosyncratic as he wishes.

Sexual climax eventually bursts the magic mental bubble that an individual creates around himself when he masturbates. For a little while, he may have experienced a great deal of pleasure and dissipated some of the tensions that led him to masturbate in the first place. But he is once again confronted with the reality of his nonsexual tensions and the unrealistic way he sought to reduce or escape from them. He knows he has temporarily set aside his usual sense of reality in order to get pleasure from his body. And the very knowledge of what he has done arouses a fear that tends to undermine the pleasure he has experienced.

Everyone must survive in the world. Such survival is enhanced by the capacity to relate to others and to satisfy one's basic needs through interacting with them. But when a person masturbates and uses his mind to carry himself away from fulfilling social interactions, he arouses the fear that he may be interfering with his capacity to survive. Whether he is aware of it or not, a person may also fear going so completely into the private pleasures of sexual intimacy with his own being that he might be unable, or unwilling, to exert any self-control over the expression of his impulses. Or he may fear the loss of control over his own consciousness in the service of the fantasies that accompany his masturbation.

One of Sue's recollections from her early adolescence illustrates why masturbation cannot avoid being problematic—however pleasurable—for anyone whose mental development has advanced to the stage of self-awareness.

It was one of my first teen-age parties. How good I felt about the trim way I looked as I left the house in my new low-heeled oxfords and neatly tailored plaid woolen dress. I expected to find my girlfriends dressed in similar outfits, but when I arrived, I found they had suddenly donned sheer, frilly fabrics and shiny, high-heeled, patent-leather pumps. And all of them had touched their lips with false color. Then the dancing! How gauche and totally unprepared I was for that! Somehow, I stumbled through the evening, deeply desiring, yet dreading, each boy's approach. And certainly none of them asked me to dance a second time after I'd so awkwardly tripped over their poor feet. By the time I left the party, I felt tortured and humiliated.

When I got home, I was desperate. Making sure that everyone in the family was safely asleep, I turned the living room lights low, leaving just a soft, romantic glow. I threw myself down on the couch, grabbed at my aching flesh, and reenacted the drama of the evening—trying to undo what had really happened, trying to make the Buster Brown shoes into glass slippers and the sturdy cloth of my plain dress into a gossamer of silk.

Slowly I fondled my breasts, my stomach, my upper thighs, clutching at my groin until I began to feel as if I was twirling across a stage, alive with passion and grace. I became the popular star of a magnificent film, in which all the members of my supporting cast coordinated their dancing movements to mine and focused their admiring eyes on me. While I masturbated, I became both the giver and the receiver, the manipulated and the manipulator—trying to make up to myself for all the love and acceptance I felt I had been unable to get from others.

And, of course, I came out on top. I was always on top in the fantasied sexual escapades I reeled off in my "home movies." I was on top, I was all-powerful, I could have it all ways—acting out both man and woman, both lover and loved one, the seeker and the sought-after. I was the playwright, the stage director, and the audience as well. No one was involved in the performance but me. It was all my own show! And I went to great lengths to embellish the characters and the setting in which they performed, drawing out the drama with suspense and staging all aspects of the production with exquisite finesse.

As director, I used whatever props were at hand to enhance the effects. The special, fresh, leathery smell of my new shoes conjured up a late 1930s musical or a Cinderella's Ball, where my clumsy big feet were transformed and floated lightly over the floor. And I was led by the strong sure loins of the Prince Charming of my dreams. Feeling his firm grip about my delicate waist, I made a mental switch and, simultaneously, his strength became mine as I pressed my muscular male limbs tighter and closer into the soft yielding flesh of my beautiful partner.

My new dress served as well. And while I worked myself up to a sensual pitch, I rewrote the entire scene in which I had worn it—from my grand entrance, through everything I said to people in the room and everything they said to me, to my final exit—a scene from which I departed in a blaze of glory that was somehow magically timed with the height of my orgasmic release.

But when the curtain fell and the play was done . . . what a feeling of letdown! What a sense of emptiness, of total separation from others! The stark reality of those ugly shoes and the simple dress jarred me into remembering the actual party. Tremulously, I pulled myself off the couch, smoothed the pillows, and went quietly to my room.

In my own bed, I felt even more despondent. I knew that I had only been fooling myself when I masturbated. Although I felt wasted, I wanted to repeat my fantasied scenario. Perhaps I could make it even better this time. I had no fear of being discovered in my own room. But I was terrified that if I gave in to it all over again, I might slip permanently away from the difficulties of that unpleasant reality which I had so unrealistically hoped to overcome.

MOTIVATIONS FOR MASTURBATION

Like all behavior, masturbation is motivated. And like Sue, people are often motivated to masturbate because they feel the need to make up for some lack in themselves. They may feel deprived of sheer sexual gratification. They may yearn to love and be loved by someone. Or they may feel unable to accomplish the things they would like to do. And as Sue's experience shows, a person can be motivated by the need for sexual pleasure, love, and achievement all at the same time.

Such needs can be met only through relationships with other people. Lovers must be sought and found. Loving and sexually fulfilling relationships must be cultivated and maintained. The skills a person wants to develop must be learned and mastered through patient effort, commitment, and risk. Action and accomplishment in the real world are the only satisfying ways for people to fulfill their potentials. This truth is easy to acknowledge but extremely difficult to apply. Everyone is tempted to evade it, as Sue tried to do by imagining herself to be a graceful movie star, although she knew very well that she was still a gawky teen-ager.

Certainly, the challenge to fulfill oneself in the real world is fraught with many pressures, obstacles, and emotional dangers. Some people find it particularly difficult because they did not have enough love and acceptance during childhood. And parents who pamper and overindulge their children can cause them, too, to lose their self-confidence. Other people may doubt their capabilities because they feel they were deprived of cultural advantages or economic security as children. Still others may have developed unrealistic plans for themselves that would be impossible for anyone to achieve and lead inevitably to frustration.

Regardless of why or how people feel deficient, their decision to masturbate means they are *not* trying to repair the deficiency through purposeful social activity. Turning inward, they may use masturbation as a way of deriving both sexual and nonsexual fulfillments that actually require relationships with other people in order to be wholly gratifying.

For some people, masturbation may become a habit to which they turn for solace whenever they are rebuffed or feel apprehensive about something. Others, however, may withdraw in this way only occasionally, when they are under the most acute emotional stress.

There is a vast range of individual differences in the ways people translate their motives into masturbatory behavior. No standard psychological formula can be automatically applied to each case. Understanding depends on a detailed knowledge of the individual's particular history and personality.

INHIBITIONS AGAINST MASTURBATION

Sue's example illustrates the motivational dynamics of someone who began to masturbate secretly, repetitively, and chronically in early childhood. But some people move in the opposite direction, by giving up masturbation completely and by vigilantly preventing themselves from indulging in any form of sexual self-stimulation. The consequences, although very different, can be equally destructive to one's sense of self, as the following vignette shows.

The first time I masturbated with genuine pleasure was in the fifty-second year of my life. Sue was in the hospital, awaiting a minor operation. I had visited her earlier in the day. Although I knew her ailment was not serious, I left the hospital feeling very worried about her. We had rarely been away from each other throughout our marriage. And even this brief and involuntary separation was very difficult for us to bear.

When I crawled into bed that evening, I felt wretched, lonely, and sorry for myself. I was so used to the comfort of her bodily presence that I felt severely disoriented. Our double bed suddenly seemed vast and desolate. I tossed and turned on it, searching for a spot where the peacefulness of sleep might take hold of me. But I could only find an aching emptiness wherever I burrowed.

After a while, I stretched out on my back, determined to face my misery and to cope with it. My right hand started reaching for my genitals. And I suddenly realized how conditioned I was to using sex as a means of reducing my nervous tensions.

This realization put a temporary halt to my hand—and to the pleasurable sensations that were beginning to fill my groin. Relieving such tensions during sexual intercourse with Sue had always seemed acceptable to me. Somehow, giving her pleasure, helping her to relieve tensions, had always made it permissible for me to give myself pleasure and to relieve my own tensions. But the idea of doing those things for myself and by myself alone seemed unnatural and frightening.

I continued to lie there stiffly in the dark, my eyes turned inward for insight that might release me from the oppression of myself. I knew that I had never let myself masturbate as a child. Not openly and in the full light of day. Instead, my adolescent history of masturbation was a furtive affair of the night, restricted to wet dreams that seemed to happen despite my pious determination to prevent them.

In young adulthood, I maintained that pose of piety with spartan vigilance. It made me feel superior to others, who, in my eyes, had to "resort" to masturbation while I could get along without it.

In the army during World War II, I remember listening with great condescension to another soldier's account of his masturbatory practices. Evidently, his favorite method was to capture a fly, remove its wings, and let it walk around the tip of his penis until he was driven to ecstatic exasperation. Then, while the fly's feet were still in contact with his throbbing flesh, he would bring himself to a climax.

Later, on a troop ship crossing the Pacific to New Guinea, I let myself give in to my acute need for sexual release. Buried in the hold of the ship, cloaked by its absolute darkness, I "beat myself off"—without dreams, without gentleness, and without pleasure. I just grabbed my aching penis like an inhuman brute and raped myself in a quick frenzy.

Naturally, that experience was not emotionally satisfying. Although it drained me of some tension, it made me feel even more inadequate than I had felt before—inadequate because I had "succumbed" to it and had not been "strong" enough to do without it.

My subsequent development in adulthood led me to understand the mental games I had been playing about the absolute virtue of not playing with myself. Eventually, I saw that my striving for purity and perfection masked extreme fears of masturbation. In my case, those fears originated from incestuous cravings toward my mother. It seems that I equated masturbation with the open expression of such taboo motives. By refraining from masturbation, I was hoping to rid myself of those dangerous desires. And, to bolster my ego, I mentally transformed this deep inhibition of my sexual functioning into an exceptional feat of self-control.

By the time I sorted out what masturbation meant to me, I was already happily married. And the fullness of my sexual relationship with Sue left me no yearning or temptation to masturbate.

Still, I felt I had never quite resolved my conflicts about it, for all the insight I had attained. After all, insight feels quite hypothetical and abstract unless it is put into practice. I had never had a truly satisfying and anxiety-free masturbatory experience. And I couldn't help but feel that such an experience was essential before I could fully accept my own being.

All of these thoughts rumbled through my mind as I lay in bed alone—missing contact with Sue and, at a deep, deep level, missing contact with my innermost self. I gradually became aware of the fact that this deep-seated alienation from my own sexual being was the root cause of the desolation I felt whenever I was alone for any length of time. I sensed intuitively that I had always been unable to enjoy complete solitude because I had never learned to enjoy solitary sex. Actually, I was uneasy about being alone because I was afraid I would be tempted to masturbate. I realized I could never feel permanently self-contained and at peace with myself until I indulged that temptation and allowed myself to experience my body as a source of undiluted pleasure.

THE POSITIVE VALUES OF MASTURBATION

No matter how permissive or repressive a person's upbringing may have been, the complex nature of masturbation leads everyone to question whether and to what extent it is good or bad, right or wrong. To make a satisfactory evaluation for himself, a person needs to be aware of the feelings aroused by his masturbation or his lack of it. He also needs to become aware of the moral and social values that guide his reactions to his own behavior.

We feel it is important for people to search themselves as fully and honestly as possible for the answers they seek about the meaning of their own masturbation. Throughout this book, we provide both general guidelines and specific examples about the relationship between motives and masturbation that may be helpful to people in their quest for self-understanding and in their attempts to change unwanted patterns of behavior. But the reader alone has the ability and the responsibility to see how those guidelines and examples may fit his own situation.

For us, the question of whether masturbation is good or bad depends primarily on whether or not a person is using it to develop his capacity for sexual love. We believe that the basic goal of human existence is to create, nurture, and enhance life. We also believe that love is the best means by which life can be brought into the world, safeguarded, and perpetuated.

Parental acceptance of a child's masturbatory behavior helps the child to feel loved; and the more lovable he feels, the more fully he can love others. As a child matures, his parents should always be accessible for honest and compassionate discussions about whatever questions he may have about masturbation. In that way, parents can help their child to develop positive attitudes toward his gender and sexual functioning. Such self-accepting attitudes, in turn, prepare a child for making an adult transition in the focus of his sexual loving from solitary masturbation to intercourse.

An important aspect of a loving environment is that it allows for and fosters reciprocity. Children need to learn not only to *receive* love but also to *give* love. Children who learn such reciprocity through interactions with their parents are likely to carry it with them into relationships they eventually develop with mates of their own.

We believe that loving sexual relationships provide the greatest feelings of pleasure that adults can experience. Through such relationships, people can best fulfill themselves emotionally and sexually, while also helping others to do the same. Throughout the long span of their lives, however, people may not always have someone with whom to share and express their feelings of sexual love. At such times, as Irv's experience shows, it is important to be able to feel enough spontaneity, self-esteem, and freedom from guilt to enjoy the sexual pleasure and emotional solace of masturbation.

Since masturbation is more personal and private than any other sexual act, it is the most intimate contact an individual can have with himself. Approached as a unique medium for self-revelation and self-acceptance, masturbation can be of crucial value in a person's search for the realization and enjoyment of his individuality.[6]

Thus, even people who are involved in a committed and loving relationship may benefit from solitary masturbation as a way of keeping in touch with their innermost selves. And lovers may develop more mutual trust and understanding by including self-stimulation in the flow of their lovemaking, letting each other see the full range of their sexual behavior and sharing the inner experiences that go with it.

PART I
The Experience of Masturbation

To appreciate the significance of masturbation in human development and intimate relationships, it is first necessary to understand both the physical and the mental components of the masturbatory experience—orgasm and fantasy. For that reason, we explain the physiology and the psychology of orgasmic release, pointing out its importance for health and its usefulness in overcoming sexual fears and problems.

Typically, people use fantasies to enhance their excitement while bringing themselves to a solitary orgasm. But they may also create fantasies for mental masturbation, while refraining from any kind of physical self-stimulation. Since masturbatory fantasy reflects a person's motives and conflicts, it can become a vehicle for self-insight and conflict resolution. By understanding the meaning of their fantasies, people may develop, as we illustrate, a greater ability to fulfill their needs for sexual love and satisfying accomplishment.

Reading about how other people fantasize and have solitary orgasms may bring to mind your own masturbatory experiences. Perhaps you never before tried to sort out their various meanings for your life. Now, if you wish, you can derive such understanding by reflecting on your own experiences and drawing on the concepts we present.

Chapter 1
ORGASM

Before I had my first wet dream, my knowledge of the orgasm was purely hypothetical. Most of what I had learned about the facts of life was taught to me by other, slightly older boys—far from expert informants. Of course, they pretended to know much more about the subject than they really did. And in my embarrassed ignorance, I accepted their crowing commentaries without ever presuming to question the authenticity of their information.

But nobody ever told me what it *felt* like to come. I had read about it in pornographic stories, which portrayed it as the most desirable of pleasures. Those descriptions led me to believe that there was something very daring, and very dirty, about it. And my buddies always referred to it with awed, hushed, or snickering voices.

The reputed pleasures of coming fired my imagination. I had no personal experience by which to gauge just how enjoyable an activity it could be. Of course, I had experienced erections. But when they occurred, I mustered all my will, distracted my attention with a "wholesome" book or daydream, and waited for the crisis to pass.

And the crises did pass—for a longer period than now seems credible to me. But my painfully manufactured virtues were abruptly shattered when I reached puberty.

My first orgasm came upon me very unexpectedly, seizing me in the middle of the night. I had gone to bed as usual. And I fell asleep easily enough. Then the alchemy of dreaming began to work, transforming me from a sexless child into a sexy and powerfully attractive man.

I dreamt I was at the seashore of a tropical island. The beach was deserted. I was sprawling lazily on it, basking in the sensuality of the exotic scene. After a while, I sat up and looked back at the jungle. While I was looking, *she* stepped gracefully out of the trees and onto the beach. She was tall and tawny, wearing a sarong and a ravishing smile. Her hips swayed languidly as she walked, her full breasts bulging against the flimsy cloth that contained them.

As she moved closer to me, I could see the details of her face: her fleshy lips, her gleaming teeth, the smooth brow carved above her dark, flashing eyes. I couldn't believe it, but she kept on walking, showing every intention of wanting to make contact with me. Yes, by God, she was coming over to make love to me! But how? What would I do? What should I do? A bolt of anxiety shot through me.

I remained sitting where I was, trying to be as calm as possible. Soon she was at my side. I gasped from the overwhelming nearness of her beauty. She seemed to sense my awkwardness, because she didn't do anything to me right away. She just sat down and smiled, her eyes filled with understanding and tenderness. But her thigh was close enough to brush against mine. That passing touch was enough to make me feel giddy with desire.

And to lure an erection out of me, I could feel it start to uncoil—slowly, while the pit of my stomach flooded with excitement. My hands trembled as I pressed down on the sand to shift my weight away from her. But she wasn't easily put off. She touched my arm, inviting me to gaze directly into her eyes. I knew it was no use trying to resist her. She couldn't speak my language, anyway—but her look didn't need any translation. So I nodded to her.

She leaned over and kissed me full on the lips, her velvet tongue purring with passion. Without a pause, she moved on, her mouth circling my chin, my cheeks, my eyes, maddening me with soft, burning kisses.

Unable to stay passive any longer, I reached out to her. As I hugged her, my erection grew and grew, pressing uncomfortably against my bathing suit. Feeling just as hemmed in by her sarong, she rose up and flung it off, releasing the fullness of her breasts and the sloping roundness of her buttocks.

The sight of her nakedness drove me absolutely wild. I tried to shed my bathing suit, but my hands were shaking too much. She helped me, her sure fingers easing it over my pulsing cock.

In a blind impulse, I rolled her over on her back, mounting her on the way. Pinning her down with my penis, I pumped and pumped and pumped away. Pumped and pumped and pumped until . . .

I woke myself up with my groans and the force of my ejaculation. I kept groaning, as my semen spurted out into my pajamas. My hands kept pulling at my penis until I had pulled out the last spurting jet there was to pull.

I collapsed on the pillow, my belly, genitals, and thighs oozing with a wet, hot, stickiness. That was it, I said to myself, still panting. I've come. That's it. That's *coming*. God, I thought, it's scary. This stuff, coming out of me—how? From where? And I didn't want it to happen. No, no, I didn't! Is that the way it is every time? What a mess I made! How can I hide it from my mother? It's all over these goddam pajamas. And the bed, too. How could I possibly explain it to her? But it did feel good, didn't it? Will it happen to me again? No, it can't! I won't let it!

But it happened again and again. That first wet dream turned out to be only the beginning of a whole series of them. And I never in my life felt so close to going hopelessly insane as I did during that run of wet dreams. Night after night, I vowed to myself that I would sleep peacefully the whole night through, keep my hands away from my pecker, and dream good, clean, righteous dreams. Then I would go to bed, making sure that I was on my back and that my hands were outside the blanket.

But without fail, an erotic dream would begin to take shape in my sleep. Invariably, I was the object of a beautiful woman's seductive and irresistible passion. And before the night was over, I would find myself waking up with a start, my hands pulling at my penis and my pelvis pumping away at the mattress. To make matters infinitely worse, my mother would occasionally appear in my dreams as the seductress; and I would not wake up until after I had begun having an orgasm with her.

For a while, I lived in horror of myself and in terror of being detected by my mother—not only as a wet-dreamer but also as her imagined sexual partner. Each morning, I tried to clean up my mess the best I could, sometimes even trying to wash off the splotches of dried semen on my sheet. But I did have to put my laundry in the family hamper. I lived in constant fear that my mother would confront me with the evidence of my nightly handiwork. I could almost hear her say, "Irving, what happened to your pajamas?"

She never did confront me or even allude to my nocturnal emissions. And I chose not to regard them as acts of masturbation. I insisted on telling myself that I was victimized by some kind of mysterious ailment, from which I literally prayed each night to be delivered.

ORGASM AS CHOICE

Human beings are born with the capacity for orgasm, which remains present throughout their lives.[1] But anyone who wants an orgasm has to work actively toward it, no matter how much he may want to deny his part in attaining it. Even infants and toddlers have to initiate, direct, and sustain their own masturbatory behavior if they are to reach an orgasm. Such a focused activity implies that the child has chosen to do it, although he is not yet mature enough to perceive it as a deliberate decision. But once a person has developed the psychological awareness that he is the source of his own masturbatory behavior, he cannot help recognizing that he is using his mind to initiate the process of having an orgasm.

The first eruption of an orgasmic climax in the middle of your sleep is certainly an experience you are likely to keep in mind for a long time. It is commonplace for adolescent boys to have nocturnal emissions. Adolescent girls may also find themselves propelled out of sleep by an orgasm they have stimulated in acting out an erotic dream. And many adults of both sexes may continue to use this form of masturbation.[2]

We refer to this nocturnal sexuality as masturbation, because orgasms do not simply happen. Even a dream-induced orgasm is willed by the dreamer, who uses the cover of sleep to realize wishes for which he is reluctant to assume full and conscious responsibility. In this way, the wet-dreamer plays a mental trick with himself, pretending that the very wishes he seeks to express and to gratify in his sexual dreams are not really his own.[3]

As Irv's case illustrates, the script of a wet dream may be created by the dreamer to further reinforce his belief that he is not responsible for his sexual behavior. Irv imagined himself being seduced by a woman under conditions in which he felt he *had* to respond. He was trying to absolve himself of any personal responsibility for indulging in masturbation. He continued to construct his subsequent wet dreams, as well as his waking fantasies, in a similar manner—always seeing himself as the object of some woman's irrepressible desires.

To the extent that people wish to shed personal responsibility for their sexual behavior, they can tell themselves that they are not responsible for masturbating while asleep. But masturbation is always a deliberate act of a person's will; even during sleep, a person is capable of exercising some control.

An extreme example of such self-control was described to us by a sex therapist. One of his patients, a devout Catholic in his early thirties, sought help because he was worried he would not be able to have an erection. Due to the religious taboos against masturbation, he had been a "good" boy all of his life and had never even touched his genitals. In the course of therapy, he revealed that he was plagued by erotic dreams in which he saw himself being seduced by an attractive woman. But he was determined not to give in to his desires to have intercourse with her, even in his dreams. As he felt his penis starting to grow erect, he would wake himself up; and he would wait until his arousal subsided before he allowed himself to go back to sleep. In that way, he prevented himself from ever having a full erection or a nocturnal emission.

Since the patient had great respect for the therapist, he responded well to the reassurance and support he was given. With the therapist's "permission," he needed only three weeks to permit himself to have erections and to masturbate to orgasm while fully awake. Having accepted that degree of responsibility for his sexual desires and functioning, the patient was able to contemplate the possibility of marriage, a commitment he hoped someday to make.

Taking Responsibility

To have an orgasm, a person must take complete control of his mental functioning and, paradoxically, use it for the purpose of losing control over it. First, he must arouse, sustain, and intensify his excitement. Then he must voluntarily put an end to his foreplay and let himself be carried away by the cresting waves of his climax. An orgasm dissolves and blasts away all the distinctions people ordinarily make between what is mental and what is physical. It may alter a person's consciousness to the point of permitting him to feel temporarily free of thoughts, images, and all the other workings of his mind. In surrendering totally to an orgasm, he experiences "mind-blowing" ecstasies.

In making love to himself or someone else, a person has to learn how to focus his sexual tensions in the genitals. But as he reaches the height of his excitement, he must relinquish all efforts to control his sexual behavior and let his pelvic movements and bodily reactions be guided entirely by the involuntary reflexes that are set off by the onset of orgasm.

Stages and Functions of the Orgasm

Masters and Johnson, whose studies were focused on the physiology of the orgasmic response, also call attention to the key role of volition in both the arousal of sexual tension and in the surrender to orgasm. They found that adult men and women go through the same four basic physiological stages in attaining an orgasm. These stages develop in the same predictable sequence, whether brought about by masturbation or intercourse.[4]

The initial "excitement" phase is indicated by the erection of a man's penis and the moistening of a woman's vagina. The second, or "plateau," stage is characterized by increased blood engorgement of the sexual organs and muscular tension. During the third phase, in which the orgasm actually occurs, it is essential for a person to mobilize both his physical *and* his psychological strength from the stockpile of sexual tension, until his total energy can be directed toward the leap into a sexual climax. The orgasmic stage is characterized by a wave of rhythmic muscular contractions in the genital organs. For women, these contractions occur primarily in what is called the "orgasmic platform," the outer third of the vagina and the tissues surrounding it; the uterus also contracts as it does during labor and childbirth. In men, the contractions of the seminal vesicles, the prostate gland, the urethral bulb, and the penis itself force the semen out under pressure, causing the ejaculation. After the orgasm has occurred, the person enters the final, or "resolution" stage, in which there is a release of blood from the engorged organs and blood vessels, a decline of muscular tension, and a sense of emotional relaxation.[5]

Wilhelm Reich, a psychoanalyst who pioneered scientific research on the orgasm in the 1920s, defined a person's health in terms of his capacity for orgasm. Reich considered the orgasm to be the natural means by which people derive pleasure and relaxation from their bodies while ridding themselves of tension and frustration. He believed that learning how to have enjoyable masturbatory orgasms could help people experience the fuller pleasure and release obtainable through orgasms in heterosexual intercourse with someone they love.[6] Subsequently, Albert Kinsey found that women who had had solitary orgasms before marriage achieved orgasmic satisfaction and release more easily in their marriage than women who had never had an orgasm on their own.[7]

Orgasms can help people to integrate their bodily sensations, emotional feelings, and mental reactions into a unified sense of themselves.[8] This coherent and positive sense of self can help them to feel good about their lives. In particular, enjoyable masturbatory orgasms can lead a person to accept his genitals as good and desirable rather than dirty and repellant. We know a girl of eight, an extremely energetic and self-assured child, who keeps telling her mother over and over again, "Oh, Mommy, you can't imagine how wonderful it makes me feel whenever I touch myself down there."

Orgasms enable people to discover, accept, and feel good about their bodies and their sexual functioning. By masturbating to orgasm, people can explore their own particular areas of sexual sensitivity and responsiveness. The knowledge gained through these explorations can be helpful in seeking sexual gratification with others.[9]

The ability to produce an orgasm for and by oneself may also increase an individual's value of his separate identity and his personal adequacy.[10] Knowing that they can enjoy and satisfy themselves on their own, people can develop self-reliance and avoid becoming overly dependent on the favorable reactions of others to them.

Vicky, a young woman in her midtwenties, recalls how she masturbated from the age of six, by rubbing herself back and forth against the trees she used to climb on the isolated farm where she grew up. Her masturbatory orgasms made her feel very strong, tuned in with the powerful forces of nature. Vicky told us that she always felt extremely fortunate, and special, to be able to provide such magnificent feelings for herself. These sensations helped her to sustain a positive image of herself despite the loneliness of her childhood years.

SPECIAL QUALITIES OF THE SOLITARY ORGASM

The decision to have an orgasm alone, without the stimulation—or possible inhibition—of a partner, means that one need not please anyone else or take another person's needs into consideration. Masturbating in one's own private time and space, one can shut the door on everything but his own pleasure; adrift from any anchorage in external reality, he can sail into every current of his sensuality.

When they masturbate, people can time and coordinate their mental and physical manipulations to their exact specifications. They can dwell on this titillation or that, on one fantasy or another. They can play back the reel and start all over again. Or, they can keep going on, searching for newer and greater highs in both the foreplay and the orgasm. But, precisely because of this solitude, the masturbatory orgasm is often followed by an aftermath of disorientation, emotional let-down, and a sense of loneliness and separation from others.

The physical surrender necessary to orgasm has its mental counterpart in the shift from controlled thought to mindless oblivion. As one moves toward orgasmic climax, the physiological changes induce a mild state of anoxia, a temporary lack of oxygen in the brain. At the point of orgasm, consciousness may become very clouded. How fitting it is that the French refer to the orgasm as *la petite morte* or *la morte douce*—"the little death" or "the sweet death."[11] Such profound mental and physical changes cannot help but arouse at least some apprehension in everyone. But they may be perceived as especially overwhelming or frightening when the orgasm is induced and experienced alone.

Fortunately, with repetition and familiarity, orgasms tend to lose their capacity to arouse anxiety. Eventually, most people learn that the loss of mental and physical control is temporary; they can quickly regain mastery over themselves. Certainly, the ecstatic pleasure of an orgasm may counteract the anxiety endured in attaining it. Such pleasure may be so intense as to give a person the transcendent feeling of being at one with the universe.[12]

Nobody is animated by exactly the same configuration of motives, thoughts, body movements, and feelings each time he has a masturbatory orgasm. Changes in these factors can lead the same person to respond very differently to his solitary orgasms.

Nick, a graduate student in his late twenties, shared with us the marked contrasts in feeling that he experienced when he masturbated to relieve nonsexual tensions and when he did it for sheer sexual pleasure: "When I masturbate to get rid of school tensions, it's almost a hollow, mechanical feeling. There's no emotional release and I feel more tired. There are times, like during exam periods, when I feel lots of bodily pressures that are more related to my general state of anxiety than to sex. My orgasms at those times are not satisfying at all. It doesn't even feel like I have a full ejaculation. My testicles don't rise up as they ordinarily do. And it even feels as if there are some sperm left over that haven't been released.

"When I do it for sexual impulses, the feelings are much clearer. I feel mellow and can lie back and enjoy the release. It's easier to get into a sexual fantasy and it seems to carry me along on a wave of sensuality that leads to orgasm. It's not necessary to concentrate or focus. And my ejaculation and the emotional relief that follows it are much more intense."

Childhood Experience and Orgasmic Release

As Nick's case illustrates, the positive effects of a solitary orgasm depend on how fully people can masturbate for sexual pleasure alone. Ideally, this ability grows out of a past in which the child has learned to accept and to take responsibility for his sexuality. After all, the capacity for orgasm, like other human potentials, develops within a context of learned experience. And children who have learned to initiate and to get pleasure from their orgasmic reactions will not be afraid to have and to enjoy orgasms later on in life.

Unfortunately, many people do not grow up with such an ideal attitude toward their sexuality. Many have learned to be so fearful and rejecting of their sexual impulses that they do not permit themselves to masturbate or to have solitary orgasms.

These fears have been traced to child-rearing patterns in which the child associates the expression of his sensuality with the threat of punishment from his parents. To feel safe, and to avoid disapproval and rejection, these children may decide to give up or to minimize the expression of their sexual drives and orgasmic potentials.

In our society, people rarely grow up without having encountered some negative reactions to the expression of their sexuality—if not from parents, then from teachers, relatives, or playmates. To the extent that a child accepts those social constraints and makes them his own, he will inhibit his orgasmic responsiveness, even when he is masturbating in complete privacy. It is for this reason that so many people are reluctant to accept responsibility for their masturbation. Instead, they prefer to regard it as something that just happens to them. Often, they experience themselves as somehow "drifting" into masturbation without being aware of having made a clear decision to do it.

In addition to their socially learned constraints, people are also subject to the inherent fear of the mindlessness that occurs, as we have described, at the moment of orgasm. That fear alone can lead a person to feel conflicts about having an orgasm. For to bring himself to orgasm, a person has to do so despite the fear of the mindlessness that he inevitably arouses within himself during the process. Despite the fact that orgasms can be pleasurable and fulfilling, the fear of orgasm may be so great that it interferes with a person's enjoyment of masturbation. Among children treated in psychoanalysis, these fears have been represented symbolically in dreams of explosions, infernos, and erupting volcanoes. One girl portrayed her fear of a masturbatory climax in a dream about a huge wave rising out of the ocean, which threatened her and warned her to flee.[13] Other girls have reported feeling menaced by their orgasmic sensations when they had actually masturbated, seeing them as signs of craziness or delirium.[14] Reacting to such anxieties, these children either stopped masturbating or learned to interrupt their masturbation in order to avoid reaching a climax.

Substitutes for Masturbation

Wilhelm Stekel, a pychiatrist who wrote the first major psychoanalytic work devoted entirely to the meaning of masturbation, said that some people may develop nervous habits that symbolically represent an outlet for the chronic and self-imposed frustration of their desires for masturbatory orgasm. Stekel gives a variety of examples of such symbolic behavior: nose-picking, ear-probing, nail-biting, skin-scratching, and mannerisms with the fingers or the tongue. We know a sixty-year-old woman who swears that she would never touch her genital area. But she incessantly probes and irritates her ears, bringing about infections in them. The persistent scratching of an itch in the ears may be a substitute for stroking the genitals to orgasm.

Similarly, children may use bed-wetting as a means of expressing masturbatory desires that they are afraid to indulge directly. In such cases, the "uncontrollable" release of urine is the equivalent of the sexual "letting go" that accompanies an orgasm.[15] Children often confuse sexual arousal, and its accompanying genital sensations, with a desire to urinate. One seven-year-old girl, who slept in the same room with her parents, wet her bed every night. But when her mother menstruated and her parents did not have intercourse, she was continent.[16] Another girl of six feels the impulse to run to the toilet and urinate every time she is stimulated by seeing a picture in a magazine or movie in which men and women are kissing and expressing love.

This confusion between urinary and sexual stimulation may continue to manifest itself in adult life. One woman, who had never masturbated or experienced an orgasm until she was almost thirty, told us how upset she was when she first tried to have an orgasm by masturbating with a vibrator. She was not sure if the sensations she experienced were really an orgasm or if she had urinated. Eventually, she learned how an orgasm felt.

Sex therapists have reported that some women are afraid of giving up enough self-control to have an orgasm, because they fear they will also lose control over their bladders and urinate.[17] Sometimes such women can attain an orgasm only after being encouraged to let go completely when they masturbate and relax control over their entire pelvic region—even if it means wetting or soiling themselves.[18]

Effects of Repressing Masturbation

Selma Fraiberg, a psychotherapist, describes a woman of thirty-five and two girls of seven and eight who complained about a complete loss of sensation in their genitals.[19] Their common symptom could be traced to a repressed desire to masturbate and the fear of orgasm. All three patients had similar dreams of searching in attics and empty houses for something precious that they had lost. They also dreamt repeatedly about a child who took flight from a fire or explosion. In the course of their treatment, it became apparent that these fires symbolized feelings of intense sexual excitement for them.

One of the girls wet her bed and had coughing spells. Very frequently, she felt an urgent need to go to the toilet because of the "itchy and tickly" feelings she experienced, even when she only had "a couple of drops" of urine to eliminate. When asked if her feelings were connected with anything else, such as touching her genitals, she reacted with astonishment, disgust, and loathing. "It's wet there!" she protested, emphasizing that she didn't like to touch herself.

As her treatment progressed, the girl was able to recover what she called "good feelings," which she could identify as diffusely localized in the genital area. She contrasted these "good feelings" with the painful tension she experienced when she had an urgent need to urinate. But these "good feelings" would appear and disappear periodically. Whenever she felt that her masturbatory impulses were too strong, her good feelings disappeared and the tension of her urinary urgency or her bed-wetting would return. Or she would have severe coughing spells that began with a "tickly feeling in the throat," and caused a tightening of the muscles in her genital area. As her therapy helped her to understand why she developed these symptoms, she would lose them and regain feeling in her genitals.[20]

People of all ages rely on their masturbatory orgasms to comfort them at night and to bring on sleep. One fifty-year-old man, who is divorced and living alone, suffers from severe back pains because of a chronic case of rheumatoid arthritis. "I masturbate at night as a way of knocking myself out and reducing my tension." His orgasms relax him enough to permit him to fall asleep. Sometimes, he says, just "the idea" of having an orgasm is enough to put him to sleep. Another married man in his late twenties described the masturbatory orgasms of his childhood and adolescence as "a kind of nightcap," which he could always count on for relaxation at bedtime.

By contrast, many people suffer from insomnia because they associate going to bed with the temptation to masturbate. Stekel claims that such people prevent themselves from falling asleep because they fear they will have erotic dreams and nocturnal emissions. By keeping themselves awake, they suffer doubly: from lack of sleep and from lack of sexual gratification.

Stekel describes a woman who consulted him because of sleeplessness.[21] She fell asleep easily, but would wake up with a start, oppressed by feelings of dread, her heart pounding. Then she tossed about in bed for hours, unable to fall asleep again. This woman had masturbated up to a few months before the onset of her insomnia. But she had read and heard from various sources that masturbation could ruin a person's nervous system; as a result, she was full of self-reproach and tried to stop. Although she did not get much sexual satisfaction from her husband, she had felt fine as long as she could masturbate. Once she began her self-enforced abstinence, she had difficulty sleeping through the night. And she attributed that difficulty to the fact that she had, indeed, ruined her nervous system by masturbating.

In psychotherapy, she revealed some of her "gruesome" dreams about love affairs with strange men. Just before or during her orgasm, she would wake herself up abruptly, always finding her hand in contact with her genitalia. Even in her dreams she did not want to "sin," so she punished herself by waking up. And she would not let herself fall asleep again because she had to make sure she did not masturbate.

In the course of her treatment with Stekel, this woman realized that she had affection for her husband and did not really want to have extramarital affairs. As she accepted the sexual limitations of her relationship with him, she gradually overcame her guilt about masturbation. Eventually, she made the conscious choice to satisfy her sexual needs for herself; and she began to sleep properly again.

The basic problem underlying the various psychosomatic symptoms we have described is the fear that people have developed about taking responsibility for gratifying their own sexual inclinations. Ironically, their disowned and repressed impulses continue to motivate them and to create tensions that can only be reduced by open sexual gratification. But instead of satisfying their sexual needs directly, they use disguised, indirect ways of venting their tensions. As a result, they develop symptoms that actually create more stress for them. Then, they have to endure and worry about those symptoms, while remaining just as anxious about facing the motives underlying them. But they do not have to accept personal responsibility for their stress, because their problems now seem to be caused by a physical illness, over which they feel they have no control.

Overcoming Sexual Repression
Psychotherapy

Fortunately, people can learn to recover these repressed sexual impulses, to accept them consciously, and to find satisfying ways of expressing them. Freud developed psychoanalytic therapy as a vehicle for helping people in this endeavor. The cases quoted from Fraiberg and Stekel show how psychoanalytic therapy can be of vital help to people who suffer from the fear and repression of their masturbatory impulses.

But the outcome of psychotherapy ultimately depends on the patient's desire to change and his willingness to assume responsibility both for his motives and for the way he deals with them. Even the most highly motivated patient is likely to be afraid of facing what he has worked so hard to hide from his own awareness. After all, he had put those motives out of his consciousness because he was so fearful of accepting and expressing them. It is only natural that he should resist dealing directly with them in therapy.

Therefore, deep-seated changes do not occur quickly or easily in any form of psychotherapy that is aimed at the recovery of repressed motives. Such changes generally come about only after a patient has struggled long and painfully with both his fears and his resistances. Naturally, the degree of competence of the therapist is also a crucial element in the outcome of this avenue to personal change.

Bioenergetic Therapy

In a radical departure from Freud's purely verbal method of treatment, Reich started the field of bioenergetic therapy, the forerunner of all subsequent approaches to sex therapy. Guided by his belief that body and mind function as one, Reich found that, as patients worked through their emotional blocks, muscles that had been rigid and tense for years relaxed. Similarly, deeply buried emotional feelings could be consciously recalled and expressed, when the chronic muscle tensions—the "body armor"— associated with them were dissolved by massage. Reich's approach combined psychotherapy with massage, exercise, and training in breathing. While helping patients to articulate and gain insight into the origins of their sexual repressions, he also worked on their bodies, loosening the muscular rigidities that represented and maintained the feelings they had repressed.

Reich's bioenergetic approach aimed not only at the removal of symptoms but also at basic change in the patient's personality. Bioenergetic therapy, like psychoanalysis, was conceived as a fairly long-term procedure, often requiring several years. Patients were not felt to have completed therapy until they succeeded in shedding both the mental and the physical manifestations of their sexual repressions; until, in Reich's terms, they were free enough to have the fullest possible orgasmic release with a partner of the opposite sex.

Sex Therapy

Since Reich's time, therapists specializing in sexual problems have been developing procedures intended to implement goals that are considerably more limited than those that guided his work. This new type of sex therapy is brief in duration, seeking to help patients overcome their current sexual problems as quickly as possible, within several months, at most.

In 1959, William Masters, a gynecologist, and Virginia Johnson, a psychologist, pooled their specialties in a remedial orientation that launched the modern approach to sex therapy.[22] Turning from research to practice, and working as a therapeutic team, they began to see couples who complained of sexual incompatibility—for example, because the wife was inorgasmic or the husband suffered from premature ejaculation, retarded ejaculation, or impotence. Over the years, their methods have been modified by other sex therapists, such as Helen Singer Kaplan,[23] who is both a psychiatrist and a psychologist. These other therapists work either as individuals or in teams, with either couples or single people.

While practitioners in this field may differ somewhat in their techniques, their fundamental approach tends to be similar. Generally, they still make use of the psychodynamic principles articulated by Freud, talking to patients to impart insight about the possible motivational bases of their symptoms. However, they use such dialogues primarily in discussing the reactions of patients to the behavioral exercises they are given to practice at home—exercises designed specifically to eliminate their particular kinds of sexual dysfunction.

For example, a patient who has conditioned herself, out of fear, to avoid touching her genitals is deconditioned from that habitual avoidance by following a set of exercises that instruct her on how to touch herself. And while losing her fear, she develops the ability both to enjoy self-stimulation and to derive orgasmic pleasure from it.

Therapists recommend that patients find a variety of ways to achieve a masturbatory orgasm. This variety helps people discover what turns them on the most, how to gain control over their genital arousal and response, and how to abandon themselves to orgasmic pleasure with a partner.

As people progress through such exercises, they are told to notice any anxieties and resistances they feel. In their therapy sessions, they discuss these reactions, seeking to understand their psychological origins. Therapists also encourage patients to share their feelings and insights with the sexual partners they may have. Eventually, they are encouraged to masturbate in their partner's presence and to manually stimulate each other in ways which are specifically aimed at overcoming their particular problems.

To help people free themselves of whatever feelings of guilt, shame, or anxiety they may bring to these masturbation exercises, therapists typically encourage them to alter their negative orientation toward pleasurable self-stimulation. Patients are urged to switch from feeling they are doing a bad thing *to* themselves to feeling they are doing something good *for* themselves.

Self-Help

The approaches used by sex therapists are being popularized in magazine articles and books, many of which offer detailed, illustrated, step-by-step programs designed expressly for the purpose of helping people to help themselves. But such publications are not entirely new.

As long ago as 1930, Dr. Helena Wright, an English gynecologist, published a book, very daring for its time, giving women frank and explicit instructions on how to masturbate to orgasm and how to transfer that ability to having an orgasm during sexual intercourse.[24] Dr. Wright's instructions turned out to be consistent with the results that Masters and Johnson later obtained in their research. Their observations exploded the myth that there is a difference between a "clitoral" and a "vaginal" orgasm. They found that both the clitoris and the vagina have essential functions in every female orgasm; the effects of those organs cannot be separated from one another.

Dr. Wright describes how a woman should run her fingers back and forth between the clitoris and the mouth of her vagina, treating the two areas as one. She stresses that the band around the vaginal entrance that extends for about an inch inside is the most sensitive part of the vagina. This is the area Masters and Johnson call the orgasmic platform—the place where a woman's orgasmic contractions first appear. By gently and rhythmically stimulating herself in and around the edges of her vagina, a woman can bring herself to orgasm. Once a woman is capable of giving this kind of satisfaction to herself, Dr. Wright suggests that she teach her husband how to do it to and for her.[25]

While a large number of current articles and books on sexual self-help focus on the problems of inorgasmic women, many of them offer specific instructions that can be very helpful to men. Some men achieve orgasm by masturbating too quickly or in rigid, stereotyped ways that undermine both the pleasure they can give themselves and the effectiveness of their sexual functioning during intercourse. Some men touch, stroke, or fondle only a limited area of their bodies or their genitals. Others may even avoid touching themselves altogether; some may only be able to have an orgasm by rubbing up against objects, furniture, or other things such as gymnastic equipment.

Dr. Barry Lubetkin, Clinical Director of the Institute for Behavior Therapy in New York City, expresses his amazement at the number of men he interviews who even resist *looking* at their genitals when they masturbate. "It's almost as if by not looking at the hand on the penis, they can delude themselves into denying responsibility for what they are doing."[26] He also points out that men who have premature ejaculations often masturbate to orgasm too quickly—perhaps because they are so guilty about their behavior—and they do not even let themselves build up a full erection. Thus, they never adequately learn how to identify the sensations in their genitals that signal when ejaculation is about to occur.

To avoid ejaculating before reaching a full erection, Dr.

Lubetkin advises men to lengthen the time they devote to masturbatory stimulation and to take more pleasure in slowly building up their arousal. He also suggests that men look directly at their genitals while they masturbate, permitting them to associate their feelings with the degree of erection they see. Thus, they can become more familiar with their bodily responses.

Dr. David Kass and Fred Stauss, authors of *Sex Therapy at Home*,[27] suggest that men massage the insides of their thighs, rubbing all around their genitals, which they should caress lightly, at first. Slowly increasing their pressure and speed, they should try to vary both as often as is pleasing to them. They describe where a man can find the sensitive ridge that runs along the underside of his penis. This ridge is often the center of excitement. By lightly rubbing this ridge just below the head of his penis, a man can discover the area that produces the greatest sensations of arousal and pleasure for him.

Kass and Stauss urge men to be inventive, to try various positions, sitting, standing, and lying down. At the onset of orgasm, men are advised to moan, groan, and make as much noise as they want; to allow their bodies to toss and turn; and to experience the fullest possible sense of release and enjoyment.

Instead of turning to sex therapists or manuals, some people are helping themselves and others by forming groups to discuss and resolve their common problems. These leaderless "consciousness-raising" groups may be exclusively female or male, or may be mixed. They are organized and conducted solely by the participants themselves, without any professional to direct them. The shared responsibility and mutual support involved in these groups often help individual members to take the responsibility for changing their own unsatisfying sexual behavior. The changes made by one person in the group can inspire other participants to follow suit in changing themselves.

One woman in her late twenties, who had never masturbated in her life, and had never had an orgasm during intercourse, told us what a thrilling experience it was when she was finally able to have an orgasm after being encouraged by the women in her group. These women had gotten together to help each other work out both their sexual and their vocational problems. When this woman started going to the group, she was having difficulties in her marriage. Her self-esteem was at its lowest ebb because she felt she was sexually inadequate. She had been in psychotherapy for years, and she still couldn't come.

Within the group, she was continually encouraged to think more highly of herself. The women told her that they experienced her as a wonderful person, who fully *deserved* the pleasures of an orgasm. Some women even demonstrated how to masturbate to orgasm, with their clothes on, while the rest of the group watched. Finally, she decided to let herself masturbate on her own, using a vibrator lent to her by a friend in the group. Her orgasm was so moving that it overwhelmed her. In fact, she was afraid to tell the women about it, feeling that she might jinx it and prevent herself from ever having another orgasm.

Continuing to masturbate privately, she had orgasms each time she tried for one. Eventually, after a few weeks of successful practice, she felt the courage not only to reveal what she had been doing but also to masturbate to orgasm in front of the group. And the women applauded and celebrated her accomplishment.

Leaderless groups, like sex therapy and self-help books, are aimed at helping people assume responsibility for their sexual desires and their preferences in gratifying them. All of these approaches provide the social support, factual information, moral legitimacy, and emotional acceptance that some people need to counteract their lifelong attitudes against exploring their bodily feelings, giving themselves sexual pleasure, and taking responsibility for caring enough about themselves to surrender to the joys of orgasmic release.

Learning how to have an enjoyable masturbatory orgasm is a truly liberating and fulfilling experience for anyone who has been unable to have it. However, most people—and most remedial approaches to sexual dysfunction—are not primarily interested in cultivating solitary orgasms as the ultimate expression of sexuality. People seeking help in achieving masturbatory orgasms primarily want to use their solitary experiences to develop their potential for having orgasms with a sexual partner.

Although a solitary orgasm may not be as rewarding as an orgasm reached in sharing love, masturbatory orgasms give people more sexual fulfillment and release than having no orgasms at all. Furthermore, the emotional freedom to have solitary orgasms is essential for the psychological and physical wellbeing of people whose circumstances restrict them to coming alone. For growing children, and for adults without partners, masturbation may be the only available outlet for expressing their sexual desires.

For people who have loving relationships and who want to improve them, masturbation may be helpful in overcoming deeply buried sexual fears and inhibitions. For those people, the remedial methods that are becoming available may undo years of suffering and open up new vistas of gratification and contentment. Indeed, the very availability of those methods heralds a new era in the social acceptance of sexuality.

Chapter 2
FANTASY

Besides the physical rewards of orgasm, masturbation offers another source of pleasure: fantasy. Fantasy is one of the most miraculous of all human capacities. The ability to influence the flow of inner experience is given to everyone. People can invent, shape, alter, and direct the contents of their minds. They need not be bound by any known reality in creating the range and richness of their fantasies. In fantasy, people can recall the past as it was or as they wish it might have been. They can conjure up the future as it is likely to be, or as the most improbable projection of their wildest hope. Through the eye of the mind, people can envision happenings that go beyond the limits of time and space. They can be and become anything and everything that suits their fancy.

While masturbating, people can combine the magical fulfillments of fantasy with the pleasurable flow of their physical stimulation. The ability to make such combinations seems to offer quick, easy, and complete gratification for all of one's wishes. The climax itself reinforces the very fantasies that helped to bring it about. Knowing that they work for him, a person may continue to use them whenever he masturbates. In this way, fantasy arouses a sexual reaction; and the sexual climax reinforces the further use of fantasy. Eventually, people learn to count on that fantasy-masturbation cycle as a reliable means of satisfying both their sexual and nonsexual desires.

USES OF FANTASY

The fantasies that accompany masturbation reveal the vast range of human motives. People of all ages use masturbatory fantasies to express their major psychological needs at different periods of development.[1] The actual content of a person's fantasies indicates the nature of his goals, desires, conflicts, and frustrations; and the characteristic way he deals with his needs and problems is expressed in the story line that threads its way through his imaginary scenarios.

Because people have many different needs at the same time, their masturbatory fantasies always blend both sexual and nonsexual imagery. Depending on which motives are most pressing at a particular time, one kind of imagery may predominate.

When the impulse to masturbate is primarily sexual, the fantasies tend to be sexual too. They may also include some representation of the nonsexual motives the person is attempting to satisfy through his fantasied sexual behavior—for example, the need to prove his adequacy, to inflate his ego, and to dominate or submit to others. Similarly, when people masturbate mainly to bolster their sense of personal worth and competence, the dominant themes of their fantasies may center around some intellectual, vocational, or artistic accomplishment. But they coordinate their fantasied achievements with images and symbols that reflect the quality of their sexual desires.

Expressing Sexual Motives

When people experience real and acute sexual deprivation, they may conjure up an enticing variety of willing partners to stimulate and channel the movements of their self-embrace. They can invent handsome strangers, re-create the passions of previous lovers, or anticipate encounters with lovers they hope to have some day. This kind of anticipation of future sexual relationships is especially widespread during adolescence and young adulthood, when people use their masturbatory fantasies to increase their self-confidence and reassure themselves about the adequacy of their sexual functioning.

Ralph is a premedical student in a small eastern college. He and Mary, both seniors, have been going steady for almost a year and are planning to be married after graduation. They have done a great deal of necking and heavy petting, but Mary has been reluctant to go all the way before their wedding.

Ralph has never had intercourse either. He had masturbated a lot as a child, but he was shy and had not gone out much with girls. Although he puts on a show of being sexually informed and experienced, he is just as scared as Mary about what will happen when they finally do make love.

One night, Ralph returned to his room after a really hot session with Mary. When he got into bed, he began to feel a tremendous tension in his groin. Just thinking about her gave him an erection. He tried to ignore it and go to sleep, but he had trouble keeping his hands away from his genitals. Ever since he has been going with Mary, he has hated to masturbate. He has wanted to wait for the real thing. But, that night, no matter how hard he tried to avoid it, he couldn't resist touching himself.

As he got more and more into it, Ralph felt much better, gradually letting himself drift off into a reverie. In his fantasy, he had finally convinced Mary to go away with him for a weekend. Speeding along the country roads in his powerful sports car, they seemed to melt into each other on the soft leather seat. He drove to a magnificent colonial inn. It was just the kind of charming atmosphere that Mary adored. She could not help but show her admiration when he flashed a ten-dollar tip at the man behind the desk, getting them a choice room without an advance reservation.

Soon Ralph was stretched out beside the pool, watching Mary swim gracefully along its length. When she climbed out of the water, she bent over and gave him a soul kiss. She had never taken the initiative to kiss him like that before. Without a word, they both sprang up and floated off to their room. Suddenly, Mary was standing before him naked. The beauty of her body was more overwhelming than anything he had ever envisioned. She seemed to have overcome all of her former apprehension. Taking her into his arms, he guided her toward the bed, kissing and fondling her all over—making sure she enjoyed every minute of it.

By this time, Ralph had fully aroused himself beneath the covers of his dormitory bed. He felt he couldn't possibly contain himself any longer. But when Mary's face flashed back into his mind, he slowed down his hand to hold back his excitement. Once again, he saw them together in their lavish room. She was really letting herself go. Sensing her desire, he started to thrust upward into the blanket, drawing out every ounce of their pleasure. When he felt she was ready to come, he rolled over and pumped away against the mattress, finally letting himself have his ejaculation.

Ralph's fantasy illustrates how the complexity of a person's motivation is reflected in the imagery of his fantasies. Ralph masturbated primarily out of sexual frustration; basically, his fantasy was an expression of sexual wish-fulfillment. The form that his sexual fantasy took reveals the nature of his sexual wishes. He had Mary come on to him in a way she had never done in real life. He used his consideration of her sexual needs to create a picture of himself that was worthy of the fine person and excellent doctor he hoped he would be. By portraying himself as tender and capable of holding out so they could have their orgasms together, he was countering his anxiety about having intercourse and wishing himself as sensitive and experienced as the husband he had read about in marriage manuals.

In addition, Ralph wanted to prove he was far more dashing and potent than he really felt himself to be. The nonsexual symbols in his fantasy enhanced his self-image in this way. Driving to a posh hotel at top speed in his own expensive sports car gave him both the daring and the flair with which he hoped to win Mary's admiration. Thus, Ralph blended both the sexual and the nonsexual imagery in his fantasy in an effort to assure himself that he could satisfy Mary sexually, and to guarantee his desirability as a good provider with social status and prestige.

Expressing Nonsexual Motives

People can also use masturbatory fantasy to overcome the anxiety aroused by pursuing their nonsexual goals. In their fantasies, they can face and work through conflicts they anticipate. As they masturbate, they can imagine themselves acting in the way they know is necessary to reach their goals, a way that may require more poise, initiative, or directness than they can usually summon when other people are around. In this way, their sexual pleasure becomes linked with this new and challenging behavior, giving them the confidence they need to try out the behavior when other people are around. By continuously pairing the reward of their sexual release with the positive outcome of the fantasies associated with it, they hope to experience a similarly favorable outcome when they try to satisfy their desires in the world.

John is a junior in high school. He had always wanted to be a politician. He told us that, even in elementary school, he often masturbated while imagining himself as the featured speaker at a political meeting. He never failed to impress himself and his colleagues with his imaginary charisma and oratory skill. He could run off an infinite number of fantasies—complete with sound tracks of the speeches he delivered—while lying in bed. His colleagues always gave him standing ovations. At the very climax of their applause, his penis was aquiver with satisfaction, and the image of his competence made his entire being tingle with pleasure.

This year, John actually ran for president of the student council in his school. But the opportunity to deliver a real campaign speech, in front of a live audience, aroused his anxiety. He described how he rehearsed the lines of his speech over and over again as he masturbated, imagining the approving smiles on the faces of all the pretty girls who had rushed to sit in the front row of the auditorium so they could be close to him. Every time he reached the peak of his sexual arousal, a resounding ring of applause reinforced his self-confidence.

John was trying to reduce his anxiety by repeatedly combining the fantasy of his well-delivered speech with the reward of his masturbatory orgasm. By making the speech a less fearful and more pleasurable event, he reinforced his expectations of success rather than of failure.

Reducing Fear

People have used masturbatory fantasy to overcome a variety of fears. As they masturbate, they imagine themselves in the situation they fear. By thinking about what they fear while simultaneously experiencing the pleasurable release of masturbation, they gradually cease to be afraid.

A man who had been severely shocked in childhood by a

major operation was able to reduce his persisting fear of it by masturbating while recalling what he had originally experienced. By repeatedly associating his operation with the sexual pleasure of masturbation, the formerly frightening event took on an erotic flavor. As he saw the old trauma in a new context of sexual excitement and gratification, the man helped himself to master his fears.[2]

Sustaining Morale

Because masturbation and fantasy can have positive effects on a person's morale, they can sometimes be literally life-sustaining. People in hospitals or prisons can use masturbatory fantasy to create interludes of physical enjoyment and emotional comfort that help them to feel better while being confined, and also help to sustain their hopes until they overcome their illness or are released. True, their fantasies of health or freedom may ultimately be unfulfilled. But as long as a person can keep his hopes alive, he can feel some zest for his own life and a commitment to maintain it.

During the war in Vietnam, a U.S. naval pilot was shot down over North Vietnam and imprisoned for more than six years in a compound near Hanoi. Deeply religious, and a devoted husband and father, he was almost fifty at the time he was freed. When questioned about how he was able to tolerate the frustrations of his imprisonment, he replied that being able to masturbate and to have fantasies gave him courage during those long and miserable years. "It's important to fantasize in life, generally," he said, "but when you're in prison, it's most important." To endure the hardships of his captivity, he used masturbation to get into fantasy and to carry on a "love affair" with himself, obtaining sexual gratification while he preserved a favorable sense of the worth of his own life.[3]

Most people do not live under such confining or harrowing conditions. They do not have to use masturbation and fantasy as the only basis for satisfying their sexual desires or for feeling good about their lives. Most people have the freedom to fulfill their lives through loving relationships or some activity that expresses their particular interests and talents. However, it is risky to put yourself on the line, to run the risk of failing to accomplish something you want. It is even riskier to face your emotional vulnerability in trying to form a deep relationship with someone else. While taking these risks, people may feel the need to bolster their egos with fantasies of sexual magnetism the worldly achievement.

Bolstering Self-Esteem

People often try to gratify both their sexual hunger and their ambitious strivings by imagining themselves as making love with movie stars or prominent people in other fields. Men and boys frequently report masturbatory fantasies in which they project dreams of glory by imagining a beautiful woman coming on to them because of their success and power. In a very popular fantasy, men see themselves as Hollywood producers who can attract any starlet they desire. Others imagine having sexual relations with several women at once. A man may even go to the extreme of portraying himself as a sheik with a flourishing harem.[4]

Women also imagine themselves as sexually and socially irresistible. In their fantasies, they may be not only gorgeous but also intelligent, sensitive, compassionate, and famous. One woman of forty-five recalls how she used such portrayals of herself even when she was a young child. In her self-glorifying fantasies, she would see herself arousing her kindergarten crush. By imagining that she was the prettiest and smartest girl in the class, she got him to choose her as his partner in all the games they played. All through adolescence, the boys of her dreams clamored for her because of her unique sexual prowess and intellectual maturity. As she grew up, in her fantasy every male's experience with her invariably turned out to be the most thrilling and satisfying sexual encounter of his life. No other female could match her feats of seduction, stimulation, and gratification. Typically, she left her imaginary partners yearning breathlessly for the next chance to make love to her.

Escaping from Achievement and Relationships

Such fantasies often contribute to the pleasure people derive from masturbation. But the respite these fantasies offer can become a problem if people rely on them too often as a way of escaping from the difficulties involved in developing their abilities and their capacity for loving relationships. Some people may "lock" themselves very deeply and chronically into some combination of masturbation and fantasy in an attempt to deny their feelings of inadequacy about their bodies, their skills, their relationships, their ability to compete, or their level of social achievement. They may cling to their masturbatory fantasies with tenacity, seeking to extract from them the reassurance and validation they feel unable to get in their daily lives. In time, their private masturbatory worlds may become an alternative to their public lives, where they have been unable to find the satisfaction they want.

Mike, a recent college graduate, described his persistent indulgence in such a pattern of masturbation and fantasy. He never felt good enough about himself to believe that women he considered attractive and desirable could be interested in him. Although he hoped to have a prominent career in industry some day, he was afraid he wasn't smart enough to apply for the executive-training program in the large New York City department store where he worked as a salesclerk. In talking to us, he expressed his feelings of dissatisfaction with both his job and his social life.

Every Saturday night, he and a few friends from the store went to singles bars, hoping to meet women. To keep up with the other guys, Mike felt he had to get at least one woman's telephone number before the night was over. He was not very discriminating, since he had no intention of following up with an actual call. Instead, he used his brief contact with the women to get material for his fantasies, which he used to compensate for his sexual inadequacy and his inability to pursue the career he really wanted.

Usually, Mike came home tired, a little drunk, and feeling horny. Before falling asleep, he acted out a sexual fantasy with the woman whose number he had gotten. In his recurrent plot, he was the extremely wealthy and handsome president of a multinational corporation. The woman he phoned was sexier and more attractive in his imagination than in real life. Thrilled to hear from him, she readily agreed to join him at his penthouse apartment. As Mike began to touch himself, the woman immediately appeared at his side. She gently removed his hand from his penis and slowly began to soothe and fondle him, making him feel like the most powerful and desirable man alive. Without his having to move a muscle, she stimulated him to heights of passion he had never actually experienced.

Realizing that his fantasies had brought him neither the woman nor the position he wanted, Mike tended to feel even more inadequate after masturbating than before. So he tried to get rid of those feelings in the same way he usually tried to overcome his sense of failure, by going out again and again, getting more and more telephone numbers, and ending up with only one more image for his masturbatory dreams.

Mike's repetitive use of masturbatory fantasy reflects his tendency to avoid taking genuine responsibility for fulfilling his desires, which would have meant changing a lifelong pattern of giving in to his feelings of inferiority. Instead, he rationalized that the women who had given him their numbers would turn him down if he actually called. He was only a salesclerk. Why would any woman want to go out with him? In his fantasies, on the other hand, he could aggrandize himself by playing an important executive whose allure was so great that he needed to give nothing of himself to attract gorgeous women, who were only too eager to take the initiative for giving him exquisite sexual pleasure.

Thus, Mike's extravagant fantasies discouraged him from seeking real success. By building up a grandiose fantasy about himself, which was so discrepant from his actual life, Mike felt that anything he could accomplish in reality—any relationship he might have with a woman, or any job he might get—must fall short of his expectations and would not be worth the trouble

For many people, finding successful solutions to the challenges they choose in life is neither easy nor free of emotional stress. People have to be careful to set goals that they are capable of achieving. Between the conception and the completion of any project, a person will meet many uncertainties and ambiguities. To bring his work to fruition, he must be willing to accept an outcome that may be much less grandiose and perfectionistic than it was in his fantasies.

Some people may feel bitterly disappointed at having to face whatever limitations are reflected in their emerging accomplishments. For a person in this frame of mind, self-expression ceases to be pleasurable. Instead, it may take on an oppressive aspect, something more to be avoided than approached. Reacting in this negative way, people may abandon their activities, or they may discard, and even destroy, their work. Destroying a project or abandoning plans may seem preferable to feeling the pain of achieving something that falls short of their desire for absolute perfection.

However, once the process of self-expression is begun, a person needs the feeling of successful completion; he denies this to himself by abandoning his activity. He now needs physical release from his blocked energy and from his anger with himself; he also tries to find some way of repairing his self-image. Responding to these needs, he may turn to masturbation and fantasy as a means of giving himself immediate and transient relief. But in this motivational state, sexual excitement is not a physical accompaniment to the emotional vitality a person sparks within himself by pursuing a real relationship or working on, and completing, an activity. Rather, he arouses himself sexually in a deliberate effort to overcome the frustrations he feels as a result of stopping himself from fulfilling the original goals he set out to achieve.

One afternoon I was cutting out the pattern for a dress. It was much more complicated and expensive than anything I had worked on before. I wasn't quite fourteen, but I was trying to keep up with my sister, who was twenty-four. Wanting to prove to my parents that I was just as capable as she was, I had begun to sew all of my own clothes.

Letting my mind wander, I felt a thrill of delight in picturing how gorgeous and impressive my new outfit would be. Just then, my scissors slipped, making a huge gash right in the middle of the cloth. Instantly, a familiar craving spread over me—that "wet itch" between my thighs. I wanted to touch myself, just for a moment—just long enough to make it all seem as if nothing bad had happened. But I tried to hold off. I wouldn't give in.

I stared at the fabric. Maybe, if I moved the skirt, I could place the sleeve next to that ghastly cut. But that would make the design go the wrong way. Oh damn! I touched myself for a second, pressing my thighs together, letting them rub just enough to give me a little "rush." Then, a vague sense of anxiety began to gnaw at me.

Oh, God! Nothing I ever did seemed to turn out right. I was hoping to wear that dress to the party this weekend. Now it was ruined. Feeling sorry for myself, I finally gave in. Right where I was standing, I let my hand drop toward my crotch.

As I touched myself, I was in the store where I had bought the material, walking from counter to counter, running my hands along those beautiful bolts of cloth, touching the smoothness of the silk, feeling the rough textures of the tweeds, the crisp taffeta, and the caressing velvet.

Letting my fingertips graze over the surface of my clothing, feeling the hint of flesh through my woolen skirt, I thought of my drawn-out deliberations in the store. Which fabric would be best? Whatever I chose, it had to be smart. It had to be different—but not too unusual.

Moving closer to the dining-room table, I put my hand beneath my slip, drawing it up along my thigh. Very slowly. No! Here I go, giving in again. I didn't want to do it, but . . . . Pulling my hand away, I placed it on my neck, slowly fondling my way down to the opening in my shirt collar.

In the store once again, I went from counter to counter, getting dizzy from the profusion of things that were available. I was in the mood for something floaty and feminine. Maybe I should try silk.

I kept thinking about all the luscious shades of silk as my hand groped beneath my shirt for the comfort of my breasts.

How could I fix the mess I'd made? My nipples tightened, making me reach beneath my skirt once more, stroking softly along the smooth silkiness of my underwear.

The tingle of gooseflesh brought me back to the scene in the store, rekindling my enthusiasm as that amazing bolt of silk caught my eye. What a striking combination of colors! The shades of red were perfect for my complexion.

Glowing with the heat of my fantasied image, I thrust my hips against the dining-room table. Furtively, I bunched up my panties and let my fingers slip inside. God, it felt so good.

The saleslady handed me the cloth. Draping it against my thighs, I admired myself in the mirror, rubbing my crotch unobtrusively. Yes, this was definitely the right one.

Transfixed at the dining-room table, I permitted my fingers to linger a bit longer inside my panties. Flitting up and down along my vagina—circling toward the front—around and around a miraculous spot that suddenly seemed to melt, moistening the tips of my fingers.

It was the same wet gush I had felt in the store. Self-conscious about the dampness in my panties, hoping the saleslady wouldn't notice, I threw the material back on the counter and ran to the other side.

The flush of my excitement increased. Grabbing a scrap of the silk from the dining-room table, I ran into my bedroom. Removing my underpants, I let myself go completely. My fingers combed wildly through my pubic hair. As they penetrated the darkness, my illusions lit up my mind.

Look at that green, that soft blue, that sunny gold . . . and the violet! Trembling, I rushed around the counter, my quivering fingers gliding across the slithery textures of the silk. They were all so magnificent! I wanted each and every one of them. How could I choose? Getting panicky, I almost ran out of the store. But I was lured back by that special bolt of red. It was definitely my thing. I always looked great in red.

There in my bedroom, I stared hypnotically at the scrap of silk that lay shimmering before my eyes. Leaning my weight on my left elbow, I dug my knees into the bed. Pumping and pulling with my right hand, I went on and on in rhythmic thrusts. Closing my eyes, my face twitching, my mouth contorted in a groan.

"I'll take that red silk," I blurted to the woman behind the counter. I was shaking in a frenzy as she wrapped it up and placed the package in my hands. I flew out of the store and hailed a cab. As we drove through the streets of New York, I was magically adorned in the elegant dress I had made. Arriving at the party, I could hear music. As I threw open the door, everyone turned and rushed over to me. I was the center of attention. The boys couldn't wait to reach me. Pressing in, they pushed closer and closer against me, their passion matching my own. Matching the fiery red dress, I was like a volcano, ready to erupt from the heat of my own inner radiance.

Digging my knees deeper into the bed, I pumped and I pulled, harder and harder. Every muscle in my body flexed, I squeezed out the last drop of pleasure until I finally made it! Waves of electricity circled in concentric rings from the core of my being. I floated off, into an infinite space. Drifting out of my body and out of my mind, beyond colors, beyond tensions, beyond thought. Where everything was cool, empty, and white. My lids hung loosely over my eyes. A peaceful vacuum in my groin had replaced that maddening itch.

Shoving the piece of silk away, I rolled over to rest. But a faint queasiness took over and kept me from relaxing. How confused and depressed I felt. Why did I keep doing this?

Dragging back to the dining room, I winced at the brilliance of that messed-up silk. How could I ever repair the damage I had done? I was almost paralyzed by despair. Maybe I should just hide it away in the bottom of my dresser drawer. Forget about it, as I'd done with so many other things. But what would my mother say? I'd spent so much on that material. If I had more time I could redo it. I decided to put it away—for later.

As Sue's example shows, some people create and try to maintain impossible standards for themselves. Reluctant to accept their own limitations, they may actually limit their potential output to a shadow of what it could be. Sue often preferred to do nothing rather than something that seemed flawed in any way.

Although she was doing a good job on her dress, Sue aroused her own anxiety by wanting to produce something more impressive than her older and more accomplished sister could have done. Worried about her actual ability to do that, she began to escape from her work into fantasy, imagining how perfect her dress would be. But how could any real dress compare with the magnificence of the one in her fantasied image? She was bound to feel that anything she could make would fall short of her extravagant desires. Instead of relieving her anxiety, her fantasy only helped to increase it. Seized by that increased anxiety, she let the scissors "slip." Then she had a good excuse not to finish the dress and not to face her limitations.

Once Sue convinced herself that the dress was spoiled, she felt no incentive to go on or try to repair it. Instead of facing her despair and dealing with the motives that caused her to slip, she used her purposeful accident to justify her masturbation and compensatory fantasy. Sue's anxiety was a natural signal that something was bothering her. Her competitiveness with her sister made her tense about placing the pattern so perfectly on the cloth. And wanting so much to outdo her sister made her incapable of evaluating her own work more realistically. Actually, she was able to do a very good job for someone of her age, but her competitive motives led her to strain beyond her level of ability and prevented her from appreciating what she could do.

Because she wanted so much love and approval from everyone, Sue couldn't see that she really was capable of making a dress that would enhance her appearance and gain her some praise from her parents and friends—even if it wasn't the most fabulous dress that was ever created. If she had allowed herself to feel that any dress she made would be nice, she would have been motivated to repair the damage she had done and finish the dress in time for the party. Instead, she tried to banish the reality of what had happened, glory in her image of perfection, and bury her disappointment in a frenzy of sexual self-stimulation.

Even Sue's inability to choose just the right fabric was

another result of her need for perfection. She wanted to avoid making any choice, no matter how good it may have been—because any choice inevitably placed some limits upon her. Yet we all have to make choices and decisions; and the very necessity of choosing among alternatives places an automatic limitation on everyone's freedom.

But within that fundamental limitation, as Sue eventually found later in life, there is still plenty of freedom to find realistic and attainable goals. By giving up the fantasy that it is possible to have it all ways, a person can make the most effective and gratifying use of his freedom and his abilities. Of course, the external conditions of a person's life may severely restrict the range of accomplishments that are realistically open to him. But even under such social conditions, a person can try to find something he is capable of doing. Focusing on what is possible, rather than what is not possible, is the best route to fulfillment and the avoidance of feelings of inadequacy and frustration.

Sue's case is not unique. The drive to transcend all personal limitations is widespread in American society, with its emphasis on endless success. As a result, many people feel it is important to be top dog in whatever they do; they strive to outdo each other in earning money, recognition, status, or anything else that requires individual competence and winning out over other people.[5] But such unlimited and unrealistic expectations inevitably lead to feelings of inadequacy. When such feelings arise, a person may, as Mike did, shy away from contact with any people or situations likely to reveal his limitations, thereby finally settling for much less than he was really able to attain and enjoy.

Expressing Sadomasochistic Tendencies

Of course, everyone has ambitions he has failed to fulfill, and failure is difficult to bear. A person who feels defeated may search for an alternative triumph. This is another reason why people with frustrated ambitions may turn to masturbation and fantasy; it provides a safe and secret way of being defiant or vindictive toward others, or of usurping their power. Thus, the drive to be successful, regardless of its human costs, the desire to beat others in the competitive race for achievement, may be transformed into sadistic masturbatory fantasies of beating or inflicting some form of violence on others.

When someone masturbates as a way of dealing with his hostile feelings toward others, he cannot help but turn his anger upon himself. For he has only his own body and mind to work with. Someone with the opposite need to express hostility toward himself may do it through fantasies of self-punishment. But since a person splits himself up into both the actor and the acted upon during masturbation, he inevitably takes the part of both the sadist and the masochist—both the giver and the receiver of his destructive impulses.

A psychiatrist has described a patient whose method of masturbation, and the fantasies accompanying it, provide an excellent example of this combination of sadism and masochism.[6] When he masturbated, he took pleasure inflicting pain upon himself with a scrub brush. He claimed that this masochistic behavior made him feel more alive. But as he masturbated, he had fantasies of beautiful girls, who were tied up so that he could carry out sexual "things" with them. Those sexual things consisted of pumping water into their vaginas.

The man connected these sadistic fantasies with his mother's practice of giving him enemas when he was a child. By hurting himself while he masturbated, he was taking on his mother's aggressive role and abusing himself just as she had done when she gave him enemas. The women in his fantasies were a symbolic substitute for his mother. By making them helpless, he was trying to make his mother seem harmless; and the pain he inflicted on these imaginary women was a way of getting back at his mother for what she had done to him.

Disavowing Sexual Responsibility to Avoid Guilt

Reich describes the case of a self-deprecating man who masturbated during childhood and adolescence while sleeping in the same bed as his mother. Because of his guilt and his fear of being detected, he masturbated in a very frustrating manner. He squeezed and rubbed his penis, but was careful to hold back his ejaculation. Later in life, it was only when having a masturbatory fantasy of being beaten by his mother that he could have an emission. In his fantasy, he experienced his penis as boiling hot; after it had been hit several times, he felt that it would explode and his bladder would burst open.

The patient came to understand that masturbation made him so guilty that he needed this fantasy of being beaten to bring about his orgasmic release. If his mother's imaginary beating made his penis explode and forced him to ejaculate, then it was she, not he, who was responsible for his sexual gratification.

This man's case shows how a person can induce climax in a roundabout way, making the fantasied punisher responsible for his orgasm, thus exonerating himself. Reich believed that the passive fantasy of being beaten allows people to continue masturbating without guilt and without taking responsibility for their own behavior. By having such a fantasy, it is as if a person is saying, "Beat me so that, without making myself guilty, I can release myself." [7]

Superficially, sadistic masturbatory fantasies may appear to be motivated by opposite needs from masochistic ones. However, when a person imagines hurting others in the process of giving himself erotic pleasure, he may also be seeking to disavow personal responsibility for expressing his sexual impulses. Like Reich's masochistic patient, a sadistically inclined person may hold the objects of his own sexual desires to be responsible for arousing him. Thus, he feels hostile toward his imagined erotic partners and has a need to punish them for having "forced" him to be sexually expressive and to experience the guilt that such sexual expression stirs in him.

As we said, the patient who imagined pumping water into the vaginas of beautiful girls was getting back at his mother symbolically by harming them; but he was also punishing the girls for being the mental stimulus to his masturbation. In this case, it is as if this man were saying to them, "I am hurting you because you are responsible for making me release myself."

This man and Reich's patient are clear examples of severely repressed sexuality motivating sadomasochistic tendencies. However, all people in our society undergo some sexual repression as they grow up, building a reservoir of unconscious sexual desires that continue to press for open expression. While people wish to disavow personal responsibility for having such desires, they still experience a need to gain release from their tensions. They also have a need to be absolved of whatever guilt is stirred up by such release.

Because of these needs, everyone has at least some yearning to have others absorb the guilt involved in expressing his repressed sexuality. As a result, everyone has some sadomasochistic inclinations—which they tend to portray in fantasies of having people seduce them into erotic activities, or of seducing other people whom they find sexually alluring. True, such fantasies may not include such dramatic infliction of pain as in the cases we have presented. However, any seduction is implicitly hostile to some extent, since it is aimed at forcing a person to do something he might not otherwise do.

The prevalent use of sadomasochistic fantasy in our society is borne out by recent studies. Many of those interviewed—both male and female—admitted that their masturbatory fantasies included the expression of varying degrees of explicit violence being inflicted upon themselves and others. Their fantasy themes also centered around having sex when they forced someone else to submit to them, as well as when they themselves were forced to submit to others.[8]

While they may not masturbate in a physically painful manner, some women can arouse themselves only by creating fantasies of being raped or of having no choice but to submit to a man who has complete power over them.

Regina, a psychiatric social worker in her midthirties, told us that, as a child, she always felt masturbation was wrong and should be kept secret. Her mother was very tense about any body contact or physical expression of feeling. She was compulsively clean and made her children feel that their bodies were something to be ashamed of. "My mother was crazy about masturbation and the whole issue of sex. She told me not to do it because I'd get hurt or diseased. It was even worse for my brother, who is now mentally ill and institutionalized. Once, when he had a 'blackout' in high school, she said it was from his masturbation."

Regina never revealed her masturbatory fantasies until she

was in her midtwenties and went for psychotherapy after she and her husband broke up. It has now become clear to her that, in several of her fantasies, she was abdicating responsibility for her sexual feelings and her masturbation.

In one fantasy, she was alone in her parents' apartment. The landlord would come storming in, demanding the rent. To make sure that they would not have to pay it, she "semiresentfully" gave in to his sexual demands. In another version of the same theme, she saw herself in church, praying together with a priest. As she aroused herself by masturbating, she pretended that the priest was putting his hand up her skirt and playing with her while they prayed. Regina could see how unrealistic these fantasies were. She had been brought up in a nonreligious Jewish home. Her family had always been financially comfortable and, since they owned their apartment, they never even had a landlord.

In one of her most vivid adolescent fantasies, Regina was with her father (with whom she always felt she had a "private romance"). They were sitting in the balcony of a theater—"an audience of two"—looking at a glass-enclosed stage. The scene was a classroom, with several seven- or eight-year-old boys. (Her mother was actually a schoolteacher at the time.) Regina saw herself brought in on a stretcher, wrapped up in cellophane. While she remained quietly stretched out, all the boys made love to her. As she and her father watched this scene from the balcony, she saw herself performing fellatio on him.

By imagining herself as having such contact with her father, Regina's fantasy reflected some sense of responsibility for expressing her sexual desires. But she was afraid to take full responsibility for her intensely sexual feelings for her father. And she was equally guilty about arousing herself by imagining such an act—which she never would have initiated in reality. Therefore, she simultaneously portrayed herself as helpless, laid out on a stretcher and wrapped up in a hygienic package, submitting to the sexual advances of boys much younger than herself. The fact that her mother was a teacher, who might have observed such a scene, also represented Regina's indirect way of expressing hostility toward her mother while, at the same time, trying to prove her own sexual innocence. By performing this drama on a glass-enclosed stage, Regina was trying to separate the sexual side of her personality from her self-image of purity and naïveté. Her fantasy represents a typical adolescent conflict between wanting to deny the existence of one's sexual desires and wanting to take some action to satisfy them.

MENTAL MASTURBATION

Some people have developed such strong prohibitions against the physical aspects of masturbation that they renounce the possibility of sexual self-stimulation. However, through fantasy, the impulse to masturbate can be expressed in purely mental terms. Some people who never masturbate physically delude themselves about their purity and remain oblivious to the masturbatory nature of their mental activity. Other people, having given up physical masturbation, often think they've given up its psychological functions as well. Actually, both kinds of people engage in what we refer to as "mental masturbation." [9]

Sometimes, the fantasies used in mental masturbation have an explicitly sexual content and are accompanied by erotic sensations in the genitals. Often, however, the fantasies contain no explicitly sexual imagery; nor does the person creating them experience specific genital sensations. But the grandiose images of nonsexual accomplishment conjured up may give him a generalized feeling of bodily well-being and self-satisfaction.

In mental masturbation, people do not touch their bodies; they use only their minds to caress images of themselves. A person may portray himself in a successful past he never experienced, in a past he regrets and tries to "rewrite" although he knows it can never be undone, or in a glorious future he has no possibility of actually fulfilling. This type of fantasy does not try to solve problems. Rather, the entire aim and effect of a person's mental masturbation is to provide immediate pleasure by aggrandizing himself far beyond the boundaries of his actual life and limitations.

As a child, I saw myself as the very model of a model nonmasturbator. But what does it mean *not* to masturbate? Well, first of all, it means keeping one's hands strictly away from one's genitals. And that's not an easy prohibition to enforce—not as a growing child with growing genitals. Not as a male child, whose blooming cock and balls are hanging out so openly, tenderly, invitingly. Just waiting, yearning, aching to be touched.

But not Saint Irving the Abstainer. Others, ordinary mortals, could touch, pull, rub, tickle, and jerk. But I resisted that fleshy, tantalizing temptation. Leaving my mere body behind, I floated into the lofty cloister of the Mind, intangible, impeccable, and, above all, untouchable.

So I became one of the untouchables. In my mind's eye, that made me very special—a member of the highest possible class. It made me, so I thought, uniquely virtuous.

I gave up bodily masturbation only to become a mental masturbator. I went at it with passionate devotion, pouring into it all the sexual energy I blocked from physical expression. And I lavished on my fantasies the kind of tenderness and appreciation I might otherwise have put into the fondling of my penis.

Of all the ways I found to discharge my masturbatory tensions, none served my purpose better than writing. Of course, not all writing is a sublimated form of mental masturbation, nor are all writers mental masturbators in disguise. But the writer is, by definition, someone immersed in the rarified atmosphere of his own mind. He is permitted, encouraged, and sometimes even rewarded to enter that inner space and to remain within it.

It took me quite a long time to give myself over to the indulgence of writing. I was so drawn to it—wanting so much to abandon myself to it—that I was afraid to let myself get into it at all. I was like a deep-sea diver who is tempted to go on and on, intoxicated by the very vastness of the ocean's depths. Or like an astronaut who is magnetized by the allure of the Universe and who toys with the idea of drifting off forever into its infinite vistas.

Little by little, I overcame my fear. I let myself write more and more, permitting myself to go off regularly alone and privately play with my mind. And I enjoyed that form of play immensely. Since I had made playing with my penis a taboo, I could let myself play openly, at last, with what I had made a phallic equivalent—my mind.

Substituting my head for my genitals, I could freely arouse and stimulate it without anxiety or apprehension. As thoughts arose in my mind, I could gaze with unabashed delight upon them; coddle and cuddle them; draw them out and extend them; modify and polish them; turn them over and over to heighten every nuance of esthetic pleasure and self-appreciation from them. And finally, seizing the fountain pen that symbolized my pen-is, I let my ideas burst forth on paper in inky streams of ejaculation.

When people masturbate physically, they must assume some responsibility for consciously deciding to engage in that behavior. The necessity of arranging the time, the place, and the privacy for physical masturbation forces people into some awareness of what they are doing. Mental masturbation, however, can be carried out under any circumstances—in the solitude of one's room, in the company of a loved one, at school, in the movies, or even on a crowded subway. Because it is so much easier for people to avoid awareness of what is happening when they do not actually touch their bodies, they can indulge in mental masturbation without feeling responsible for it.

Engaged in solitary, boring, and mechanical tasks, many housewives put themselves into trancelike states of rumination, imagining themselves in professional fields far beyond their capabilities. Other people, feeling trapped in monotonous jobs, may envision themselves in situations where they are free to determine all the conditions of their lives.

In itself, mental masturbation is a perfectly harmless and prototypically human form of self-solace. While it may seem futile, it expresses what Eugene O'Neill implied may be a universal need for "pipe dreams," the illusions people maintain solely for the purpose of sustaining their self-esteem. Yet people know, at some level of awareness, that their self-enhancing fantasies are illusory, since they are so unlike the reality and constraints of their day-to-day lives.

Motivated to inflate their self-images by impressing others, people often exchange pipe dreams as if they were sharing information about actual accomplishments or realistic intentions, using one another as mere props to stimulate their mental masturbation. Many people who frequent bars do so for the opportunity to brag about their imaginary prowess and exploits. While they may appear to take seriously the pipe dreams other patrons tell them, they often have no genuine interest in the people they are talking to. Other settings provide similar opportunities for mental masturbation in public. People crowded together at huge cocktail parties, openings for art exhibits, conventions, and professional meetings often use those occasions for an intense and continuous exchange of self-flattering fantasies.

Everyone has an emotional vested interest in pretending to himself that he believes his masturbatory fantasies. For only by believing in them can he use his fantasies magically to endow himself with attributes or achievements he lacks in reality. Understandably, people deeply resist facing the truth of the personal limitations that originally motivated them to create their compensatory fantasies. It is almost as if they fear the loss of something crucial for their morale and social functioning, even though that "something" is no more substantial than a figment of their imagination.

While deceiving himself into believing his fantasies, a person tends to lose sight of what he can really do. Instead of using his energies to work toward attainable goals, he is likely to spend an inordinate amount of time in fantasizing achievements that he cannot possibly attain; instead of accepting the strengths he actually has and building on them, he may fantasize himself as having attributes that can never be his. Thus, he deprives himself of the fulfillments and satisfactions that can only come to a person who does what he is in fact able to do.

Attainable Goals and Insight

Painful as it may be to confront their masturbatory illusions, doing so permits people to gain self-insight, psychological maturity, and a greater ability to enjoy life in the here and now. Of course, the tendency to create such illusions can never be completely overcome, since it reflects an unending and ever-recurrent human need to feel good about oneself and to be deemed worthy in the eyes of others. However, people can learn to recognize their masturbatory fantasies and to use them to resolve their ongoing emotional conflicts.

A person's masturbatory fantasies are symbolic reflections of his self-perceived inadequacies and frustrated desires; they can show him how he is trying to escape from the realities of his life. He can then see the futility of his magical thinking; and he may be better able to accept the fact that no amount of wishful thinking can produce the traits he feels he lacks or the success he yearns for. With that awareness, a person can better put his full effort into making the best possible use of his real endowments, directing them toward realistic objectives. As Professor Jerome Singer of Yale University concludes, after twenty-five years of research on daydreaming: "Even our more fantastic daydreams may . . . point up the incongruity between our current reality and our hopes, thereby giving us a chance to decide on a more effective approach to a life situation."[10]

PART II
Masturbation and Child Development

If he is to become a loving and productive adult, every child needs to develop four basic characteristics of personality:

Understanding and Competence. *A child must learn to understand the value of sexual loving for his own happiness and well-being, and he needs to develop an awareness of how he functions physically and emotionally. He must also learn enough about the world to provide him with the competence and skills necessary to live and work effectively on his own and in society.*

Self-Acceptance and Acceptance of Others. *By developing a positive image of his body, his gender, and his intellectual and creative abilities, a child will feel adequate to love and be loved by others. He will also be prepared to deal with the problems of living, seeking realistic solutions to them rather than blaming himself or others for his inherent limitations.*

Individuality and Relatedness. *A child has to develop a sense of his own individuality, feeling the confidence and self-reliance to separate himself emotionally from his parents and to take responsibility for his own life. At the same time, he must develop the capacity to relate cooperatively with others and, eventually, to form a fulfilling relationship of sexual love with a partner of his own choice.*

Release and Containment. *A child must learn how to release and to contain the tensions generated by his sexual and nonsexual motives. Through release, a person gratifies his needs and desires, expresses his uniqueness, and experiences pleasure and a zest for life. Containment is required to modulate the expression of his impulses and desires in ways that are consonant with his own welfare and that of others.*

Learning how to develop a satisfactory balance between release and containment permits a person to attain the fulfillments of sexual love and personal achievement within the limitations of his society.

Of course, it takes time for these four characteristics of personality to crystallize. They emerge gradually as a child grapples with the particular challenges he is required to face at different stages of his development—for example, weaning, toilet training, separating from one's parents, coping with school and competition, and the onset of puberty.

In the following chapters, we discuss how a child's reactions to such challenges are reflected in his masturbatory activity, and how, in turn, that activity may affect his ability to develop the four basic personality characteristics we have described. At the same time, we show how the reactions of parents to their child's masturbation may help him to meet those challenges in ways that contribute to the continuing growth of his personality.

In reading through these developmental chapters, you have a chance to reconstruct your own history of masturbation, comparing and contrasting it to the examples we present. Naturally, you will not be able to remember your complete masturbatory history. Nor will you be able to use everything you do recall for the purpose of changing your personality. However, you may be able to discover a great deal about how your own childhood approach to masturbation influenced your personality development. You may also see how it is possible for you to continue developing in desirable directions by resolving conflicts about masturbation that you acquired early in life.

If you also happen to be a parent, such understanding and change in yourself could certainly have a positive effect on the children you are rearing. In addition, you may succeed in furthering the development of their personalities by applying what you learn from the guidelines we offer to parents for open and constructive communication with children on the subject of masturbation.

Chapter 3
INFANTS AND TODDLERS

An infant comes into the world as a vibrant sexual being, with deep needs to be fondled and loved. A newborn baby's skin is highly sensitive to the quality of touch; and his entire body yearns to be petted and stroked. Infants may show their capacity for love in an unmistakably sexual manner. Many boys are born with erections. "Having an erection is a natural function," says William Masters in *The Pleasure Bond*. "No man learns to have one; he is born with that facility. As a one-time obstetrician, I can tell you that there's many a baby I've seen with a full erection before his umbilical cord was tied and long before he got around to nursing. . . ." Because their genitalia are much less obvious, it is difficult to detect similar signs of sexual arousal in baby girls. But, Dr. Masters claims, "There's not a woman . . . who didn't lubricate in the first twenty-four hours of life. It isn't something she had to learn. It's simply that sex is a natural function like breathing or eating."[1]

Love and sex are naturally interwoven in the fabric of human functioning. From the beginning of life, a person is immersed in feelings of sexual love. The very conception of a child involves sexual intercourse between a man and a woman; when their intercourse is freely desired, it reflects the most intimate expression of love that people can share.

Women who go through natural childbirth often compare the emotional "high" of their delivery to the sexual feelings they experience when they have an orgasm.[2] Some women who previously had difficulty experiencing orgasms report that they developed the ability to have orgasms after they had given birth to a child.[3] In fact, there are many similarities in the physical and emotional aspects of birth and the female orgasm.[4]

Nature contributes to this phenomenon by providing a hormone that aids both processes. This beneficial hormone, oxytocin, is secreted during childbirth, stimulating the muscular contractions of the mother's uterus during delivery and helping it to return to its original size after the baby is born. Oxytocin also facilitates a woman's uterine contractions when she has an orgasm, and its secretion is essential for the release of a mother's milk during breast feeding.[5]

When a newborn infant sucks at his mother's breasts immediately after delivery, their interaction is a perfect illustration of the harmonious physiological and psychological reciprocity between mothers and their offspring. The infant's sucking not only enables him to feel the emotional comfort of his mother's sensuous warmth and nurturance, but it also helps his digestive and respiratory systems to start functioning properly. At the same time, the baby's sucking gives comfort to his mother, too, by stimulating an increased flow of oxytocin throughout her system, which causes further uterine contractions and hastens the readjustment of her internal organs to their normal condition.

Since there is a definite physical and emotional similarity among the feelings that can be aroused in a woman by intercourse, birth, and feeding—the three processes essential to conceive, deliver, and sustain life—it is only natural for a woman to feel sexually "turned on" to her own baby.[6]

Although a man cannot directly experience the joy of childbearing and breast-feeding, the actual conception of his child is proof of a man's capacity for procreation. Surely, a man can feel as validated as a woman by holding in his arms a life that he has helped to create.

The reciprocal aspect of the love that flows between men and their offspring is exemplified by the fact that fathers, too, can get deep sensual satisfaction from playing with and caring for their babies. Through the physical expressions of his love and his participation in the care of his infant, a father can satisfy his need to be tender and nurturing.[7] He can reexperience the sensuality of the loving relationship he once enjoyed with his own mother—or he can experience it for the first time, if it was missing in his own infancy.

The importance of warm, loving, parental care cannot be overestimated. It aids in the adjustment of the baby's respiratory, digestive, circulatory, and neurological systems, helping him to adapt to the world and increasing his chances for survival. Intimate tactile contact has a positive effect on both the physical and mental rates of a child's growth; it enhances his motivation to explore and learn about himself and his environment, increasing his ability to be more socially responsive as he matures. Loving acceptance of an infant is also likely to foster his ability to trust others and to acquire a basic sense of emotional security.[8] By accepting their baby's masturbation as a natural expression of his need for love, parents can help him to acquire a positive, lifelong orientation toward sexual loving as a holistic integration of erotic and affectionate feelings.

UNDERSTANDING AND COMPETENCE
Infant Self-Stimulation

A baby's desire for sexual self-stimulation blends with the satisfaction of his innate curiosity about himself and the world. Just as that curiosity motivates him to reach out and touch the objects around him, it also leads him to explore his own body. Soon he discovers that he can create extremely enjoyable bodily sensations by himself. While in his crib playing with a toy or examining the texture of his blanket, an infant may accidentally rub those objects between his legs. Sensing how good it feels, he gradually learns that he can use such things to stimulate his own sexual pleasure. Then he may pick up a toy for the specific purpose of squeezing it against his genitals, often moving it or himself rhythmically to heighten his gratification.

While being bathed, many babies discover the erotic possibilities of contact with water, the wash cloth, or the tub itself. One mother told us how her baby girl loved to rub the bath sponge against her genitals. Another mother said her infant daughter loved to place her pubic area against the stream of water as it ran out of the faucet. Baby boys often enjoy sliding back and forth on their bellies, rubbing their genitals against the smooth surface of the tub.

Parental care inevitably contributes to a baby's awareness of the pleasure that can be derived from the genitals. While parents change their infant's diapers, their tactile contact—however brief and emotionally neutral—helps the baby to localize sources of pleasure in his body.[9] Considering how often one cleans and washes an infant, one can see how much genital stimulation he gets from his caretakers. An infant may also be erotically aroused as he is carried about from place to place; and he may try by himself to duplicate the caressing rhythms he experienced while being swayed in his parents' arms or while being pushed in a carriage.

As they get older and begin to crawl or walk, babies become more and more familiar with the objects and people around them. Moving from room to room, touching and experimenting with all sorts of things around the house, they discover new methods of masturbation. Toddlers of both sexes learn to attain sexual pleasure by rubbing their crotches against the legs of furniture or even against the leg of another person. One sixteen-month-old found that she could wrap her legs around a post of her playpen and stimulate her genitals by pulling her body up and down on it. If taken out of her playpen, she would toddle over to the leg of a chair or table and repeat the same behavior.[10] Other toddlers soon discover the special joys of riding on the rocking horse and may spend long periods of time arousing themselves sexually as they rock.[11]

Because of their need for nourishment and their innate sucking reflex, infants immediately discover that their mouth and lips are a major source of sensual pleasure. As a baby sucks on his mother's nipples, he is stimulating one of the most erotically sensitive regions of her body. But his sucking also stimulates a similar and reciprocal arousal of erotic pleasure in himself. Researchers have found a close relationship between the arousal of erection in baby boys and the normal function of feeding. Strong sucking arouses the reflex for erection,[12] and this relationship between sucking and genital sensations appears to exist for baby girls, too.

When Deborah's daughter was about six months old, she frequently put her hand on her crotch and softly rubbed her genital area while she was nursing, smiling contentedly at the experience. Deborah's son also started to fondle his genitals at about the same age when he was being breast-fed. At that time, he didn't actually take his penis in his hand and rub it rhythmically, as he did later on when he started walking; but he did press on it frequently and move it about while he was nursing.

Quite apart from using their mouths during feeding, many infants spend hours sucking on their thumbs, fingers, rattles, pacifiers, or anything else they can find. Freud regarded this type of "pleasure-sucking" as the earliest expression of infantile sexuality, a satisfaction totally independent of the purpose of feeding. He felt that intense and rhythmic thumb-sucking can produce physical reactions of mounting tension and release similar to those experienced during orgasm. Because babies often combine pleasure-sucking with rubbing other sensitive parts of their bodies, such as their breasts and genitals, Freud concluded, "It is by this road that many children go from thumb-sucking to masturbation." [13]

In using their hands to explore their own bodies, babies soon find other openings that yield great pleasure when they are stimulated. For example, an infant may put a finger into one of his ears. Finding that it feels good, he may continue to probe it intensively, with a concentration similar to the kind he shows in sucking.[14]

But the erogenous regions between an infant's thighs offer even greater enticements for tactile self-stimulation. The genitals far surpass all the other erogenous zones in erotic sensitivity. Since the tissues involved in the baby's normal toilet functions are also directly connected with the ones forming the genitals, babies are erotically stimulated in the very process of elimination. So it is natural for them to learn that their genitals are ideally suited to pleasurable self-stimulation. Once they have learned that, they are inclined to center their masturbatory activities on their genitals.

Some babies begin to masturbate regularly when they are only one or two months old.[15] Others start at a later age. Of course there are individual differences; and some babies may show no signs of masturbatory behavior at all. But most babies engage in some form of genital self-stimulation by the end of the first year of life.[16]

Genital masturbation during infancy is not only normal, but it also helps a baby to make the mental connections between his desires, his self-initiated activity, and his reactions to it. Masturbation helps the baby to understand that when he performs a particular action, he will have certain corresponding sensations. Because those sensations are so enjoyable, he learns how to control and coordinate his actions to produce the specific effects he desires. So in addition to his other sources of learning, the baby's own sexual stimulation helps him to understand that his behavior can *cause* certain definite *effects*. In this way, masturbation contributes to his dawning awareness of his ability to get what he feels is good for himself; and it helps to provide him with the sense of competence he needs to cope with the problems of his developing life.

Parental Reactions

Parents can confirm their baby's perceptions about masturbation and reinforce his growing ability to recognize the effects of his own behavior. By accepting his masturbation and acknowledging how pleasurable it is, they show their baby that the erotic sensations he feels are also regarded as good by them. This acceptance reassures the baby about the accuracy of his own reactions to his personal experiences, encouraging him to continue exploring the objects of his curiosity, including his own body.

Unfortunately, some parents simply repeat the harsh treatment they received, imposing on their own children the same threats and punishments that their parents imposed on them. Having had their own hands slapped as a deterrent against masturbation, they may automatically slap the hands of their children when they masturbate.

Such blatant punishment for infantile masturbation is no longer as widely practiced today as it was when masturbation was considered a physical and moral evil by both medical doctors and the general public. Now, parents who feel like stopping their babies from masturbating are likely to do so by diversionary rather than punitive tactics. For example, they may quickly replace a diaper on a naked infant who has begun to touch his genitals while being changed; or, they may entice the baby to withdraw his hand by offering him a toy. Other parents may simply take hold of the baby's hand, as if expressing an affectionate feeling, and proceed to remove it—ever so gently and subtly—from his genitals; or, they may engage the baby in a game of pat-a-cake, diverting him from his sexual play with himself.

Such methods of distraction are certainly not as emotionally shocking to a baby as direct and hostile punishment. Still, a child knows where he stands with openly punitive parents: he has no doubt about what they want of him and what their attitudes are toward self-stimulation. The baby who is distracted, however, receives no such clear message. Instead, he is subjected to a psychological state of mystification, which reflects the ambivalence of his parents. By not calling negative attention to his masturbation, his parents appear to be accepting it. Yet by distracting him from masturbation, his parents indicate that they are not accepting it. So the baby is uncertain about what they really want him to do with his masturbatory urges. Should he have them at all? If so, should he express them? When and how should he do so? Distraction is so devious an approach that it doesn't even permit a child to bring such doubts into focus or to resolve them. By never calling attention directly to a baby's masturbation, parental distraction encourages him to refrain from dealing with sexual questions as he grows older in a way that could satisfy his curiosity about them and increase his understanding.

Similarly, some parents find it difficult to adopt a frank and straightforward acceptance of their baby's genitals, referring to them only when it is absolutely unavoidable. At such times, they may use a vague and indefinite "it" or "down there." [17] Alternatively, parents may attempt to desexualize their baby's sex organs by giving them "cute" names: a boy's penis becomes a "wee-wee" and a girl's vagina becomes a "poopy." Parents may continue to use such babytalk long after their children are past infancy.

In these ways, parents may discourage their baby from learning about his own sexual functioning. Brian Sutton-Smith, a leading child psychologist, has observed: "If a child concludes that his sexual behavior and feelings—even his genitals—are taboo subjects, never to be mentioned, he will find it difficult to understand these matters." [18] Without realizing it, by obscuring their baby's understanding of his sexuality, parents may also be squelching his motivation to understand many other aspects of his functioning. Babies and toddlers who feel it necessary to avoid sexual curiosity may suffer from a corresponding lack of curiosity and interest in the world around them, impairing their spontaneous enthusiasm for learning.

Many parents have told us that they grew up with all sorts of misconceptions about their masturbation and their sexual functioning. As a result, they felt confused and inhibited when they wanted to express their adult feelings of sexual love. These parents are often eager to avoid making the same mistakes with their own children. Understandably, they may find it extremely difficult to overcome the insidious effects of their negative childhood experiences. As one mother said, "It nearly drove me crazy to do it, but my doctor told me just to let it pass. So I did." [19] Another young mother confessed to us that she avoided making any comments to her babies about their masturbation because she didn't want her own guilt feelings to come across to them. Although she never did anything to stop them, she kept on wondering if she was *supposed* to do something about it. "Do I let it go—as I do—or should I say *something?* I want to do the right thing, but I don't know what that is. It's still so taboo. None of the parents I know ever talk about it."

Fortunately, with sufficient motivation to change, it is possible for parents to give their children more positive orientations to masturbation than they acquired in their own childhood. Deborah and her husband, Jan, are examples of contemporary parents who have tried to avoid transmitting their own parents' negative attitudes toward masturbation. Although they both grew up in very puritanical environments, they are trying to rear children who delight in, rather than fear, the expression of their capacities for sexual love.

Jan spent his childhood in Switzerland, where his father was the stern principal of a Calvinist school. Every night, Jan's father came into his bedroom for an "inspection," making sure that he had his hands outside of his blankets. To keep them warm, Jan would have preferred to put his hands inside the covers. That way, he could also fondle his genitals—which was, of course, exactly what his father wanted to prevent. Eventually, his father's intensely negative attitude toward masturbation, and his nightly vigilance in enforcing it, made Jan feel acutely guilty.

Having rebelled against his father's prohibitions long before he met Deborah, Jan was determined to prevent his own children from experiencing the guilt about masturbation that had plagued his own childhood.

Deborah was raised in North Carolina in an equally repressive atmosphere. All through her adolescence and early adulthood, she continued to believe in the preachings against masturbation that she had learned in the religious training of her childhood. She grew up feeling very inhibited, deprived of both masturbation and sexual play with other children, and she was unable to masturbate to orgasm until she was over twenty years old. Before she met Jan, Deborah had begun to realize how much her sexual inhibitions were costing her in terms of her ability to enjoy life. When she came to New York to live on her own, she sought the help of a psychotherapist, hoping to undo her fear of expressing herself sexually. By the time she married Jan, Deborah shared his determination to bring up children who would have a positive attitude about their masturbation and their feelings of sexual love.

While she was changing her personal orientation toward sexual expressiveness, Deborah had a dream that had a profound and decisive impact on her. In that dream, she was an infant once again. While her mother was changing her diaper, Deborah tried to shove a stuffed toy elephant into her vagina. She could see the yellow, flowered print on the elephant very clearly. Suddenly, her mother seized the toy and threw it away, making Deborah feel that she was doing something very, very bad. Some time after this dream, Deborah actually asked her mother if she ever had a toy fitting that description; her mother told her that she did, indeed, have just such an elephant when she was a baby.

Of course, Deborah could not recall the admonitions against masturbation that her mother may have expressed when she was an infant in diapers. However, she did realize how deeply oppressed she had been by her mother's negative feelings about masturbation, feelings that she had picked up very early in her life. As a result of her self-insight and her relationship with Jan, Deborah was able to react very differently to her own children; and she talked glowingly about their sexual explorations as well as her delight in watching them. When her babies masturbated, Deborah wanted them to know that *she* knew what they were doing and that it was fine. So she acknowledged her awareness of the babies' behavior and feelings by telling them, "I know that feels really good. It's nice to touch yourself."

SELF-ACCEPTANCE AND ACCEPTANCE OF OTHERS
Self-Image

In exploring and fondling his own body, an infant gradually builds a mental representation of its form and function. This bodily image becomes a crucial and lasting component of a baby's sense of himself.[20] By deriving pleasure from his self-stimulation, a baby begins to perceive his body in favorable terms. By seeing his body as a source of joy, he can experience himself as somone who possesses the capacity to satisfy his needs. Such awareness enables a growing child to develop a sense of personal adequacy and faith in himself. Eventually, as his interpersonal relationships evolve, he can approach other people with the same acceptance and confidence that flows from his positive body-image and his acceptance of himself.

According to Dr. Mary Calderone, Director of the Sex Information and Educational Council of the United States (SIECUS), parental attitudes that affirm the joys of sexual self-stimulation can help a child to develop a favorable sense of his own body.[21] But the ability of parents to convey positive feelings depends on how they feel about their own bodies and bodily functions. For example, one study of patterns of parent-child interaction showed that mothers who enjoy their own bodies and the experience of sexual intercourse tend to have more favorable and permissive attitudes toward their children's masturbation and their expression of sexual curiosity. In contrast, mothers who have anxious concern about their bodies and their sexual functioning tend to be less accepting of their children's masturbation and sexual behavior.[22]

As Alexander Lowen, a psychiatrist who follows Reich's approach, has noted, parents communicate their own sexual attitudes through the direct physical contact they have with their babies. "The quality of physical intimacy between mother and child reflects the mother's feelings about the intimacy of sex. If the act of sex is viewed with disgust, all intimate body contact is tainted with this feeling. If a woman is ashamed of her body, she cannot offer it graciously to the nursing infant. If she is repelled by the lower half of her body, she will feel some revulsion in handling this part of the child's body." [23] Lowen claims that infants of mothers who are afraid of intimacy will sense that fear. They may interpret their mother's fear as a rejection of themselves. So such babies may develop fear and shame about their own bodies and their normal bodily functions.

Similarly, Wardell Pomeroy, a sex therapist who was an associate of Kinsey's, says that a child continues to absorb his parents' attitudes about their own bodies and sexual functioning until he leaves home to start his own adult life. For example, when a father covers up his penis with a show of embarrassment if he happens to be in the presence of his young toddler, he is communicating a lack of acceptance of his own genitals, whether he realizes it or not.[24]

Gender Identity

Sexual self-stimulation and self-observation are significant factors in the formation of a baby's image of his sexual identity.[25] Actually, an infant begins to acquire a sense of his gender from the moment of his birth, as a result of both his own perceptions and the way his parents respond to him, and that sense of being a boy or a girl grows as the child develops his capacity to process information about his anatomy and the responses of others to him.

A boy's penis is clearly observable. An erect one is even more apparent, and a boy can explore its range of appearances by stimulating it himself. At the same time, he experiences a variety of feelings that go along with his self-stimulation. Over time, he learns to connect what he does with what he sees and feels. These connections lead him to develop a stable mental image of his penis and the feelings its stimulation can arouse, even when he is not directly observing or touching it.

Baby boys begin to "see" themselves as individuals with an

appendage protruding and hanging from the body: something that is extremely sensitive to touch, that can get bigger and smaller, and that moves around whenever they crawl, walk, or shift the position of their bodies. The genital movements that accompany a boy's bodily movements can create erotic sensations. Very often, a baby boy's awareness of the involuntary erection and detumescence of his penis is discovered as he acquires the ability to walk and as he gains mastery over his voluntary bodily movements in an upright position. So sheer motility may contribute to a boy's sexual self-image.[26]

Because a baby girl cannot so directly observe her genitals, it is not as easy for her to develop a mental image of their appearance. In fact, even doctors often find it difficult to determine, while observing a baby girl, which part of her genitals she is actually stimulating. Of course, girls also develop an awareness of the pleasurable sensations that emanate from their genitals when they touch them. But their visualization of just where those feelings are coming from is bound to be more uncertain.[27]

Girls have to poke and to probe their genitalia in order to learn about them. Sometimes, they may go to great lengths to get a visual image of their genitals. Deborah's daughter was an exceptionally active and agile baby. When she was only six months old, she loved to crawl across the floors without her diapers on. Often, she would stop, sit up, and spread her legs wide apart. Bending her head way down between her legs, she would try to get a good look at her genitals. Most of the time, she lost her balance and fell over. But whenever she could remain sitting up, she rubbed her vagina with a very pleased expression on her face.

Although a baby girl may lack clarity about the visual aspects of her genitals, she can develop a tactual and kinesthetic awareness of how it feels when she touches her clitoris or the lips of her vagina; and this awareness of the differing sensations she derives from manipulating those areas becomes an enduring part of her self-image.

Thus, at an early age, baby boys and girls begin to evolve perceptions of themselves as sexual beings with a specific sexual gender. As they grow, the details and complexity of their sexual self-images reflect the developmental changes that occur in the appearance and functioning of their genitalia and its surrounding organs. In the second year of life, babies crystallize a clearer picture of themselves. As an integral part of that process, they may become very active in exploring their bodies. Consequently, there may be occasions when a toddler is exceptionally preoccupied with genital play and stimulation.

Dr. Eleanor Gallenson and Dr. Herman Roiphe have made careful observations of babies in a research nursery at the Albert Einstein College of Medicine. They found that boys and girls between the ages of fifteen and twenty-four months normally experience heightened genital sensations and awareness, engaging in increased genital handling and frank masturbation. They attribute this increase to the maturational changes that occur in a baby's mental awareness and in his ability to exercise muscular control over his bladder and bowel functioning—even if his parents have made no direct attempts at toilet training.[28]

Effects of Parental Disappointment

Strong parental preference for a child of one sex may create problems of gender identity for a baby of the opposite sex, which can have a very negative effect on his ability to accept himself. Sometimes parents are so committed to their prenatal wishes that they remain emotionally resistant to completely accepting the reality of their baby's sex. While they may name and rear the baby in a manner that is culturally appropriate to his gender, they may subtly continue to communicate their disappointment to him.

As a reaction to the conflicting messages that are communicated to him, an infant may try to avoid contact and involvement with his genitals. It is almost as if such a baby correctly reasoned that his genitals were the principal criteria of his sexual gender. By shunning his genitals, he minimizes his own and his parents' attention to their existence, thus coming as close as he can to denying his sex and to satisfying his parent's wish that he be other than what he is. This may give the baby the sense of pleasing his parents and keeping them from being reminded of his actual gender. But his own sexual suppression prevents a child from acquiring a favorable image of his own body and from enjoying its erotic pleasures.

Irv was finally able to trace his inhibitions about masturbation to the fact that his mother had hoped he would be a girl instead of a boy. He sensed her wish as a rejection of what he was, so he tried to accommodate her by not stimulating or paying attention to the parts of his anatomy that defined his gender —his penis and testicles.

For her part, Irv's mother delighted in keeping his hair in flowing curls and letting him hover about at her side until he was old enough to go to school. It was only after he was an adult on his own that Irv could question his mother about his childhood and confirm the fact that she had, indeed, wanted him to be a girl.

Renouncing his genitals meant a renunciation of the sexuality of his body and of any pleasure he could take in stimulating it. As a result, as he grew up, Irv shifted the locus of his self-stimulation to his mind, using his imagination to fantasize situations in which he could be an all-powerful male in social, intellectual, and creative pursuits—but never in explicitly sexual ones. In that way, he cultivated and retained his gender identity as a male, while avoiding the erotic implications that go with maleness. So while submitting to his mother's wishes through sexual abstinence, he defied her by secretly affirming his desire to be the boy that he was.

Other children, like Sue, react in the opposite way when they feel they do not meet their parents' expectations. Rather than refraining from masturbation, she got into it intensely; and her pattern of sexual self-stimulation shows how she was motivated to use extremely private and secret masturbatory activity to compensate for the unconditional love and acceptance that she felt she did not get from her parents. As far back as Sue can remember, she always realized that she was an unwanted child—"an accident." She also knew that if she had to be born at all, her mother would have definitely preferred a boy.

Sue's early masturbation represented an attempt to retaliate against her mother's disapproval of her gender. Even if everyone else in the world disapproved of her because she was a girl, she would at least give herself the love and acceptance for which she yearned. Wanting so much to be the boy her mother desired, she even adopted a position for her repetitive masturbation that could be considered "masculine," lying on her stomach and pumping her pelvis against the mattress, as if having intercourse with someone lying beneath her. Later, Sue showed her conflict about being a girl by having masturbatory fantasies of being a man who was making love to a woman. And it took her a long time to accept herself as a person who was worthy of love, although she was "only" a female.

Since a baby is able to discover a great deal about what it is like to be a boy or a girl from his or her genital self-explorations, it is particularly important for an infant to feel free to explore and stimulate his own body without guilt or inhibition if he is to develop a positive image of his gender. A baby who learns that every part of his body is good—including the particular genitalia with which he happened to be blessed—is likely to develop a feeling of desirability, which later helps him to feel good about both giving and receiving sexual love.

Many parents tend to perceive their baby girls as less sexual than their baby boys. Dr. Margaret McHugh, Assistant Professor of Pediatrics at New York University Medical School, told us that parents seem to be less upset by their sons' masturbation than they are by their daughters' masturbation. She also found that even young, college-educated parents tend to deny the sexual nature of infants of both sexes. While some of these parents agree, theoretically, that infants have sexual needs and feelings, they are likely to see their own babies as exceptions.

Seeking to help parents develop more informed and positive attitudes toward their infant's sexual anatomy and functioning, Dr. McHugh carefully examines the baby's genitals in front of his parents, during her first contact with the newborn infant. She shows the parents all the details of the male and female genitalia, identifying them by their proper names and explaining their functions. She tries to break down the stereotyped attitudes that parents may have about the differences between boys and girls, emphasizing the sexual nature of *all* babies.

Dr. McHugh continues to include this type of genital examination as a routine part of her regular infant check-ups. As the babies develop more self-awareness, she identifies the details of their genital structures for them as well as their parents. She even has the toddlers feel their own genital parts as she labels them correctly. If a toddler is capable of talking, she encourages him to repeat the words after she says them.

Children react very positively to this approach. Dr. McHugh feels that her type of routine examination helps a baby to accept his sexual organs and functions as a natural part of his life. Through such experiences, a toddler becomes relaxed about having a doctor look at and touch his genitals; and in his later development, if the need for it should arise, he will be less fearful of medical examinations of his genital region. Dr. McHugh particularly emphasizes the desirability of this type of examination for little girls. It helps them to understand the complex nature of their genitals and reassures them about their normalcy. At the same time, it creates a positive attitude that prepares girls for the frequent pelvic examinations they must have as they mature.

Parents may also benefit greatly from sharing this experience. Both mothers and fathers can rid themselves of old fears and misconceptions about the male and female genitals and improve their feelings about their own sexual functioning. They can then approach their baby's sexuality in a more accepting and less fearful manner, helping him to gain increased self-acceptance.

INDIVIDUALITY AND RELATEDNESS

The close, loving, and reciprocal involvement between a newborn child and his parents characterizes the kind of emotional relationship that helps him to feel good about being alive. Because of its deep gratifications, both parents and children are inclined to cling to their mutual attachment. However, to become capable of functioning happily as a separate and mature individual in his own right, a child needs to give up the intensity and exclusiveness of his original attachment to his parents. For their part, parents can assist in their child's individuation by giving up the depth of their attachment to him.

Naturally, both the child and his parents may find it difficult to go through the process of emotional separation, and that process is likely to extend throughout all the years of child development. But as they succeed in letting go, they reap its benefits as reciprocally as they once enjoyed their symbiotic attachment. Thus, a child acquires the ability and confidence to form loving relationships of his own choice and to fend for himself in the world outside his parental home; and his parents gain the satisfaction of seeing him fulfill his potentials, just as they have fulfilled their own.

Weaning

Weaning a baby is a major step that parents take in the long process of helping their child to acquire a sense of self-sufficiency. But weaning also tends to be a stressful process, since it breaks the reciprocal cycle of pleasure that an infant has been sharing with his mother since birth.

So when a baby is required to give up sucking as a mode of gaining nourishment, he may feel acutely frustrated. For he loses not only the erogenous delights of sucking but also the emotional closeness of being cradled lovingly in his mother's arms. Reacting to such frustrations, an infant may begin to suck more frequently on his thumb or other objects. He may also begin to masturbate more avidly, seeking to give himself the kind of genital stimulation and gratification he naturally experienced while sucking on his mother's breast or on a bottle. Or he may do both—suck on things more and masturbate more.

In most cases, these reactions to the frustrations imposed by weaning tend to pass as a child reconciles himself to the permanent change in his mode of feeding and as he receives praise and social rewards for learning new ways of eating and drinking. Some children, however, seem to fight a rearguard action against weaning. They may try to cling to their bottles, and if they are already inhibited about touching their genitals, they may develop a tendency to use oral self-stimulation as a substitute for genital masturbation.

Since masturbation is one of the first self-fulfilling activities that an infant initiates without outside help, it can help him to become self-reliant and responsible for his own feelings. Thus, it is one of the first and most important means by which a baby begins the long struggle to become psychologically independent. A baby masturbates as an autonomous and independent person, expressing and satisfying his own desires. The resulting gratification rewards him for acting independently and for being who he is, and he can take pleasure in his separateness, with his own particular body, mind, and gender.[29]

Encouraging or Discouraging Self-Reliance

It is important for parents to validate their baby's individual existence, confirming his intrinsic goodness, his ability to care for himself, and his right to fulfill his own needs. Having been validated in that way by his parents, a child is better able to validate himself; when he is alone he can look inward and hold himself to account for what *he* thinks and feels. Through this kind of self-validation, a child gains confidence in his ability to give and receive validation in relating to others.

When parents disapprove of a baby's masturbation, they deny his right to have and to express his own needs. Implicitly, they regard and treat him as a mere extension of themselves; they force him to react to himself the way they want him to feel and behave. In that way, parents can discourage their child from developing a sense of himself as a unique individual who deserves to gratify his feelings of sexual love and whose desires are worthy of respectful acceptance by others.

By stifling their baby's need to masturbate, parents may also make him feel afraid to satisfy his own needs in other areas of his life. Fearing to be self-reliant, such a baby may find it difficult to relate to strangers, and he may experience great anxiety about being separated from his parents, even for very short periods of time. The more negatively parents react to a baby's self-stimulation, the more inadequate he may feel about his ability to cope with his own life. As a paradoxical result, he may want to masturbate more frequently than he might otherwise have done, in order to give himself solace and reassurance.[30] Reacting against such attempts, his parents may further squelch him, making him feel less capable of gratifying his own essential needs.

It is often agonizingly difficult for parents to know exactly how much responsibility to give their baby in dealing with a specific aspect of his life. A great deal of trial and error is involved in developing the delicate balance between meeting a baby's needs and meanwhile encouraging and permitting him to learn how to satisfy his own needs. But masturbation is an activity for which a baby must assume full responsibility from birth onward. And nobody on earth—not even his parents—can possibly get inside a baby's being to tell him when he feels the desire to masturbate or how he should enjoy doing it.

Because they may be unaware of their motivation to cling to their babies as love objects or as a substitute for their own sexual gratification, some parents may stimulate their babies in a seductive manner. Kathy, a woman in her late twenties, has no recollection of childhood masturbation. For several years after she was married, she was unable to experience an orgasm through intercourse with her husband. It wasn't until her mid-twenties that she allowed herself to masturbate; and it was only through masturbation that she was finally able to learn how to have an orgasm. Although she has no memories of masturbating as a child, Kathy does remember that she was an ardent thumb-sucker; and she clearly recalls how her mother used to rub and rock her buttocks as she lay face down in her crib. While her mother rocked her, Kathy experienced erotic feelings in her genitals. Her mother kept up this habit of rocking Kathy to sleep until she was eight or nine years old, and Kathy continued her habit of thumb-sucking until she was twelve.

Curious about whether she had ever masturbated as a toddler, Kathy recently asked her mother if she had ever seen her doing it. Her mother told her that she had seen her touching her genitals as a baby; but she had distracted Kathy by putting a toy in her hand whenever she touched herself. As a result, she prevented Kathy from fulfilling her own needs through masturbation. In this way, Kathy was kept dependent upon her infantile habit of thumb-sucking and on her mother's sexual stimulation. Because of this dependency, she remained emotionally tied to her mother all through her childhood. When she reached adulthood, Kathy discovered that she had not learned to fulfill her own needs, and she could neither masturbate nor respond orgasmically in a relationship of sexual love.

RELEASE AND CONTAINMENT
Orgasmic Capacity of Infants

As an indication of their needs for sexual stimulation and gratification, some infants seem to masturbate with the specific intent of giving themselves orgasmic release. Babies as young as four months have been observed having masturbatory orgasms; and they are capable of putting forth a great deal of concentrated effort to achieve a sexual climax. Sweating, flushing, panting, and grunting, an infant may get almost blue in the face on his way to an orgasm. Sometimes a baby may grimace or develop a fixed, glassy-eyed, far-away stare. He may also appear oblivious to everything around him and react with extreme annoyance if anyone tries to interrupt his activity. After his climax, he may look pale, exhausted, and perhaps fall off to sleep.[31]

Dr. Milton Levine, a pediatrician with many years of experience, has noted that there is a difference between a baby's genital play, or the mere pleasurable stimulation of his sexual organs, and real orgasmic masturbation. Dr. Levine writes that "the greatest satisfaction and certainly the occurrence of an orgasm during masturbatory activity is dependent to a large degree upon repeated manipulations which have a specific rhythmic form." [32]

Researchers at the Kinsey Institute have observed baby boys while they were masturbating to orgasm. Although they were less than one year old, their orgasmic behavior was strikingly similar to that of mature men, except, of course, for their lack of an ejaculation. As they approached orgasm, their tension mounted visibly. Rhythmically thrusting their pelvis back and forth, their convulsive spasms at the point of climax were sometimes accompanied by weeping and by wild thrashings of their arms and legs. After they reached climax, their erections subsided and they lapsed into a calm and peaceful mood.[33]

Just like older children and adults, babies may use their masturbatory orgasms to release pent-up tensions that they are unable to discharge in other ways. A baby's orgasmic experiences may further enhance the value of infantile masturbation as a rehearsal for his subsequent functioning in sexual intercourse. Having frequently experienced the physical and emotional release of a masturbatory orgasm as a baby or toddler, a person may find it easier to let himself go and have a similar orgasmic release when he grows up and eventually makes love with another person.

Parents often have difficulty in accepting the fact that their babies are actually capable of having and wanting such intense orgasmic experiences. In the past, even physicians have been known to mistake the orgasmic spasms of masturbating babies and young children as symptoms of epilepsy or some other type of neurological disorder.[34] Of course, not all babies who masturbate actually stimulate themselves to the point of orgasm. Babies differ widely in their inclinations; while a baby is born with the capacity for orgasm, he may not feel motivated to use it until some more mature stage of his development. Orgasmic reactions among infants may be more the exception than the rule.

But masturbation—with or without an orgasm—is a perfectly wholesome expression of a baby's sexuality. Stekel found that children who masturbate frequently are often healthy, energetic, and intelligent.[35] Similarly, Dr. Levine has written that many of the most active masturbators among his patients had beautiful bodies, with good posture and excellent muscle tone.[36] Another pediatrician, Dr. Harry Bakwin, having seen many infants whose parents were worried about their masturbatory behavior, reports there is no reason to believe that infantile masturbation leads to disturbances later in a child's life.[37]

Learning Self-Control

Of course, every child must learn how to contain his sexual impulses as well as how to release them. Eventually, children do have to adapt to social customs and laws that punish the display of sexual behavior in schools and other public places. So parents have to teach their children about containing their masturbatory impulses, as they become old enough to understand its necessity and capable of exerting such self-control. Meanwhile, before a child has to learn such social prohibitions, his parents need not be concerned about imposing them on him. In general, as Reich has said, a child's own inherent capacity for sexual self-regulation is the best guide for the expression of his masturbatory inclinations. Parents who trust their children to be self-regulating in the sexual area may also be helping them to learn how to govern themselves in all other aspects of their lives.[38]

Inevitably, babies are also required to contain the tensions of the nonsexual needs that they cannot immediately gratify either by themselves or with the aid of their parents. Sometimes, a baby may be troubled by the discomforts of a beginning illness, which has not yet erupted in a fever or other obvious symptoms that his parents can readily detect or do anything to relieve. Or he may suffer from the emotional distress of being prevented from playing with objects that might hurt him.

Thus, while learning how to be emotionally expressive, babies must also learn how to be patient, to tolerate frustration, and to modulate the release of their emotions in ways that are not destructive to themselves or others. A baby who has no doubt about being loved and who has enjoyed the freedom to regulate the gratification of his own masturbatory desires is best prepared to tolerate such inescapable nonsexual tensions and frustrations. Naturally, he may protest, cry, or become temporarily enraged when he is in pain or cannot have something he wants. But he is less likely to lapse into long periods of emotional withdrawal or despair than a child whose parents have not given him the feeling of being securely loved and who have greatly inhibited his masturbatory behavior.

Chapter 4
EARLY CHILDHOOD

I was lying in the dark. Pretending to be asleep. Waiting. Faint noises creaked in the hall. Was that him? I thought I felt something brush by. And Daddy was coming, too. He always came home from his long business trip on Christmas Eve. A faint line of light glowed on the stockings we'd hung from our closet door. I had to beg Mommy to give me one of her real long silk ones. It had a run but it would hold more than mine. How I hoped Santa would bring me lots of goodies. That song about him was still ringing in my ears. It had played on the radio all day long. I couldn't stand it. Where were they? Maybe if I "did it" they'd get here sooner.

Does Santa really know if I've been bad or good? I've been a good girl, haven't I? Even though Mommy yells so much. Good enough for him to bring me a new bike. Can Santa really see if I'm awake? What if he knew what I was doing? But it feels so-o-o-o good. How can anything that feels so good be bad?

No! Santa can't really see everything. That's only make-believe! Daddy doesn't know what I've been doing, either. He's never said anything to me about it. Would Mommy be mean enough to tell?

Was that the door? I wriggled and squirmed in my bed. Wondering what I'd get. Slowly, gently, I rubbed myself. It felt delicious. Better than all the Christmas candies. But as I rubbed, I got more and more confused. Was my sister trying to say that Santa was really Daddy? That couldn't be! Then why did she hang up her stocking? I couldn't understand. I was getting so itchy. Rubbing faster and faster. Oh, where were they? Slowing down a little. I didn't want to miss the first sound of footsteps. But I had to go deeper and deeper under the covers. I sure didn't want Santa to catch me!

It was so warm and cozy under there. With my nightie pulled all the way up, I could stroke my bare chest and stomach. The sheets were so silky against my skin as I slid back and forth along the length of my bed. Oh, how beautiful. I felt as pretty as the doll I'd asked for when I was sitting on Santa's lap.

My hands tingled along the inside of my thighs. My fat round bottom magically melted away. I was the graceful, twirling ballerina dancing around that huge department-store window. Pressing my fingers between my legs. Sliding and pulling. Back and forth. More and more. I was twirling and twirling. Faster and faster. My ruffled skirt flying out like puffs of cotton candy in the wind.

Suddenly, a noise startled me. Footsteps? The floorboards in the long hall squeaked. Oh, God! He was coming . . . he was coming! Who would it be? I was so excited I almost wet myself. But no, I wouldn't do that! I was a big girl. Quickly pulling my hand away from my legs, I inched my way up to the top of the bed and put my head back on the pillow as if nothing had been going on. But I kept the blankets tightly clasped about my face so I could hide what I'd been doing from Santa.

Yes, that noise was definitely footsteps. It sounded just like Daddy, when he came down the hall at night to tuck me in and give me a nice big hug and kiss. But never on the lips. Even though I aimed for his. He always told me it wasn't healthy for people to kiss on the mouth. They could catch germs. Silly! Daddy couldn't have any germs. He was such a good, clean man.

I could see the shadows. Someone was coming. On tippy, tippy, tiptoes. So quiet and still. I didn't dare to budge. The shadows stretched out, getting bigger and bigger, fuller and darker. It must be Santa with his big belly and bushy beard. And his jolly face! I could see him hopping down the hall, all dressed in red, carrying his sack of wonderful toys. Oh, I couldn't stand it! I just had to give myself one more juicy little squeeze before he hopped into my room. With all those covers, he'd never see.

I shut my eyes very tight as I squeezed myself once again—really good. Streaks of bright red flashed behind my eyelids. And rings of white fur swirled around. It must be Santa! But I was afraid to look. I was supposed to be asleep. Or he wouldn't leave anything.

But how could I resist? Slowly, I opened my eyes. Just enough to take a safe little peek. The red and white was gone.

It was all black. Could he leave so fast? I looked toward the door where the stockings were hung. Was that a hand lit up by the crack of light? I thought I saw a hand. And maybe an arm. An arm covered with the thick rough sleeve of Daddy's overcoat. And there were the ripples of his wavy hair wiggling in the shadow on top of the closet door.

No, I didn't really want to see. I closed my eyes again—tight, tight, tight. I couldn't look anymore. But I heard sounds of scratching paper mixed with the shuffle of footsteps. And then it was all gone.

Opening my hopeful eyes, I searched the wall for some sign. Was that lump over there my new doll? And those crazy shapes stretching across the door—could it be the shadow of a tricycle? Rolling over on my belly, I grabbed myself again. Yes, I grabbed and I grabbed and I twisted and squirmed. It didn't matter now. It was all over. No one would see.

Daddy got here first. But maybe Santa would still come. No, he wouldn't. My sister was right. But see—Daddy always remembers. He's much, much better than Santa. Yes, Daddy always remembers, even when he has to work so hard. Pumping and pulling, I laughed and I cried. Not caring what happened anymore, I let myself go. It was feeling better and better down there. Wonderful. I was sure Daddy brought me some beautiful presents from his trip on the road. I could see myself in the morning. Ripping open the packages. Reaching down into that long stocking. Tasting my sweet candy treats. Running into Mommy and Daddy's room. Crawling into their bed. Pushing Mommy out of the way, I'd snuggle up close to Daddy. Giving him a big, wet, welcome-home kiss—right on the lips. And I'd show him everything that Santa had brought.

Understanding and Competence

Sue's four-year-old Christmas fantasy illustrates the veritable explosion of mental capacities that children experience during this period of development. Nobody actually knows precisely when and how toddlers shift from being unaware of the workings of their minds to being aware of them. Typically, however, that alteration becomes dramatically manifest between the ages of two and five, as children develop the ability for representational thought. After that development, children can visualize and manipulate images and words that symbolically represent people, places, objects, and events with which they are not in direct contact.[1] When a child *realizes* the existence of his own ability for such mental representation, he has taken the most important developmental step in his whole life. That realization makes it possible for him to use his mind deliberately, and to develop a sense of personal responsibility for the ways in which he uses it.

While they are hatching their minds, children also experience a flowering of physical competencies, enabling them to translate their thoughts and intentions into purposeful action. They learn to walk steadily and then to run; to use their hands with agility and precision; to coordinate their sensory perceptions with their bodily movements; and to articulate their mental states through the use of spoken language. Consequently, they can do what they want with ever-increasing effectiveness.

As they improve their ability to speak fluently, children can communicate better not only with others but also with themselves. They can now conduct private, upsoken dialogues, similar to Sue's—inner conversations with themselves in which they can reflect on their experience, evaluate it, and learn from it to change their subsequent behavior. Thus, children inevitably bring their emerging sense of self-awareness to their masturbation; they can no longer masturbate without connecting themselves in thought and fantasy to what they are about to do, are doing, and have done.

Adding Fantasy to Masturbation

When children first discover their imaginative skills, they may revel in the creation of fantasies for the pure joy of "making believe." In their play with each other, they often act out and verbalize the content and flow of their inner scenarios. In the same period, children learn that they can "play with themselves" while they play with their minds. Then, they can purposely use the psychological activity of their imaginations to embellish the sensual pleasures of their physical masturbation.

Children also learn to use their masturbatory fantasies to obtain emotional release from the tensions and anxieties of growing up. The contents of a child's masturbatory fantasies reflect both his prevailing desires and the ways he would like to satisfy them.[2]

Sue's scenario shows how a child's fantasies may portray the imaginary gratification of all of his needs. She used masturbation as a means of getting everything she wanted for Christmas, letting her mind range freely to supply her with the parental love and approval for which she yearned, the material things she craved, and the various roles she aspired to play. And while her mind was doing her bidding, so were her hands.

A child's ability to masturbate independently and to give himself intense physical and mental pleasure cannot help but impress him with the fact that he is actually doing something he wants to do—all by himself. As he repeatedly chooses to masturbate, he inevitably realizes that he must also be the one who is creating the particular fantasies he has at that time. Of course, a child may frequently feel unwilling to accept full responsibility for the fact that he makes the decision to masturbate and to spin his own fantasies. Sue attempted to justify her masturbatory behavior to herself as a magical way of getting both Santa and her father to arrive sooner. And even as she tried to convince herself that she had drifted into it unintentionally, she controlled it as long as there was a possibility of being discovered when Santa or her father came. However, as soon as Sue felt she could no longer be caught, she abandoned herself completely and wholeheartedly to her self-stimulation—showing the level of mental sophistication and duplicity she had already mastered.

Sources of Guilt

Theoretically, knowledge of his own responsibility for his masturbatory activities need not be oppressive to a child. On the contrary, his full acceptance of that responsibility could greatly accelerate the growth of his emotional maturity and enhance his enjoyment. However, as the conscious awareness of his own thoughts and feelings increases, a child also acquires the ability to judge the thoughts and feelings of others. Perceiving the reactions of others toward him, a child learns what is considered right and wrong, and what is socially expected of him; and he begins to evaluate himself in the light of those standards. Thus, a child gradually forms an enduring conscience of his own.

Unfortunately, many children seem to pick up negative parental attitudes toward masturbation very early in their lives, just as Sue did. Once adopted by the child as his own, such disapproving attitudes are bound to arouse feelings of guilt whenever he stimulates himself sexually. Reacting to his guilt, a child is inclined to keep his masturbation a secret from his parents and everyone else.

There is another profound source of guilt that children learn to associate with masturbation: the social prohibitions against their incestuous feelings. Typically, a child's psychosexual maturation at this age arouses his sexual interest in his parent of the opposite sex. Simultaneously, he tends to experience feelings of rivalry toward his parent of the same sex. Freud felt that this matrix of feelings—the Oedipus complex—has an instinctual basis, as indicated by the taboo against incest that prevails in all societies throughout the world.

Children may express the entire mixture of their Oedipal feelings in a single masturbatory fantasy, as shown by Sue's imaginary desire to jump into her parents' bed and push her mother aside so she could snuggle up to her daddy and give him a big, wet kiss right on the lips. Fearing the disclosure of their incestuous wishes, children tend to be very secretive of the masturbatory fantasies that portray them. Often, it is their Oedipal desires, rather than the purely physical aspects of their masturbation, that stirs the most acute guilt among children.[3]

Motivated by their instinctive and intensifying needs for sexual love, children generally go on masturbating despite the guilt that blights its enjoyment for them. Although she worried about being "bad" because she masturbated, Sue's behavior clearly shows how much she wanted to continue masturbating. Realizing that her mother strongly disapproved of masturbation,

Sue sought to keep herself safe from punishment by hiding her masturbatory practices. At the same time, Sue's secrecy was also her indirect way of defying her mother's prohibitions.

However, Sue's secretiveness spoiled the pleasure of her masturbation, since it reinforced her guilt and her sense of inadequacy about feeling unable to confront her mother with the hostility she felt toward her. Such spoiling of one's own enjoyment illustrates how a person can use masturbation to take out on himself the anger he is afraid to express directly to others. By crimping his own pleasure, a person punishes himself for engaging in a taboo activity—and for having taboo thoughts.

No child is immune to feeling some concern about the incestuous and hostile content of his masturbatory fantasies. A child of four is already capable of recognizing the intent of such fantasies; and he cannot help but anticipate some retaliation for his desires. In some cases, this guilty concern, rather than causing children to stop masturbating, may actually stimulate an increase in masturabtion and fantasy. Through such increased masturbation, some guilt-ridden children may try to reassure themselves that their genitals are still intact and capable of giving them sexual pleasure.[4]

However, the more a child masturbates to relieve himself of guilt about it, the guiltier he is likely to become. Eventually, the cycle of guilt and fear of parental retaliation may become so oppressive that a child finds it too harrowing to go on masturbating. Or a child may feel completely overwhelmed by guilt stemming from the incestuous wishes that motivate his sexual desires. So, as Irv did, a child may refrain from even *beginning* to masturbate; and he may vigilantly repress and inhibit his masturbatory inclinations throughout childhood, suffering chronically from sexual frustration.[5]

Understandably, children may want to avoid or deny the pain of guilt arising from their masturbation. Nevertheless, guilt is in some ways a helpful emotion, since it signals a person's failure to follow his own standards of right and wrong; an enduring conscience is essential to everyone's social functioning and personal well-being. A child learns his standards of right and wrong from his family and society, but once he adopts the moral values of his culture, he is in a position to monitor his own behavior. In that way, he avoids suffering social punishment and ostracism, while gaining social rewards and approval. And when a society's moral codes stress the ideals of love, kindness, and cooperation between people, a child's adoption of them motivates him to be helpful and considerate toward others.

However, if children experience too much guilt from masturbation, they may be unable to enjoy their own sexual stimulation; eventually, their negative attitudes about sexual behavior may undermine their ability to enjoy sexual relations with others. According to John H. Gagnon, the author of a text on human sexuality, one of the lifelong sources of uneasiness about masturbation stems from the fact that it is begun at a very early period of development. Because masturbation is the first form of sexual conduct, and usually done in secret, a child cannot check either his particular way of masturbating or his reactions to it against a common set of standards that affirm and support the activity. As a result, Gagnon states, masturbation "easily becomes a source of guilt and anxiety—guilt and anxiety that spread to other forms of sexual conduct." [6]

As their guilt increases, children experience an increasing need to relieve themselves of its painful effects. Fortunately, that need can be met through open communication with loving and compassionate parents. By being accessible to *whatever* their child may wish to communicate about his sexual feelings and behavior, parents can provide him with a crucial means of reducing his guilt over masturbation. By unburdening himself to his parents while receiving acceptance from them, a child can learn that his masturbatory activities are normal and commonplace among children. A child who receives such understanding and acceptance is likely to grow up feeling competent to express himself sexually to partners in his adult loving relationships.

Learning about Sexuality through Masturbation

After becoming aware of his own ability to give himself erotic gratification, a child is likely to become exceedingly curious about everything connected with masturbation. Do other children experience a similar desire to do it? Do they do it the same way as he does? How do they feel about it? What do they imagine while they're doing it? And what about his parents— is it something that grown-ups do, too?

A child's own masturbation can be an excellent starting point for helping him to satisfy his natural curiosity and to develop a greater understanding about his own and other people's sexual functioning. What could possibly provide a child with a more vivid and concrete example of sexual experience and behavior than his own masturbatory experiences? After all, through their bodily self-explorations, children start their sex education long before they can possibly ask questions about sex.

Unfortunately, however, many parents are inclined to deny or minimize their child's masturbatory activity, refusing even to acknowledge its pleasurable aspects. Parents are often afraid to make *any* reference to the erotic feelings that either stimulate or are aroused by their child's masturbation—let alone discuss and explain them. Robert Sears, Eleanor Maccoby, and Harry Levin, psychologists who did a study on child-rearing practices, report that they "did not encounter anyone who helped the children identify the *emotional* states related to sex." While parents would refer specifically to their child's feelings of anger or emotional upset when he acted aggressive or unruly, "none, as far as we could tell, said: 'You're feeling sexy, that's why you're acting like that.'" [7]

Ironically, the same parents who are willing to teach a child how to identify and cope with his aggressive impulses shy away from helping him to do the same with his loving feelings and sexual desires. By failing to confirm the pleasurable qualities of his sexual feelings and behavior, parents miss a crucial chance to validate their child's own powers of perception.

Similarly, parents have told us they are reluctant to communicate with their child about what may motivate him to masturbate or what goes on in his mind when he does it. Even such parents as Deborah and Jan, who openly accept their children's masturbation and acknowledge its pleasure, hesitate to talk to them about the mental aspects of their self-stimulation. One mother, who admitted her own curiosity about the psychological component of her child's masturbation, claimed that she did not want to pry too much because she was trying to respect her son's integrity and right of privacy. Another said that she didn't want to "put thoughts" into her child's head.

Yet most mothers are willing to let their children spend hours being influenced by the exploitative values and destructive behavior often shown on television. While he watches TV passively, a child absorbs its canned fantasies, which may stimulate him to masturbate more than he does when he is participating in some active form of play or learning. In fact, many mothers have told us that their children often lapse into masturbation as they are watching television. Dr. Ava Siegler, a child psychologist, told us she has heard young boys state: "I have a funny feeling in my penis when I watch TV." According to Dr. Siegler, the content of the material a child sees need not be erotic in nature to produce erotic feelings in the child. Children may sometimes react sexually to aggressive stimuli as well, or may use masturbatory activity to comfort themselves and reduce the intense anxiety aroused by seeing people hurt and killed.

As a result of a virtual conspiracy of silence among parents in dealing with the subject of childhood masturbation, most children have little choice but to rely on their own bodies and their private fantasies for sexual information and understanding. In the course of their masturbatory experiences, children often do try to visualize how they will ultimately be able to function sexually with others. Of course, many children inquire about sex during their mother's pregnancy or when a new sibling is born. The fact that parents can bring life into the world is an impressive demonstration of their sexual powers; their children are inclined to take an intense interest in the marvels of procreation.

But even if a child and his parents remain mute about sex, he has within himself an experiential basis for understanding the mystery of procreation. Just as masturbation may lead a child to crystallize his awareness of the incest taboo and the sexual morality of his society, it may pave the way for his understanding of the sexual facts of life. According to Alice Balint, a psychoanalyst, his own "genital excitation is the child's first clue to the solution of the secret." The pleasure a child derives from his own sexual organs during masturbation "dimly but definitely guides the child toward reality." A child may be further guided by experiencing his own genital arousal while watching his parents kiss and give physical demonstrations of their affection for each other. So children begin to suspect, from empathy growing out of their own erotic feelings, that there is some connection between the pleasurable sensations in their own genitals and the process of making babies. "Children want to partake, somehow, in the pleasures which adults give each other. But what can this good thing be? Their guesses mostly concentrate round the fact . . . that the parents sleep together. The secrecy that surrounds the doings that take place in a bedroom enhances curiosity still further. Children have no doubt that what is kept so private from them must be something agreeable, and they imagine it on the pattern of pleasures known to them." [8]

Dr. Mary Calderone agrees with Alice Balint that a child's masturbation can be both a stimulus and an aid to the development of his understanding about intercourse and conception. In fact, Dr. Calderone has recently written that parents should point out this relationship to their children, thus giving them a positive attitude toward their own capacities for procreation and sexual pleasure. "At various times in their early years, when children show interest in learning about how babies begin, develop, and are born, parents should help their children make the connection between the process of reproduction and the process of sexual pleasuring that their children have already discovered for themselves." From this point, Dr. Calderone believes it is easy for parents to go on and explain that, although people may continue to masturbate throughout their lives, "eventually they will probably prefer to experience sexual pleasure with another person." [9]

Self-Acceptance and Acceptance of Others

Infants and toddlers learn to feel good about themselves by stimulating pleasurable sensations in their bodies. But as they develop further, young children can use fantasy deliberately, to create gratifying and self-enhancing images of themselves while they masturbate.

In her fantasy, Sue tried to compensate for the negative picture she had developed about herself. While her hands fondled her body, her mental illusions fondled away her large buttocks. As she felt herself becoming as thin and graceful as a ballerina, her mental imagery gave her some of the emotional sustenance she needed to maintain her sense of personal worth; her simultaneous physical pleasure reinforced the good feelings she was mentally creating about herself.

As an integral part of such a morale-boosting process, a child may interpret the erotic functioning of his own genitals as an indication of his inherent goodness. From the time he could talk, Deborah's son expressed such a reaction to the sexual excitement of his penis. Whenever he masturbated, he felt that his penis became erect because he had been doing something good to it. "When I'm nice to it," he said, "my penis feels so happy it stands up."

Similarly, when Deborah's daughter was three, she started to smell her fingers after she masturbated, taking pleasure in the odor of her genital secretions. Sometimes, she would rub her vagina, and then hold her fingers up for her parents to smell. Recalling how fearful and inhibited she had always been about stimulating herself sexually, Deborah was very pleased by her daughter's spontaneous and self-accepting gesture. So she responded positively to the child's little game, smiling with approval and letting her know that she was offering her mother a pleasant experience. Sometimes, Deborah also added a comment about how nice a body her daughter had.

Body Image: Girls

Since masturbation is a vehicle through which children develop their gender identity, it is desirable for parents to react to their daughter's genital self-stimulation in ways that encourage her to feel good about being the sex that she is. The accepting response that Deborah gave her daughter, for example, shows how parents can help their little girls to develop positive feelings about both their kind of genitals and their masturbatory activities.

However, many mothers have not developed either the insight or the self-assurance about their own sexuality to follow Deborah's example. Jessie Potter, a faculty member of the human sexuality program at Northwestern University's School of Medicine, is quoted in Nancy Friday's book about mothers and daughters as giving this ironical summary: "If we can repress and police a young girl enough about her genitals, she'll never find them. Even if she does, she is going to have had so many negative messages, she will have been anesthetized from knees to belly button. After we've taught her that part of her body is so awful you can't even call it by name, that it smells bad and she'd better not even look at it, then we tell her she must save it for the man she loves. Women must be pardoned for being less than enthusiastic about such a gift." Thus, Nancy Friday concludes: "After such denigration of the vagina, is it surprising that so many little girls look at their brothers enviously? He has something in that area we do not." [10]

Fortunately, social attitudes toward girls are gradually changing for the better; and many parents—including fathers—are becoming aware of the importance of helping children of both sexes to feel equally good about their bodies. One such parent, who was trying very hard to get rid of his sexual stereotypes, is described in Warren Farrell's book on male liberation. That father, a participant in a men's consciousness-raising group, told fellow members about an incident in which he had to reply to his daughter's curiosity about the genital differences between females and males. One day, while he was bathing her and his older son, she asked why she didn't have the same thing between her legs as her brother. The father answered, reassuringly: "You have a *fun* spot there."

This man admitted he was taken aback by his daughter's question; and he also felt he had been too self-conscious when he answered her. "I think it showed—I think kids pick these things up." But still, he did communicate an accepting attitude toward her. "I've heard some parents tell their children 'You don't have one because you're a girl,' without mentioning what they *do* have. At least when I said, you have a fun spot, she could view her anatomy as a *positive* thing—something she could do something with and enjoy just like a man can with his penis." [11]

This parent made an excellent start in giving his daughter the emotional foundation for a favorable self-image and a positive attitude toward her sexual gender. He could also have used the occasion to give her more detailed information about her genital anatomy and her sexual feelings. Then, he could have given her further validation and acceptance by pointing out that girls can have as much fun by touching their sexual parts as boys can by touching their penises.

Unfortunately, until very recently, girls have been widely regarded as being less sexually excitable, and having a weaker sex drive, than boys. Many women remember feeling that something was wrong with them when they masturbated during early childhood. They thought masturbation was something that only boys do. Many of these women feel that the negative self-image and guilt they developed as a result of such childhood misconceptions impaired their subsequent ability to enjoy adult sexual intercourse.

However, from all the scientific evidence now available, it is clear that girls and boys have an equal need to give themselves sexual gratification. So it is important for parents to help their children to learn that girls have as much desire to masturbate as boys—and that it is just as permissible for girls to masturbate as it is for boys.

Body Image: Boys

Boys tend to have as many questions and concerns about their genitals and their masturbation as girls do. Having a penis is no automatic guarantee of happiness and self-assurance. In fact, when a boy of this age observes that girls have no penises, he may worry about losing his own. According to Dr. Benjamin Spock, it is commonplace for children of this age to "get mixed up and worried about the natural differences between boys and girls. If a boy around the age of three sees a little girl undressed, it may strike him as queer that she hasn't got a penis like his. He's apt to say, 'Where is her wee-wee?' If he doesn't receive a satisfactory answer right away, he may jump to the conclusion that some accident happened to her. Next comes the anxious thought, 'That might happen to me, too.' " [12]

Karen Horney reports that some girls may interpret the fact that they have a "hole"—but not a penis—as proof of having injured themselves through masturbation.[13] Boys may arrive at a similarly false conclusion: if they masturbate, they may lose the penis they have. A boy's castration anxiety may also be aroused by his fear of retaliation for the incestuous fantasies that accompany his masturbation.

A boy's fear of genital injury, however, may not always lead him to surpress his masturbatory urges. Sometimes, it may actually motivate him to masturbate in an effort to assure himself that his penis is still there and can function properly. One boy, who attended a nursery set up to do naturalistic studies of child development, attempted to give himself this kind of reassurance. "Once when looking at a hole between a doll's legs and talking about his awareness of the sexual difference, he started to masturbate and then ran into the bathroom to urinate." [14]

Of course, telling any boy that masturbation will hurt him physically or make his penis fall off is bound to make him fearful. Both sons and daughters of this age could be helped by getting clear, undistorted, and unbiased explanations about the sexual anatomy and functioning of boys and girls—and about the naturalness of their desire to masturbate.

At this stage, boys may also become very curious about how their penis functions—especially about the erections they get when they touch it. Why does it get so hard? How can it get bigger and smaller . . . and bigger again? One mother told us that her two boys were able to discuss such questions with their father. As a result, he and his sons felt they had "very special things" to talk about, increasing the closeness and trust of their relationship. At the same time, the information they got from their father made them feel more self-accepting and less anxious about their masturbation.

Sex Play

Wanting to explore and feel good about their developing sexuality, children of this age may seek confirmation of their own sexual experiences not only from their parents but also through sex play with their friends. Children often carry their sexual concerns with them into nursery school, where, by talking and relating to other children of their own age, they try to validate the information they have received from their parents or picked up on their own. Since both boys and girls usually use the same toilets, they have an excellent opportunity to exchange sexual observations, facts, and opinions. According to the nursery-school teachers we interviewed, sex play and discussions about sexuality are a daily occurrence in nursery school bathrooms. Often, children of both sexes look unabashedly at each other's genitals and share their reactions about them.

Parents have also described their children's sex play to us in considerable detail. One mother recalled how her four-year-old son and his three-year-old female playmate loved to amuse themselves by repeatedly pulling down their bathing suits. The boy always had an erection to show the girl. Later, when the same boy was attending kindergarten, he came home and told his mother that the girls in his class kept pulling their pants down in front of the other children. Joking about it with his mother, he remarked, "They're just like 'flashers.'"

Although some parents are now quite permissive about the sex play of their children, many of them continue to frown upon such activities. Certainly, outside the acceptance they receive in some nursery schools, children are still likely to encounter a lot of disapproval if they attempt to engage in sex play where their parents—or other adults—can observe them.

One nursery-school teacher said that the parents of her pupils semed more worried about sex play between boys and girls than they were about masturbation. Mothers of girls tend to be more worried than those of boys. Many parents are also upset by the thought of their children having sex play in secret. Yet it is the parents' own negative attitudes toward sex play that often leads their children to be secretive about it.

However, A. S. Neill, the founder of Summerhill, an English school based largely on Reich's theories of sexual love, feels: "Heterosexual play in childhood is the royal road . . . to a healthy, balanced, adult sex life." He believes, in fact, that a great deal of adult impotency and frigidity may stem from interference in the heterosexual play of early childhood.[15]

Neill's belief has found some indirect support in the laboratory studies of Harry Harlow, an experimental psychologist. Harlow separated baby monkeys from each other, depriving them of the opportunity for the sexual experimentation, play, and posturing in which young monkeys ordinarily participate. He found that those monkeys were unable to engage in sexual intercourse when they matured.[16] Commenting on such findings, John Money, a leading researcher on human sexual development, has written: "It is almost certain that human beings, like other primates, require a period of sexual rehearsal play in order to ensure the maturation and manifestation of functional mating behavior during puberty and later." [17]

Thus, sexual exploration between children may help them to establish some realistic basis for anticipating the behavior involved in mature sexuality. These playful experiments can also give children an accurate image of their own and other people's genitals, permitting them to feel more secure in relating to the opposite sex when they grow up. Finally, by learning directly from children of both sexes that they share erotic urges, sensations, and gratifications similar to his own, a child may feel less guilty about his emotional involvement in sexuality and about his masturbatory activities.

RELEASE AND CONTAINMENT
Toilet Training and Eroticism

From birth onward, a child is taught by his parents to gratify his natural impulses in ways that conform to the norms of the society in which he lives. In infancy, weaning is a prime example of how parents socialize their children to meet cultural expectations. However, a child's socialization rapidy accelerates in early childhood, when he is ordinarily expected to be toilet-trained and to refrain from masturbating in public.

Like weaning, toilet training is another inevitably frustrating discipline that a child must go through to develop greater self-sufficiency and personal autonomy and to adapt to society's demands. But gaining control over the muscles involved in urinating and defecating creates a great deal of preoccupation with body parts closely connected to the genitals. As a result, children become increasingly susceptible to erotic arousal and the desire to stimulate themselves sexually. Thus, masturbation may become more frequent at this age either as an enjoyable by-product of toilet training or as a release from its frustrations.

Many mothers have told us that their children masturbated most often during the stage when they were learning to use the toilet. While she was being trained, one little girl took the opportunity to stimulate her genitals whenever she sat on her potty chair. Deborah also observed that her son tended to masturbate in connection with urinating. Indeed, because of his early association between toilet training and erotic arousal, a child may learn to make the bathroom a haven for his masturbation, as Philip Roth showed in *Portnoy's Complaint*.

For boys, the penis, is both a sexual organ and a channel for urine. The internal pressure to urinate can be felt as erotically arousing. Besides, every time he urinates, a boy has to touch his penis, which inevitably stimulates its erotic sensitivities.

Similarly, girls may also experience sexual arousal from a full bladder; and since a girl's urethra is very close to her clitoris and vagina, she may also experience erotic sensations when she urinates.

According to Karen Horney, girls are often jealous because a boy can hold his penis while he urinates, giving him an "excuse" to indulge in masturbation, which many girls feel they do not have.[18] But while a girl does not have to touch her genitals while she urinates, she does have to touch them afterward, when she wipes herself. Girls may find that wiping as sexually stimulating; and they may give themselves some extra sexual pleasure during the process. Of course, in wiping themselves after defecating, both boys and girls have an equal opportunity to brush against and erotically stimulate their genitals.

Some parents may lead a child to believe that the main function of his genitals is for going to the toilet, and that those parts are not clean and should not be touched, except during elimination. Parents may also try to distract a child from masturbating by asking him if he has to go to the toilet whenever they see him touching his genitals. Naturally, when they are being toilet-trained, children may often clutch at their genitals because they are trying to "hold in" their urine—not because they are seeking sexual gratification. However, according to Sears, Maccoby, and Levin, "If a child is told not to touch his genitals because they are 'dirty' from going to the toilet, or if he is sent to the toilet whenever he is seen holding himself, on the assumption that he needs to eliminate, he may attach to sex some of the emotions he feels in connection with toileting: for example, disgust. Or, when sexually stimulated, he may experience anxiety that will be reflected in disturbances in toileting activities." [19]

Sometimes, a child may so resist toilet training that he develops a generalized and lasting rigidity in his pelvic region—the kind of "body armor" that Reich found in so many of his sexually repressed patients.[20] Because he becomes extremely reluctant to "let go," such a child can enjoy neither bowel movements nor masturbation. This blockage of his own erotic impulses leads him to fear that they will burst forth uncontrollably. So he tends to repress himself still more, increasing his painful and debilitating burdens of sexual tension.

Sears, Maccoby, and Levin found that mothers who had a high level of anxiety about their own sexuality were inclined to toilet-train their children both very early and severely—and they were not permissive in regard to their children's sexual behavior. These mothers seemed to keep their children under rigid control and to demand conformity to mature standards of behavior. They tended to use physical punishment fairly often, to be strict about noise and table manners, to emphasize that their daughters be "feminine" and their sons "masculine," and to be quite cold, emotionally, toward their children.

By contrast, less-anxious mothers were more permissive about toilet training and had a relaxed attitude toward their child's pleasure-seeking, they were aware of their child's needs to express himself; they generally rejected the use of punishment as a form of control; and they were willing to tolerate less mature forms of behavior in the areas of sex, aggression, and dependency.[21]

However, it is important for parents to know the difference between helpful permissiveness and potentially harmful overindulgence. In this area of child-rearing, as in all others, a balanced blend of gentleness and firmness is needed to help a child master the socialization of his biological drives. Such mastery is generally not acquired without a good deal of opposition from the child. But parents are also likely to feel somewhat ambivalent about helping their children to become more autonomous, since a child's movement toward autonomy increases his psychological separation from them.

So the process of toilet training often arouses feelings of separation anxiety that are acutely experienced by both children and their parents. Those feelings may cause children to cling to their parents; for their part, parents may be inclined to indulge such dependent behavior too much, since it gives them an excuse to act out their own freshly aroused desires to cling to their children.

Frequently, children express their resistance to toilet training—and to the increased emotional independence it heralds—by claiming that the cannot "stay dry" at night unless they are sleeping with Mommy and Daddy. In this way, a child seeks to prolong his dependency on his parents by using them to control his excretory functions. Parents who take such a child into their bed night after night are retarding his emotional growth by assuming a responsibility that he needs to make his own—and has the full capacity to do. Obviously, too, this kind of sleeping arrangement is also bound to exacerbate the Oedipal feelings of all concerned, thus compounding the difficulties they already have in reducing the intensity of their "family romance."

Sometimes a child may go to great lengths in devising ways of making his parents responsible for the mastery of both his toileting skills and his masturbatory impulses. A child may repeatedly nag his mother to inspect and clean his crotch after going to the toilet. One three-year-old boy was even more ingenious. He refused to urinate by himself or to touch his penis, claiming that it would fall off and be flushed down the toilet. So he asked his mother to hold it for him. And she complied with his request. Needless to say, her compliance only succeeded in greatly intensifying their mutual attachment, while it markedly impaired the boy's ability to learn how to regulate his own toileting and the satisfaction of his masturbatory inclinations.

By getting his mother to handle his penis, this boy succeeded in devising an unusually direct physical expression of his desire for erotic contact with her. Other children, who are less bold or whose parents are less compliant, may find more indirect physical channels for expressing the same incestuous wishes. Thus, children may learn how to use the erogenous zones of the mouth and the anus—instead of their genitals—to obtain some physical release for their Oedipal yearnings. As a result, they may develop long-lasting tendencies to use the self-stimulation of those zones as a substitute for masturbation.

I was such a passioniate little suitor, following my mother around the house like a vigilant watchdog and insanely jealous of the attention she gave to my older brother. I refused to be held or petted by anyone but her. Yes, I had a very powerful case for my Mom. I meant to keep her all to myself.

Since I assumed it would please my mother most if I could forget about my penis altogether and pretend it wasn't there, I had renounced the possibility of masturbating. My penis was strictly off limits. I allowed myself to hold it while I urinated, but that's as far as I permitted myself to go.

I soon discovered that my masturbatory urges could be expressed with other parts of my body. And I also used those substitute forms of masturbation to express my fantasies of having sexual contact with my mother.

I latched on to my bottle as my first outlet. Oh, how I loved that bottle! I carried it with me everywhere until I was shamed into hiding it. Then I kept it hidden in a closet. And I would sneak into that closet frequently, sucking away in the dark until my mouth grew weary.

Although my mother knew about my secret sucking, she never seemed to object to it. In fact, when only the two of us were in the house, she let me suck on my bottle in her presence. Those were the best times of all. Those were the sweet, quiet, dreamy times, when I had my mother all to myself, when I could immerse myself in the idyllic feeling of sucking at her breast.

When I was about four, I could see that this sucking would have to stop, since it made me feel too much like a baby. But my mother inadvertently helped me to find a new outlet for my blocked sexuality. Although my toilet training had long been completed, my mother suddenly began to take a renewed interest in my bowel movements. Each day, she would ask me detailed questions about them, showing great distress whenever I did not "produce" what she considered to be enough. Besides asking me questions, she often checked on my progress while I was actually on the toilet. She would peer into the bowl to see what I had "made." If satisfied, she smiled. If not, she would cluck her tongue and shake her head.

Soon I became constipated, and my mother gave me enemas as a remedy. Not an enema a day, but often enough to make a big thing of it for me. I hated to submit and to feel so helpless. But my mother said it had to be done, so I accepted it. After all, I was sexually attracted to her. And those enemas gave me a chance to share some physical intimacy with her.

My mother's concern was short-lived, but it lasted long enough for me to feel it was legitimate to focus my own attention on my anus and to derive intense erotic pleasure from it. Thus, I developed an anal substitute for masturbation, which I continue to enjoy to this day. In the past, I tried to fool myself about the masturbatory aspects of my bathroom habits, rationalizing my extended sittings on the toilet as a chance to catch up on important reading. But now I can admit that I just want the time and the privacy to revel in the sensuality of my bowel movements and, meanwhile, to create erotic or self-enhancing fantasies.

Growth of Orgasmic Ability

Relatively few parents realize that children of this young age are entirely capable of having orgasms. In fact, a child's developing manual dexterity and sensory-motor coordination permit him to invent a large repertoire of masturbatory variations. At the same time, he can coordinate his physical manipulations with his fantasies. Now that he has mental self-awareness, a child can masturbate with a plan, expressing his own particular desires in the ways he begins his self-stimulation, prolongs his foreplay, and brings himself to climax.

Children of this age do not necessarily attain an orgasm every time they masturbate, and they may well forget the orgasms they did have by the time they reach adulthood. But true awareness of the orgasmic experience is now possible for the first time in a child's life; some adults, like Sue, retain memories of their childhood masturbatory orgasms.[22]

Children of this age often give themselves orgasms at bedtime, in order to relax enough to fall asleep after an active day. Some become so immersed in the process that they seem lost to the world and in the throes of a mysterious ailment.

The masturbatory experience of a three-year-old girl, described by her mother to Kinsey, is a classic example of such total absorption. The girl would lie face down in her bed, draw up her knees, and rhythmically thrust her pelvis back and forth while she kept her legs in a tense, fixed position. Her forward thrusts were smooth and in perfect rhythm, except for brief pauses, during which she adjusted her genitals against the doll on which they were pressed. Pulling herself back from each thrust, her movements were convulsive and jerky. Meanwhile, the child was oblivious to everything around her and her eyes remained in a fixed stare. Her breathing was rapid and intense. As her excitement mounted and she approached the point of orgasm, she made audible gasps and abrupt bodily jerks, after which she appeared noticeably relieved and relaxed.[23]

One of the mothers we interviewed said that she had observed her son becoming very excited as he rubbed his penis against his toys or some bunched-up clothes. Another mother described being struck by the orgasmic behavior of her son's friend, whom she intruded on by chance. This four-year-old boy showed far more bodily movement and tension than she had ever noticed when she happened to see her own child masturbate. Her son usually stimulated his genitals while he was also doing other things. But his friend appeared to be concentrating entirely on his sexual self-stimulation, "as if he wanted to withdraw into his own world and be left alone."

Another woman also recalled inadvertently interrupting a five-year-old when he was in an intense state of sexual excitement. The boy was so involved in his masturbation that, despite her intrusion, he continued to rub his penis vigorously. He even shouted out to her, "Look, look at it! Touch it, touch it!"

Encountered in a child for the first time, this kind of orgasmic intensity may understandingly alarm a parent. However, parents who see a child panting, gasping, or writhing in orgasm should know enough—from their own sexual experiences—not to interfere. Otherwise they may cause him physical frustration, or they may lead him to believe that something is wrong with him. If he believes that, he may find it lastingly difficult to enjoy the full benefits of orgasmic release.

Self-Control and Social Limits

Naturally, for their own well-being, children need to learn how to impose socially appropriate controls over their masturbatory urges. Otherwise, they may incur disapproval and ridicule of traumatic proportions for masturbating in public places where such behavior is regarded as taboo. But how can parents help a child to acquire adaptive self-regulation? How can they convey a sense of the prevailing social restrictions on public masturbation without crimping a child's freedom to do it in private? How can they teach him to adopt these specific restrictions as his own without inducing a generalized guilt over masturbation?

Quite simply, whenever parents notice a child masturbating in their presence, they can take the occasion to inform him of society's ground rules concerning such behavior. At the same time, they can make sure to let him know that they completely accept his masturbation as natural, normal, and pleasurable. As A. S. Neill has said: "It may be a grim necessity to tell a child . . . not to play with his genitals in public. This advice may sound cowardly and unfair . . . but the alternative has its own particular danger, too. For if the child comes up against stern disapproval expressed in hateful and shocked terms by hostile adults, more harm might be done to him than that which derives from his loved parents reasoning with him." [24]

Dr. McHugh also believes that it is important to set limits for children about masturbating in public. While noting that children of this age may know their masturbation makes *them* feel good, she points out that they may not realize how uncomfortable some people may get from watching them do it.

Still, even a child informed about such a possibility may forget himself in public and become the object of scorn for touching his genitals. In such an unfortunate situation, says Dr. Calderone, a child whose parents have already discussed masturbation openly with him, and have given him positive attitudes about it, is less likely to be badly disturbed than a child who is not so emotionally prepared.[25]

Of course, even the most understanding parents may experience some emotional discomfort upon seeing their child deliberately begin to masturbate in their presence. If so, parents need not hesitate to advise their child to confine his masturbation to his own room. This kind of advice is likely to be just as helpful to the child's peace of mind as to their own. Why? Well, let us recount the reasons Nadine, a recently divorced mother, gave us in deciding to tell her three-year-old son to refrain from masturbating outside his room.

First, Nadine wanted to prevent an intensification of the sexual feelings that were already passing between herself and her son—feelings that surfaced when he masturbated in front of her. While she realized that such feelings were perfectly normal for both of them to have, she thought it best to avoid situations that were certain to arouse them blatantly. Second, Nadine wanted to minimize the extent to which her son would be motivated to make her a prime object in his masturbatory fantasies. If she permitted him to masturbate while she watched, she felt she would be a virtual accomplice to his behavior. As a result, she feared his Oedipal involvement with her would become too binding and that he would find it exceptionally difficult to break away from his emotional and sexual attachment to her.

The Effects of Anxiety

Insightful and accepting parents usually have no trouble getting their children to accept their request to masturbate privately. However, a child is sometimes beset by special sources of tension and anxiety which may make it difficult for him to control his masturbation—for example, an unexpected separation from one or both of his parents, a flare-up of marital discord between them, the birth of a sibling, moving to a new home, or starting nursery school. These kinds of stresses may well induce children to begin holding their genitals in a kind of continuous and compulsive manner.

As Alice Balint says, "masturbation is not a deliberate naughtiness, but a help provided by nature against yearning, misery, fright, loneliness, or the excitement induced in a child by overdone fondness." [26] Dr. Spock has made similar observations, concluding that children who handle their genitals a great deal "are usually tense or worried children. They are not nervous because they are masturbating; they are masturbating because they are nervous. The job here is to find out what's causing the tenseness, instead of attacking the masturbation directly." [27]

By masturbating compulsively in the presence of their parents, these children are implicitly sending out invitations for their help. But how can parents best respond? Dr. Ava Siegler, who directs a preventative mental health project for young children and their families, has a number of suggestions which arise out of her successful experience in helping parents cope with children under stress.

Dr. Siegler advises parents to focus on the *meaning* of their child's masturbation rather than on its occurrence. She suggests that they try to remember their own childhood thoughts and feelings about masturbation. She has found that, by recapturing their own past, parents can often become more sympathetic to what their child is experiencing. She also encourages parents to look for connections between what is currently happening in their *own* lives and the possible cause of their child's compulsive masturbatory behavior. Perhaps he is reacting adversely to some stress they have introduced into his life. For example, are the parents going through some emotional or physical crisis that may be causing them to neglect or reject the child? Is a mother showing resentment to her child because her aspirations are frustrated by the responsibilities and demands of child-rearing? Is a father too worried by his work and financial pressures to give his child loving attention? If a mother is unmarried, has she recently become emotionally involved in a new sexual relationship, which may be arousing the child's jealousy, fear of abandonment, or erotic feelings?

Dr. Siegler feels that a thoughtful examination of their own lives can help parents to identify the sources of tension that may be troubling their child. Then the parents are in a good position to talk to their child about what is going on between them. Such communication, in turn, provides the child with some understanding of the link between feeling troubled and communicating it to others through behavior. It also conveys the message that his parents are seriously interested in his welfare and in helping him to feel better. Ideally, with new lines of communication open to them, the family can cooperate in mitigating or alleviating the problems that led the child to signal his distress through masturbation.

Privacy, Not Secrecy

Actually, the very nature of masturbation tends to make it an activity that people can most enjoy in private. Without anyone around to make him self-conscious, a person is free to make whatever movements and sounds he may want to accompany his sexual self-stimulation. By contrast, if a person masturbates in the presence of someone else, he is bound to be influenced in various ways by the observer's reactions and by his own sense of what the observer might find acceptable or unacceptable.

So, like adults, children naturally prefer to masturbate in solitude. But privacy is not the same as secrecy; a child who masturbates privately need not feel obliged to keep what he does a secret from his parents or other people. In fact, he may be quite willing to discuss his private masturbatory experiences with adults who will enter into a genuine dialogue with him. And, as is shown by Dr. Siegler's work, parents can help the child identify and cope with his erotic feelings, without becoming too intrusive in the child's psychic life.

While having such talks with an understanding parent, a child may gain more confidence in controlling the expression of his masturbatory inclinations. Certainly, he does not compromise his personal integrity or his pleasure. Rather, knowing that he is free to satisfy himself privately whenever he wishes to do so, that his parents understand and accept his masturbatory behavior, and that he can turn to them at any time to share his sexual questions and concerns, a child is in the best possible position to learn how to maximize his masturbatory pleasure while tolerating the restrictions society has placed on its public expression.

INDIVIDUALITY AND RELATEDNESS

Interactions with others leave a child with little choice but to begin taking an individual stand in the social world. In relating to his parents, siblings, other relatives, and friends, he must learn how to differentiate his own thoughts, feelings, and expectations from theirs, and how to evaluate his own experience and behavior.

Separation Anxiety

At this age, many children are sent to nursery schools or day-care centers. There, for the first time in their lives, they must function without parental protection, affirm their own rights, exert self-discipline, and modulate the expression of their sexual and aggressive impulses in ways that permit them to play in harmony with their peers. It is not easy for children to make these transitions from babyhood. While they may like the *idea* of growing up, they are inclined to resist the changes that it requires of them.

The very development of a child's sense of self may trigger his anxiety about becoming an individual completely separate from his parents. Children now alternate between wanting to let go of their parents and wanting to cling to them; it is hardly surprising that this period of development is typically marked by a heightening of conflict in the relationship between children and their parents.

For his own long-range welfare, a child has to work through these conflicts and separate from his parents, both physically and emotionally, in a way that leaves him feeling good about assuming individual responsibility for himself and for relating to others. But such responsibility can be very frightening, since it puts children increasingly on their own resources and outside whatever degree of parental support they have been used to counting on during the first few years of their lives. So, when they begin nursery school and experience physical separation on a regular basis, some children turn to masturbation in an attempt to alleviate the intensity of their anxiety; they may masturbate in school to relieve their tensions and to give themselves emotional comfort.[28]

Teachers report that children tend to masturbate most frequently at nap time. Nadine's earliest memory of her own masturbation was at the age of four, when she was trying to fall asleep on her cot in nursery school. She remembers being aware of the fact that she felt "safe" doing it then, because she thought the other children were napping. She called her masturbation "choo-choo," since she did it by moving back and forth on her stomach. Nadine feels that she used masturbation as a way of reducing her nervousness.

Another three-year-old girl, described by her teacher as being very nervous, frequently stimulated herself in school through her dress. Sometimes, she lifted it and rubbed her genitals directly. When she did that, she would look down, avoiding the gaze of others, as if that prevented them from seeing what she was doing. Teachers have told us that this kind of self-comforting is particularly apparent in day-care centers, where children may spend an entire day away from home.

The Oedipus Complex

In order to overcome their separation anxiety, children may seek ways of reasserting their formerly close attachments to their parents. This may reinforce the strength of the erotic attractions they already feel as a result of their Oedipus complex. Of course, a child's yearning for sexual contact with his parent of the opposite sex may represent his wish to be a mature adult and to play that role in society. But the same wish also shows his need to stay attached to that parent. Many boys begin to have erections when they are in close contact with their mothers.[29]

119

And girls may feel a sexual excitement when they hug their fathers or sit on their laps. As we have said, such sexual attractions are often paired with a feeling of hostile rivalry toward the parent of the same sex.

In Sue's Christmas Eve fantasy, the hostility she felt toward her mother was clearly expressed in her thought that she had to beg her mother for one of her stockings, and in her fear that her mother might be mean enough to tell her father about her masturbation.

By contrast, at that point in her life, Sue remembers spending hours in her father's room, watching him work at his jeweler's bench. When he was done, he would lean back and let her play "barber" by running her fingers through his soft, wavy hair. He always had freshly roasted peanuts for her in his huge overcoat pocket when they took their Sunday-morning walks together on the boardwalk by the sea. So she let herself believe that he had a very special feeling for her. When, in her masturbatory fantasy, Sue portrayed her daddy as such a good, clean man, even better than Santa, she was expressing the kind of idealized image that a girl in the Oedipal stage may have of her father.

Sue took great care to conduct her Oedipal drama in secret; she never revealed her incestuous desires to anyone. However, there are children who may actually verbalize the content of such fantasies while masturbating in the presence of the parent they long to possess.

Bernice, a young mother married to a busy physician, told us how her three-year-old son, Larry, enacted a masturbatory fantasy "right out of Freud's notebook"—and right in front of her eyes. While having his bath one evening, Larry called her attention to his "swimming"—gliding on his belly back and forth along the slippery smoothness of the tub. "Look, Mommy. Look at my penee trick. It feels so good." Bernice described how the muscles in Larry's tiny buttocks tightened, making his "rump look like a little pear." Soon, he began to breathe heavily, his face red and contorted with intense concentration. She was startled when she suddenly realized what he was doing.

As Larry continued to glide and pant with complete abandon, he exclaimed again: "Oh, Mommy, I love to show you my penee trick. See what a big boy I am! I'm a better doctor than Daddy." His rhythmic movements continued. "I'm going . . . to invent a pill," he panted, "to make you live forever. Me, too . . . and we'll get married . . . and stay in this house . . . alone . . . for always." He raised his head and arched his back. "Just the two of us. Nobody else can have the pill . . . not even Daddy."

Letting out a final grunt, Larry stretched his body as far as it could go. Shutting his eyes, he shuddered. Then he rolled over and relaxed, revealing his reddened penis. "Oh . . . it feels so-o-o good. Isn't my penee good, Mommy?" Totally confused about how to respond, Bernice replied lamely, "It's time to get washed now, darling."

Shocked by Larry's unabashed candor, Bernice understandably felt at a loss to respond more appropriately. However, as we have pointed out, whenever a child deliberately masturbates in front of his parents, he is inviting them to give him their views of his behavior. In reflecting on this incident with us, Bernice realized what had been going on in that bathroom scene. "I can see now that Larry wasn't so naïve about what he was doing. He certainly was trying hard to impress me by exhibiting his penis and expressing his love for me. If I hadn't been so freaked out by what he did, I might have set some limits for him by explaining how impossible it was for him to ever marry me or invent such a pill. I also could have talked to him about why he didn't want to give it to his daddy. Maybe I could have helped him to be more realistic about his relationship with both me and my husband."

Bernice is not the only parent who has ignored or missed the chance to help a child to accept the limitations of his ability to fulfill such Oedipal fantasies in reality. Charlotte, a college teacher, said that, until he was about six, her son also used to masturbate in her presence while having his bath or listening to her tell him a story. He always told her it felt good, but he never said what he was thinking about while he was doing it. Charlotte confirmed the fact that it was pleasurable, but she never discussed any other aspects of his masturbation with him. Sometimes, when they were stretched out side-by-side on his bed at story time, he would even begin to rub his crotch against her body. If he continued to do it, Charlotte would move away, without making any comment.

When he was going through this stage, Deborah and Jan's son frequently came into their bed early in the morning and wedged himself between them. Once, when he was about five, he got into bed and cuddled up next to Deborah while she was alone and half-asleep. Then he started to masturbate under the covers. Although he didn't show it to her, he did let his mother know that his penis had gotten "big." Deborah responded merely by saying, "Fine."

Of course, it's difficult for parents to talk to young children about feelings as subtle and complex as their incestuous desires. First of all, most parents never had the experience of discussing similar childhood feelings with their own parents; they have had no adequate models of parental communication to follow. Besides, although they may be familiar with writings on the Oedipus complex, parents are bound to find it quite another matter to apply this theoretical knowledge in a real-life situation with their own children.

The Reverse Oedipus Complex

But there is still another—and most deeply rooted—emotional reason why parents are inclined to avoid engaging a child in an open discussion of his incestuous desires: the erotic feelings they have toward him. Just as their children may be torn between clinging and letting go, parents may also be torn between wanting their children to grow up and wanting to hold on to them. And they, too, may show their desire to remain attached by experiencing an increase in sexual feelings for their children.

It is natural for parents to experience what we call a reverse Oedipus complex—an attraction to one's child of the opposite sex. This involvement often leads a parent to withhold energy from his mate, who may respond, in turn, with feelings of jealousy and rivalry for the child's affections. It is also natural for parents to experience the sexual arousal of their reverse Oedipus complex in the form of fantasy—just as their children do. As Dr. Lonnie Barbach, a sex therapist, advises: "It is important to realize that sexual fantasies about one's children are normal. . . . Children are sexual, warm, cuddly human beings—we can feel turned on and have the fantasies, but we don't have to act them out. Acting them out can be detrimental to the child, while just having the fantasy is harmless." [30]

We agree that these fantasies are both normal and harmless. But they may make parents feel too guilty or ill-at-ease to talk candidly to their children about the sexual feelings that are passing between them. However, parents can try to use such fantasies to discover how strongly they may want to remain attached to their children. While this motivation is also perfectly natural, parents who persist in holding on to their children are not helping them to develop the individuality they need to feel confident about relating to others. If a child is to be able eventually to form and maintain loving sexual relationships with partners of his own choice, he must resolve his Oedipal conflicts and give up the possibility of having his parent as a sexual love object. Of course, it is equally essential for parents to break their sexual ties with their children, so that they can give all of their sexual love to their own spouses.

Coping with the Oedipus Complex

When a child invites a response to the Oedipal feelings he openly expresses through his masturbatory behavior, parents can accept his invitation and deal with it honestly—for both the child's benefit and their own.

After watching Larry masturbate and hearing his fantasy, Bernice could have acknowledged that it feels good to masturbate, and that it is normal for boys of Larry's age to want to marry their mothers. Then she could have gone on to say that she and his Daddy are very much in love with each other and intend to stay married, so Larry will never be able to marry her. To reassure him about his adequacy, Bernice might have added that she and his father both love him and feel he is a wonderful child. Finally, Bernice could have told Larry that, when he becomes a grown-up man like Daddy, he would be able to look for a nice wife of his own.

Similarly, Charlotte and Deborah could have told their sons

how natural it is for a boy to love his mother and to feel good when he snuggles up close to her—so good, in fact, that he may want to touch his penis. They could also have explained that parents show such loving feelings for each other when they make love and have intercourse. Of course, they could add, little boys can't make love to their mothers like that; but when they grow up, like their daddies, they can also find wives of their own to make love to. In the meantime, these mothers could have admitted, they would feel more comfortable if their sons masturbated in their own rooms.

According to Alice Balint, a parent who "does not pretend with the child and unsparingly shows him the hopelessness of his present aspirations in love" is responding in the best possible way. By telling him "boldly and frankly" that he must restrain the expression of his sexual feelings toward them and eventually find his own lover elsewhere, parents augment their child's sense of self-respect by taking his feelings seriously; and they present adulthood as a time worth looking forward to, when a child will have the chance to find love and fulfillment with his own mate.[31]

Because most parents have no intention of actually seducing their children, they usually succeed in placing clear and unmistakable limits on the sexual aspects of their loving feelings. So, even if they do not help their child to articulate his incestuous feelings and to get a verbal reaction from them, he will pick up their prohibitions against acting them out. And, he will, in due course, yield to and accept the reality of the sexual limits they have placed on their relationship with him.

Once a child psychologically accepts that reality, he can begin to give up his Oedipal wishes and move forward in the development of his own individuality as a separate person in the world. No longer so erotically preoccupied with his parent of the opposite sex, he can direct his newly released energies toward making friendships with his peers at school. No longer feeling so rivalrous toward his parent of the same sex, he can increasingly identify with him. Instead of trying in vain to displace his father, a boy begins to model himself after him, acquiring a personal sense of the strength and maturity he represents. Similarly, as a girl accepts the futility of competing with her mother for the love of her father, she identifies with the mother; and by modeling herself on the strengths she perceives in her, she strengthens her own self-image. As she consolidates her identification as a woman, she can look forward to the time when she, too, will have a man of her own as a lover and mate.

Naturally, an emotional involvement that is as deeply felt and instinctual as the Oedipal one can hardly be completely resolved all at once—or ever—by the child. Rather, he is likely to carry remnants of those Oedipal feelings with him throughout his childhood and, indeed, during his whole life. At adolescence especially, as we will see, the old Oedipal flames tend to be rekindled; and most adults carry within them some emotional immaturities that go back to their early childhood conflicts over growing up—some areas of behavior where they still want to be babied or to escape full responsibility for themselves. But a preschool child who has "turned the corner" on his former involvement in the Oedipus complex is inclined to continue in the direction of emotional independence; and he can regard going off to elementary school not as a fearsome fate but as an exciting opportunity for growth.

Chapter 5
MIDDLE CHILDHOOD

Regina's first clear memory of masturbation goes back to the age of nine, when she discovered it quite accidentally while she was playing alone in the bathroom. She had let a gold jewelry chain dangle between her legs. As it began to feel good, she continued to slide it up and down along her genitals until it felt better and better. Regina recalls quite vividly how her pleasurable sensations built up until she experienced a climax similar to her present orgasms.

"Right after this first intense experience, I became an active masturbator, doing it at least once a day. I continued to limit my activities mainly to the bathroom, because I shared a room with my younger brother until I was eleven. But sometimes I would take a chance and pile up a bunch of pillows on my bed. Straddling them, I'd hump myself against them while I imagined they were a man. But my brother frequently tried to surprise me. So I had to figure out a way of hiding the pillows very quickly. To shortcut this procedure, I tried using the smooth handle of my hairbrush instead. I found that I could get almost as much enjoyment stimulating myself by rubbing the handle against my clitoris and vagina until I reached a climax. And the hairbrush was certainly very easy to hide! It's only very recently that I've been able to touch myself directly with my own hands while I masturbate."

Kris is a tall, rather handsome physician of fifty, who grew up on the West Coast. He was completely oblivious to the sexual implications of what he was doing when, at the age of nine, he rubbed his penis against the climbing bars in the school playground as he shinnied up and down on them. Kris, an only child, was very naïve about sex in those days. Neither of his parents had ever talked to him about it; nor had he seen them show any physical signs of love and affection for each other.

"I was very short and underdeveloped all through my elementary-school years. My testicles didn't descend until I was in junior high. Because of my feelings of inadequacy, I was usually very up-tight and socially isolated in school. I often got the shit kicked out of me by the other kids, So, although I never realized consciously what I was actually doing, I continued to reduce my tensions by giving myself the pleasure of sliding on those climbing bars until I was in my adolescence."

Vicky, now a married woman in her midtwenties, was reared on a large farm in Pennsylvania. She did not masturbate with her hands, but she often rubbed her crotch up against the trees on which she loved to climb. Vicky began her "lovemaking" with trees at the age of six; and she clearly recalls the pleasurable intensity of her orgasmic feelings. With an impish smile, she told us how all the doors on the lower cabinets in her mother's kitchen hung loose on their hinges as a result of the frequent masturbatory rubbing and swinging she had done on them all during her childhood years.

Gregg, a married teacher in his late twenties, grew up in a small New England town. He masturbated regularly from the age of six; he was also eager to make sexual contact with girls. "I tried to screw my cousin when I was six years old. And I remember having fantasies about getting the girls in the fourth grade to go in back of the baseball field with me to have intercourse. I always wanted to be more grown-up than I was. When I first started masturbating, I did it until I was tired. I don't remember any sense of climax or release—just a sense of resignation that I was still a child."

But Gregg had his first ejaculation when he was only nine. His older brother told him it happened because dark-haired people matured earlier. From then on, Gregg was pretty alert about not being discovered; when he went to bed at night, he kept a "masturbation rag" handy—a pair of underpants or a T-shirt into which he would ejaculate. Then he would immediately drop it into the laundry hamper so his mother wouldn't know whose it was. Laughing at the way he tried to hide his masturbation, Gregg recalled how other boys used to brag about buying condoms so they could have a "sanitary jerk-off."

The need to give and receive sexual love is a central, unceasing, and lifelong source of human motivation. Children continue to experience and to express that need through the years of middle childhood, from about the age of six until the onset of puberty. Certainly, as these examples illustrate, those years are not characterized by a period of sexual "latency," as Freud said, during which a child's erotic feelings and behavior become relatively dormant.[1] On the contrary, as children keep growing, so does their motivation for sexual love; and they display an unslackening interest in sexual play and experimentation, while showing and satisfying an ever-increasing curiosity about sex and its functions.[2]

But the beginning of middle childhood does bring an end to the relative freedom a child has enjoyed from the constraints and pressures of society. True, his parents, as adult representatives of society, have already imposed many of its norms on him. But they have also sheltered him from the full impact of the social realities he will have to cope with successfully if he is to survive and to flourish on his own outside his family.

INDIVIDUALITY AND RELATEDNESS

By his middle years, a child has usually consolidated his concept of himself as a separate, autonomous person. Ideally, he has also resolved his Oedipal conflict and overcome his separation anxiety with a fair amount of success. But as he enters elementary school, he is faced with the need to use his evolving mental powers to develop his individuality while relating to a growing number of strangers—both adults and peers of his own age. He must now meet the challenge of establishing satisfactory relationships with a steady succession of teachers, who represent adult authority and who function in many ways as parental surrogates. Similarly, he has to learn to get along with many different children, who are often in competition with him that is analogous to the rivalry he has experienced at home with his brothers and sisters.

In fact, a child is likely to spend many more of his waking hours relating to and being influenced by his teachers and peers than he does with his parents and siblings. So these new relationships begin to take precedence over his involvements with the members of his own family, often replacing them as the center of his emotional concerns and fantasies. And a child may transfer many of his characteristic attitudes and ways of reacting toward his parents and siblings onto his teachers and his friends.

The new relationships of grade school subject a child to new social stresses. Entering the first grade, he is introduced to the "real" world and forced into the arena of serious competition. He is repeatedly tested and evaluated on his acquisition of new skills, his performance being compared with that of his classmates; and he has to perform publicly, demonstrating his level of competence not only to his teacher but to his fellow students.

Relating and Competing

For the first time in his life, a child is no longer "just playing," when he gets together with other children under the supervision of an adult. Now, in elementary school, he is "playing for keeps." The competition instigated by his education in the three R's tends to spill over into all of his extracurricular activities. Typically, children of this age also seek to impress themselves and each other with endless "proofs" of their exceptional competence in their games and hobbies. And many children become preoccupied with a concern to demonstrate their adequacy—or to mask their inadequacy—in almost everything they do.

Beset with the competitive tensions of formal schooling, many children often have an acute need for the kind of pleasurable relief that masturbation can provide. True, they may be able to "let off steam" by participating in sports and physical games. But their participation in such activities is usually carried out within the social framework of a contest between individual children or teams, thus feeding rather than damping the flames of competitiveness. And a child may experience as great an impulse to masturbate after a tense athletic event as he did before it.

Some children may feel the impulse to masturbate while they are in school. Boys often get erections when they are anxious about taking a test, performing in a game, or being called upon to read a passage from a book.[3] Girls may feel sexually aroused under similiar circumstances. One woman told us that, whenever her teachers called on her to give an answer, she got so nervous that she felt compelled to relieve her tension by rubbing her genitals against the corner of her desk as she stood up to respond.

Of course, the anatomical differences between the sexes permit girls to be more covert than boys in the way they can masturbate in the classroom. Because they can sit quietly while pressing their thighs together—imperceptibly squeezing their internal vaginal muscles—it is quite easy for girls to hide what they are doing. Some girls can even reach an orgasm without worrying about their teachers or anyone else realizing it.

A boy may also try to release his tension by moving his penis against the underside of a desk or by surreptitiously rubbing himself with the edge of a book he is holding on his lap. By withholding their urine, or by subtly rocking, boys can also give themselves secret sexual pleasure. But while girls and boys can find ways of hiding their masturbatory foreplay in school, a boy's erection is an unmistakable sign of sexual arousal that anyone can see. And since a boy usually needs to be quite overt in bringing himself to an orgasm, it is far more difficult for a boy to reach a climax undetected.

Gregg told us that when he got bored or nervous in school, he often experienced a feeling of sexual tension. "Whenever that would happen, I'd ask the teacher if I could leave the room, and I'd go to the john and masturbate."

Kris remembers reacting in a similar way. "Whenever I felt

nervous or tense in school, I used whatever excuse I could to get out of the classroom and go to the boys' lavatory. I'd slide up and down against the edge of the door to the toilet stall, rubbing my penis until I felt some relief. But I never had any realization that what I was doing was masturbating."

The Need for Approval and Achievement

Despite all the tensions it generates, school offers invaluable opportunities for personal growth and pleasure. Formal education opens up fantastically exciting vistas for every child, exposing him to the many wonders of life beyond the narrow confines of his own limited experience and environment. As a result of the mental stimulation and encouragement they receive from teachers and peers, many children can overcome the economic or cultural deprivations of their familial background. For some children, regardless of their socioeconomic class, home life may be intellectually barren or emotionally stultifying. School often provides them with the chance to relate to teachers who, even more than their own parents, may take a sincere interest in their personal welfare and development, giving them the sense that their lives are purposeful and worthwhile.

A child's fellow students are generally as much concerned as he is about cultivating a good relationship with the teacher. So children in the classroom are implicitly in the same kind of competition for the teacher's love and recognition as they may be with their siblings for the love of their parents. Yet they are required to minimize the social display of this rivalry, because they want so much to be accepted and loved by their own classmates—and because their teachers try to inculcate the values of cooperation and neighborliness.

Under these conditions, children inevitably develop contradictory feelings toward their peers. Striving to belong, they "sniff out" signs of how they compare to the rest of the group. Although they may want to love and be loved, to accept and be accepted, they are intensely motivated to be special, to stand out, and to be superior to their peers. In their urgent need to maintain and expand their self-esteem, they try to ward off failure by being the brightest, the strongest, the fastest, the greatest, or the most popular.

Fantasies of Scholastic and Social Success

While trying to hide any public display of the anxieties their conflicts arouse, children may brood privately about them and seek the consolations of solitary masturbation. And their masturbatory fantasies can help them to drain off some of the hostility and tension that results from their competitive struggles. In such fantasies, children can accomplish what they have failed, or are afraid of failing, to achieve in reality. They can vicariously obtain the success, affection, approval, and admiration they crave, even if—in reality—they feel ignored by their teachers and unpopular with their peers.

The masturbatory fantasies of this period tend to be oriented toward individualistic achievement and accomplishment, reflecting a child's worries about being on his own, building up his ego, and comparing favorably to others. Through such fantasies, children frequently try to overcome anxieties about being observed and evaluated. Often they envision some exceptional personal performance that arouses the admiration of their siblings, peers, teachers, and parents. At the same time, they may gloat in the imaginary failure of their envious competitors.[4]

The virtues of achievement were constantly stressed in my family when I was a child. Being the youngest, I wanted to surpass my older sister and brother and impress my parents that I could outshine everyone else, being the greatest at anything I did. Yet I also wanted everyone to reward me for surpassing them—to love me, accept me, and give me approval.

So, whenever I did anything well, I feared that my success would arouse everyone's envy and make them withdraw their love from me. But because I was always so anxious about losing their love, I felt an even greater desire to impress them with how clever I could be. Trying to deny the dilemma I was in, I used my fantasies to create the illusion that I could easily satisfy my insatiable and conflicting needs—that I could outstrip everyone else, make them green with envy, and still have their love.

Cultivating the magical tricks of my mind became far more compelling, far more alluring, and often far more gratifying than the sexual satisfaction I derived from my masturbation. In most of my fantasies, I depicted the desires I was afraid to express directly to my relatives and friends—such as my wish to dominate and humiliate them, or to achieve far greater levels of perfection than anyone else could possibly reach. By portraying myself as an ambitious little charmer, I tried to turn every challenge into the most grandiose heights of successful achievement.

Because my parents always seemed so busy and preoccupied about making ends meet during the Depression years when I grew up, I often felt ignored or neglected at home. So I chose school as the place where I would really shine. But I never masturbated in school. I was much too shrewd to do that! Instead, whenever I had to do something at home that was related to school, I would imagine the favorable reactions I'd get from my teachers and friends if I did it perfectly. Then I'd feel a surge of sexual excitement rise up within me.

I remember how turned on I often felt when I did the arithmetic assignments for Mr. Moss, my teacher in the fifth grade. I always wanted to get everything absolutely right so I could impress him. I thought he had a "thing" for me. Certainly I had one for him! How hard it was for me to concentrate in his class! Especially when he walked up and down the aisles between the rows of seats and stopped right in front of me. I couldn't resist diverting my eyes from the paper on my desk to steal a quick glance at his fly. When he'd lean over and point out some example I was doing well, I'd quickly turn my head and look up innocently into his handsome, approving face.

Whenever his homework was particularly challenging, I would sweat over the problems until I was sure my answers were perfect. Then I'd relieve my tensions and reward myself by masturbating. Taking my notebook into my room, I carefully placed it on my bed and spread it open to the page of examples I had just so painstakingly completed. Tossing myself down on my stomach, I'd begin to stimulate myself as I stared with satisfaction at my excellent work and imagined how marvelous I'd seem in class the following day. While I masturbated, I would continue to go over the examples in the fantasies that rushed through my mind, trying to make sure there couldn't be any other possible way of solving them. And in my masturbatory psychodramas, my "study habits" always worked!

As my sexual pleasure mounted, I'd see myself returning to school the next morning to discover that I was the only one in the class who had been able to figure out the correct answers. What a fuss everyone would make! "How did you do it? We haven't even covered that material yet!" Mr. Moss would beam, the curly ends of his dark mustache turning up with the corners of his smiling lips, while his keen bright eyes sparkled —just for me. And he would explain why my solution was so much better than the method used by Stanley, a math whizz and my chief competitor all through elementary school.

Although I was thrilled by the acclaim I received for my fantasized brilliance. I tried not to reveal the boastful pride that was bursting inside my head. My heart pounded with joy as I reached the height of my sexual arousal. But in my mind's eye, I showed the whole class, and especially Mr. Moss, that I was still the sweet, modest, unassuming little girl that everyone could love.

Sue's experience illustrates how a child can fuse the nonsexual motive of achievement with the need for sexual love into a single masturbatory fantasy of being sexually loved for an outstanding scholastic performance. Of course, a child can have such fantasies without masturbating, or even touching his body. But since most children have already learned how to combine fantasy and masturbation, they are often tempted to blend the psychological thrill of an ego-enhancing fantasy with the bodily relief and sensual delights of masturbation. In this way, children can easily funnel the tensions generated by their nonsexual aspirations into masturbatory activity; they can obtain sexual gratification while using their imaginations to transform gnawing doubts about their fallibility into grandiose accomplishments.

Since humans function holistically, a child who experiences the inherent gratifications and social rewards of intellectual creativity is also likely to feel physically enlivened and sensually stimulated. In school, the teacher is the main person to introduce the child to the joys of such creativity and reward him for demonstrating it. So it is natural for children to crave and to look for signs of their teacher's special regard for them.

Wanting to be accepted and approved by his teachers, a child may also want to be close and intimate with them. Since sex is the language of intimacy, a child may imagine being sexually attracted by and attractive to his teachers. Certainly, children often develop "crushes" on their teachers. Like Sue, they may use their teachers as sexual partners in the fantasies that stimulate and accompany their masturbation.

Of course, children are generally most motivated to have masturbatory fantasies that involve teachers of the opposite sex. This tendency is consonant with their instinctive drives and with the identification they have made with the parent of their own sex in resolving the Oedipal conflict. However, some children may have masturbatory fantasies involving teachers of their own sex; this may be particularly true for girls, since so many elementary-school teachers are women. Viewing teachers as parental surrogates, children may also want to possess a teacher's power, status, and knowledge. And what better way is there for a child to create a feeling of complete equality with his teachers than to imagine having a love affair with them?

Understanding and Competence
Reading

Learning how to read permits a child to enter vast new realms of creative delight. Once he reads, a child can enormously expand the scope and content of his imagination through mental access to whatever facet of life and the world he wants to explore. And he can continue his explorations outside the classroom without the help of his teacher or anyone else.

A child's reading can greatly enlarge the range and kind

of self-flattering images available for his use in his masturbatory fantasies. The reading materials most accessible to a child necessarily reflect the values of aggrandizement that are cherished in our society. Certainly, the stress on individualistic achievement is as widely represented in children's literature—including schoolbooks—as it is in other mass media. So a child's desire to be outstanding in school and among his classmates is often intensified by his reading of the exceptional exploits of heroes and heroines, both historical and fictional. He may become very eager to emulate them, which he can do only in fantasy. And the tensions aroused by the discrepancy between his lack of worldly achievements and the fabulous ones of his storybook heroes may motivate him to masturbate for temporary relief.

Melanie, a librarian in her late thirties, was an ardent reader all through her middle childhood. She would stay up very late at night, using a flashlight to read by so her mother wouldn't catch her and make her go to sleep. She often finished several books a week. Identifying herself with the heroines she admired, Melanie would also spend a lot of time daydreaming in her room after returning home from school. She particularly remembers the time when she pretended to be the female detective in a mystery series. Draping her nude body in a blanket, which she imagined was a chic raincoat, she would invent a romantic "caper" by elaborating on an incident from one of her books. Posing and gesticulating in front of the mirror, she spoke all the dialogue aloud. Usually, one of her hands would begin moving toward her genitals in response to her increasing erotic arousal. And she would finally masturbate in earnest, timing the climax of her story to accompany her orgasm.

Other children "rewrite" parts of a book even while reading them, letting their minds wander in response to their stimulated desires. As their eyes continue to stare fixedly at the printed page, they begin looking inward, "reading" a story they have contrived to suit their own special needs and purposes. A child may actually start to fondle his genitals while his book is open and resting on his lap.

Ben, an advertising executive of fifty-eight, described how he used to masturbate regularly in that way. "It was a real private joke for me. My parents were immigrants from Russia. So they were very pleased by my passion for reading. That's what I found so great about using reading as a 'front' for playing with myself. I would sit in my room, the lower part of my body hidden by the desk my folks got me for my schoolwork. I didn't even bother to shut the door to my room, so they could see me with my head in a book if they happened to walk by. It was easy to slip one hand down to rub my cock while I got off on a fantasy of myself doing something great. And that was easy to do with all the adventure stories I read as a kid. Tom Swift was my favorite. I could always count on him to give me some amazing ideas. Of course, I always added a few important details about how me, as Tom, would be making it with the girl next door after I had done something fantastic."

Pornography and Voyeurism

Pornographic books and magazines may be especially favored by schoolchildren as a means of satisfying their sexual curiosity and desires. And even if a child does not use such materials as a stimulus to physical masturbation, he may use them to increase his sexual education and to ignite his masturbatory fantasies.

When I was a kid, my father owned a stationery store in a small town. About the age of ten, I discovered that he carried a small stock of pornographic books and magazines, which he kept out of sight in the back of the shop. Luckily for me, there was a partition separating that part of the store from the front, where my father dealt with customers. So I had access to a buried treasure of eroticism without having to worry about being caught digging in it.

Still, I worried. I was sure my parents would put an end to my secret pleasure if they found out about it. So I decided to play it cool, doing my best to prevent them from becoming suspicious about my greatly increased visits to the back of the store.

Typically, I would saunter through the front door, a disarming smile on my lying face. "How's it going, Pa?" I would ask, knowing it was only a diversionary tactic and not really caring whether or not he replied. And his usual answer was just as perfunctory: "What can I tell you, Irv?"

Instead of dashing immediately into my private "library," I forced myself to dawdle a little, looking over the "clean" magazines and newspapers that were set on the racks against the wall across from the cigar counter. Then, I'd turn around slowly to face my father, who was usually stationed behind the counter. Perhaps I'd even yawn to show him that I was badly in need of rest. "Well, I think I'll go into the back a little." Saying that, my heart began to pump wildly in anticipation of the excitement I knew was awaiting me. But I didn't rush, although my legs felt like moving faster than I permitted them to go.

When I got behind the partition, I carefully and quietly probed my way into the pile of sexy merchandise my father thought was securely hidden. And I did my best to keep him thinking that way, restoring the stack exactly as I found it when I felt it was time for me to leave.

Selecting a few choice morsels, I squirmed into the most cluttered corner of the dimly lit room. There, I disappeared into a steaming jungle of feverish flesh. The pictures fascinated me the most, since I had never examined naked women at my leisure. Their breasts were especially alluring to me, given my long addiction to sucking on my baby bottle. But I also wondered a lot about their genitals, which were never fully exposed. All that could be seen was pubic hair. But even that gave me a giddy, sensual "rush."

I stared at the pictures until by bulging eyes were ready to pop out of my head. If my eyes had been capable of ejaculating, they might have come all over the pictures. But I didn't know anything about ejaculations then. My personal experience with genital sexuality was nonexistent. And my hearsay knowledge of human sexual functioning was almost as limited.

Without pausing to give my eyes a rest, I would switch to the pornographic stories. Even at that age, I knew the writing was awful and intended only to be sexually arousing. And I was aroused by it—very, very aroused, my penis pressing tightly against my pants.

The fondling of luscious nipples, the kissing of lips hungry with desire, the fiery tingling of heated bodies—these described sensations I could understand and appreciate to the fullest. They evoked deeply buried memories of half-awakened intimations of passion and delight. But the hard-core material—the fucking and the coming—pointed only to some unknown plane of sexual ecstasy, supremely desirable, it seemed, but still entirely foreign to me.

I might spend as much as an hour or two poring over a variety of "dirty" books and magazines. And I did feel dirty, knowing I was doing something my parents would forbid. But, even more, I experienced a delicious but anxious inner turmoil, a chaos of emotions that left me feeling both calm and tremulous, both satisfied and expectant.

Of course, I was itchy for an orgasm but I didn't even know it. As a self-styled abstainer from masturbation, I wouldn't even touch my aching penis, much less pull on it until I could have some release. Yet I repeatedly indulged in those voluptuous binges of voyeurism. And I never confronted the obvious contradiction between my immersion in the rawest, most vulgar kind of sexuality and my self-image of sexual purity. Now, I see the partition in my father's store as a symbol of the compartment I had put up inside myself, separating my thoughts from my emotions and my head from my genitals.

For many children, reading pornography gratifies more than their impulses to look at and mentally participate in the erotic behavior of adulthood; it also serves as a regular accompaniment to their sexual self-stimulation. When Nick was nine years old, he often used pornography when he indulged in masturbation three or four times a week. Making himself comfortable in his own room, Nick would select a "hot" story from the cache of erotic books and magazines he kept hidden underneath a pile of old schoolbooks he stored in his closet. While he masturbated, he would fantasize that he was making love to the women who were shown or described as participating in various sexual acts. These fantasies gave him the warm feeling and comfortable illusion that he really was loving a woman. "It didn't matter who or what she was, as long as I could love her and feel loved by her."

When Irv was a boy of ten, he had much more opportunity than most children to see frankly pornographic books and magazines. Today, however, such reading matter would be difficult for a child to avoid seeing, since it is often openly displayed in supermarkets and drugstores, in addition to newstands and bookstores. But apart from such graphic sexual stimulants as *Playboy* and *Playgirl*, a preadolescent child now has easy access to sexually titillating books written specifically for his age group.

For better or worse, pornography seems here to stay, both in its blatant and its subtle forms. If a child is strictly forbidden from reading "sexy" books or magazines at home, he can surely find them elsewhere. Such censorship robs a child of the opportunity to learn how to be responsible for himself about what he chooses to learn, think, and express. Indeed, censoring what a child reads contradicts and undermines the ideals of self-governance, individual freedom, and personal responsibility that are the goals of psychological maturity in a democratic society.

Admittedly, pornography tends to portray people as mere sexual machines and objects, rather than as human beings who are expressing deeply felt affection in loving relationships. So, rather than attempting to censor their child's reading materials, parents can alert him to the dehumanizing aspects of pornography; and they can convey their feelings about the desirability and the beauty of having relationships, like their own, in which love and sex are emotionally integrated and expressed by both partners.[5]

Writing and Manual Skills

Reading is, of course, a relatively passive medium for partaking of expressions of sexual love, although a child's mind may be extraordinarily active in translating printed symbols into erotic fantasies and feelings. But writing requires children to use their hands—or at least the hand with which they write. For children who have always felt free to masturbate, the act of writing may not hold any particular sensual appeal. But for boys who habitually block their masturbatory impulses, writing offers the special attraction of permitting them to hold an implement that may symbolize a penis. Likewise, in using a pen or pencil, children of both sexes may unconsciously feel they are stroking, fondling, and rubbing as they might do if they were masturbating. Sometimes, children may combine these symbolically sexual aspects of writing with the creation of stories in which they project themselves as a fictional hero or heroine. When that happens, children may fall in love with writing, using it as an outlet for masturbatory activity they are too afraid to engage in directly—as Irv did.

The visual and plastic arts may serve similarly masturbatory purposes for some children. Through such media, they are often able to give vent to sexual impulses they might otherwise be fearful of expressing in direct form. Working with clay and finger paints allows children to have tactile experiences that may be very expressive of their masturbatory desires, styles, or inhibitions. And some children go through periods of great involvement with coloring books, carefully filling in every nook and cranny of the prepackaged drawings. While such books severely restrict the range of a child's creative spontaneity, the scratching and stroking involved may be very appealing to children who are fearful of masturbating.

School may also encourage children to develop other manual arts, such as sewing, carpentry, and playing a musical instrument. Undoubtedly, each of these media may be a source of intrinsic delight for children who are gifted in them or who simply enjoy them. But each of those arts also offers children a chance to use their hands and fingers in ways that may permit them to express tensions stemming from their masturbatory desires. Sewing permits a child to touch, stroke, and fondle a wide variety of textures, just as carpentry involves feeling and sanding various shapes and grains of wood. The fingering involved in playing any musical instrument provides a similar outlet for handling something in a way that is sensually gratifying while it is also socially approved and rewarded.

If a child proves to be especially skillful in any of the arts and crafts, he may also be motivated to develop it as a means of heightening his self-esteem. When that happens, a child may use his "golden hands" or his "good eye" as stimulants to masturbatory fantasies of amazing accomplishments, as Sue did with her painting and sewing. For some children, producing a painting, a dress, or even a neatly written page in a notebook of homework assignments may become psychologically connected with the use of their hands and minds during masturbation. Such a child may condition himself to use the finished products of his artistic and intellectual handiwork as erotic props, as Sue did, admiring or touching them while he indulges in a session of masturbatory self-adulation.

Fetishes

Whenever any material object is used as a stimulant for masturbation, it takes on the function of a sexual fetish. And a few people do grow up as fetishists, who choose to masturbate while looking at or fondling some object in preference to any form of sexual gratification that involves interaction with other people.

While an exclusive preference for fetishism may be quite rare among adults, many children go through phases, especially in early childhood, during which they may use a blanket or some article of clothing as part of their thumb-sucking or masturbation. Some psychologists have speculated that such behavior represents a need to cling to "transitional objects," which symbolize a parent from whom a child is emotionally struggling to separate himself. One mother described how her six-year-old daughter developed the habit of masturbating. She would take her father's undershirt, roll it up, put it inside her underpants, and then lie down on her stomach and rub back and forth on her bed.

The use of material objects to enhance one's sexual excitement does not arise, however, merely from the emotional strains a child experiences on his way toward becoming psychologically separated from his parents. On the contrary, even before they can read and respond intelligibly to the mass media, American children are bombarded with advertising images that consistently link sex appeal with material things. Many ads present their message in almost these words: "If you use our product, you will become as sexually desirable as the glamorous or handsome model pictured with it." Such promises of sexual allure and fulfillment are used to promote a vast variety of products, including not only cosmetics and body deodorants but even automobiles and household appliances.

Of course, school-age children cannot rush out to buy a car they have just seen demonstrated by a sexy Hollywood star. But they can and do nag their parents to buy them similarly advertised products such as expensive toys, games, sports equipment, and stylish clothing. They may incorporate those objects into their masturbatory fantasies, seeing their newly purchased baseball glove or embroidered blue-jeans as giving them an increase in sexual desirability.

These ads may strongly affect children who feel exceptionally undesirable and inadequate, luring them into believing that the mere purchase and use of such products can substitute for fulfillments they can only get from loving relationships and actual accomplishments. But even children who feel quite adequate may be profoundly influenced by constant exposure to advertising's false prescription for personal happiness. So parents can help their children by giving them an honest account of what it really takes for a person to achieve both a loving relationship and vocational success. Parents would also do well to avoid using toys and presents as a substitute for giving a child the time, care, communication, and attention he needs to develop as a loving and capable person.

SELF-ACCEPTANCE AND ACCEPTANCE OF OTHERS
Feelings of Inadequacy: Boys

At this age, the physical changes in the size and sensitivity of a boy's genitals lead him to center on his penis as the main focus of his erotic attention—both physically and mentally.[6] In locker and shower rooms at school and camp, a boy cannot help but expose his penis to the scrutiny of his fellows, who can make comparisons and evaluations of its size and shape. Being subjected to unfavorable comparisons may cause deeply disturbing psychological problems for many boys, impairing their self-image and their sense of sexual potency. For the size of a boy's penis has been widely regarded as an indication of his virility.

Kris said his early feelings of physical inadequacy have had a lasting impact on his adult sexual life. "I always felt so self-conscious about my genitals and my physique, which stacked up so poorly in comparison to the other guys in school. I was so full of rage by the time I entered junior high that I went around writing 'fuck you' all over the school walls until I was temporarily suspended. But nobody responded to my outrageous plea for help. Neither my parents, my teacher, nor the principal ever tried to talk to me about what might have motivated my hostile behavior."

Gregg recalls that he developed similarly negative feelings about himself as a young child. Like Kris, he remembers how the other boys in school beat him up. Although Gregg had his first ejaculation at the unusually early age of nine and was far more aware of his masturbatory behavior than Kris, he still felt very self-conscious and sexually inadequate. "I always remember feeling that I was too fat as a kid and that my cock was too small to ever satisfy a woman."

Boys like Kris and Gregg may be very reassured to hear their parents tell them that the size of a boy's penis does not affect the amount of pleasure he can experience either when he masturbates or when he grows up and makes love to a woman. Quoting the studies of Masters and Johnson,[7] a parent could explain that a small penis can get just as hard as a big one and can remain hard for just as long a period of time. A boy who is worried about his penis being too small when it is flaccid may feel very much better to learn that, when a small penis becomes erect, it tends to increase in length proportionately more than an originally larger penis. Besides, when a boy eventually engages in sexual intercourse, his partner's vagina will automatically adjust to the size of his penis.

Not having this reasurring information, Gregg used masturbatory fantasies in an effort to overcome his feelings about having an overweight body and an undersized penis. He would build up his self-image by projecting himself into the role of a strong, handsome, virile man—very attractive to women, who were highly responsive to his seductive advances. He would see himself seducing only the prettiest and most physically alluring women. After a lot of hugging and kissing with such a woman, he would gradually undress her and kiss her stomach. By the time he reached the peak of his excitement, he would be having intercourse with her, usually imagining that his penis felt very warm and comfortable inside her vagina, just as he had heard it was supposed to.

Gregg also used fantasies of athletic achievement to enhance his self-esteem. In reality, he took great enjoyment in swimming and other sports that stimulated his sensuality. But he longed to be as physically mature and agile as his coaches, viewing them as better and more effective men than his own father. So he often had masturbatory daydreams of being capable of performing the kinds of athletic feats he observed among his coaches.

Feelings of Inadequacy: Girls

Since society places even more value on female beauty than on male handsomeness, girls of this age may become extremely concerned about the appearance of their bodies. Some girls worry incessantly about how their shape compares to that of their friends.

Just as boys may measure their personal adequacy by comparing the size of their penises, girls may engage in similar comparisons of their budding breasts. Because our society ascribes great sexual attractiveness and adequacy to large-breasted women, a girl may regard her bosom as the most visible proof of her desirability and sexuality, just as a boy may feel about his penis.

But the mystery created by the hidden structure of the female sexual organs may be particularly troubling to many girls of this age. Her unseen genital anatomy contributes to a girl's lack of comprehension about the origins of the thrilling sensations she experiences during masturbation; and it may arouse her fears about the bodily effects of her self-stimulation.[8] Even if a girl has already learned to locate, identify, and correctly label every part of her external genitals, she is still left without direct knowledge of the inner parts of her sexual organs. This lack of direct perception may contribute to a girl's feelings of insufficiency about her sexuality. Since they have no way of comparing their inner organs by direct observation, some girls may begin to doubt whether they are "normal" or are equipped as well as other women for sexual intercourse or bearing children.

Constance, an attractive young mother in her late twenties, was a copy editor on a newspaper before she had her first baby. As a child, she was very frail and timid. She was always worried that she had made herself so thin because she masturbated so much. Constance still remembers how shy she was about changing for swimming in front of the other girls at day camp, when she was about ten. In her eyes, they all seemed to have such beautiful bodies; their legs were strong and shapely and some of them were even beginning to develop a soft, full roundness on their chests. She was embarrassed to take off her clothes and reveal her "scrawny skin and bones."

"It wasn't only my sunken chest that made me so self-conscious. I was also worried, when I moved my legs apart to take off my panties, the girls would see those funny flaps that hung down from my vagina. I was sure they'd be able to tell how much I masturbated from that! It wasn't until I got to college and studied female anatomy that I realized I was perfectly normal. I guess my vaginal lips seemed to stick out so much in contrast to my skinny body. And I was so late in getting pubic hair that they never got covered up like those of the other girls I knew." Constance also lived in terror of being discovered as a "mad masturbator" when she went for her regular medical check-ups. But the doctor never brought up the subject with her.

"I kept on masturbating even though I was so worried about it. It felt so wonderful, and I guess it was one of the few pleasures I had as a child. Sometimes my climax felt so intense that I shook and it felt like I was having some sort of spasm. I used to get panicked at the thought that maybe my insides were getting damaged in some way. I didn't begin to menstruate until I was fifteen. After that, I finally began to fill out and gain weight. I even became popular with the boys. But I don't think I ever really felt like a completely normal woman until my baby was born."

In their attempts to feel more confident and self-sufficient, girls may also have masturbatory fantasies in which they portray themselves as being outstanding at various athletic activities. While touching her genitals, a girl may feel erotic sensations suffused over her entire body; and she may experience her own body as a very unique source of pleasure. Often, girls feel as if they are floating, flying, dancing, or skating as lightly as a feather. And they may take pride in the fact that they can manipulate their own bodies in order to control the source and degree of their sexual sensations.[9]

Maggie, a thirty-six-year-old mother of three children, recalls how she used masturbation during childhood to gain an awareness of her own bodily potentials and to feel good about being a girl. "I always wanted to be a skating star. When I was only eight, I was already quite an accomplished skater. I would keep in tune by traveling the long distance to school and back on my roller skates. In the winter, I'd rush to the rink to practice my ice-skating skills. That's the kind of skating I really loved the best. I was a tough little kid—a real tomboy—and I wanted to play on the hockey team with the boys on my block. My mother insisted on giving me figure-skating lessons. I protested, at first. But I got to love it because there were always lots of people around to watch and admire me."

Maggie described how she loved the "feel" of rubbing her legs together as she twisted and twirled over the surface of the ice, bending as low as she dared while still keeping her balance. The pressure of her movements, combined with the silky texture of her tights against the skin of her thighs, made her very conscious of the sensations in her genitals. "I always felt very sexy as the blades of my skates glided around the curve of the rink and the wind blew against my cheeks."

Maggie claims that the physical relief and emotional gratification of her masturbation had a positive effect on her skating performance. While she masturbated, she would imagine making the exact bodily movements she needed to improve her form and grace. And when she was actually skating on the ice, the sensual "high" aroused by her activity felt almost as intense as the sexual excitement she created for herself when she masturbated.

"By visualizing the physical sensations of skating while I masturbated, I learned to appreciate the pleasures my own body was capable of experiencing. The more I was able to let go and enjoy my climax, the more I overcame whatever fears I had of letting myself go while I skated. And that helped me to trust the flow of my own natural body rhythm much more."

Sex Play

Boys and girls at this stage of development do not usually wait for either their parents or their teachers to satisfy their keen curiosity about sex and its functions. Instead, they use their peers to exchange endless accounts of sex lore and mythology, including the repetition of an infinite number of "dirty" jokes.[10] Sometimes their motivation to learn about sex is so intense that they become obsessed with sexual thoughts and concerns. And, if they haven't already done so, this is the time when some boys and girls engage in mutual sex play.[11]

Gregg is not the only man we interviewed who recalls sexual experimentation with girls when he was a young boy. Nick also remembers that his first sexual experience took place at the age of six, when he played "doctor" with his girlfriend. He doesn't know where he got the idea, but Nick made believe that his penis was some kind of surgical instrument; and he rubbed it along the girl's vagina, pretending to make an incision in her body in order to perform a very essential operation.

Typically, however, boys and girls of this age are placed under considerable social pressure to avoid close sexual or emotional contacts with each other.[12] In fact, despite the recent movements toward sexual liberation, parents and educators still generally expect children of the two sexes to learn different social roles. These sex-role differences include both behavioral styles, such as modes of dress and grooming, and psychological orientations, such as interests, aspirations, and attitudes.

Thus, children of the same sex are put in the position of developing more social solidarity with one another than with children of the opposite sex. Same-sex children tend to have more frequent and intimate contact with each other, and to select each other as their first and best friends.

Having already established a friendly relationship with each other, children of the same sex may find it relatively easy and agreeable to express their mutual affection in some form of sexual play. Often, such friends go no further than jostling, wrestling, or, in the case of girls, hugging and kissing each other. But some of them may decide to stimulate each other genitally, perhaps even to the point of orgasm.

Many boys participate in some form of the "circle jerk," in which they get together for the purpose of exhibiting themselves, comparing their sex organs, proving their sexual prowess by getting an erection, and engaging in either self-induced or mutual masturbation. Sometimes, such homosexual play with their male peers may actually help young boys to feel more potent as men.[13] Because of their conditioning in the cultural emphasis that equates masculinity with sexual performance and virility, boys may gain self-assurance from such exhibitionism. By showing off their penises, exploring their ability to attain and sustain an erection, and handling each other's genitals, boys may get to accept and to feel more confidence in their maleness.[14]

Similarly, some girls also get together as partners, or in larger groups, for mutual sexual stimulation. When Deborah and Jan's daughter had her seventh birthday party, a group of her girlfriends stayed over night to sleep at her house. After Deborah had gone to bed, she was awakened at one A.M. to find the girls dancing around the living room together, completely naked. They seemed to be indulging in a joyous celebration of their own bodies. On other occasions, Deborah's daughter and one of her closest friends have gone into a bedroom and shut the door. When the girl's brother threatened to tell on her, she argued that it was none of his business. However, she has openly shared her fantasies with Deborah about wanting to get her own apartment so she and her girlfriend could live together and travel around the world.

Children who have such experiences and fantasies are not necessarily in danger of becoming permanently fixated on homosexuality. Rather, they may be all the more motivated to move toward heterosexual love, sensing in it the only way they can truly transcend the limits inherent in their own sex. For having sex play with a person of one's own sex is very reminiscent of playing sexually with oneself. Since the other child has a body and sex organs nearly identical to his own, erotic contact with him cannot possibly free a child from the familiar boundaries of his own solitary sexuality. So children who do not feel too inadequate about progressing toward the fullest possible realization of their human potentials for sexual love and procreation will feel no incentive to opt for homosexuality as a permanent life-style.

RELEASE AND CONTAINMENT
Reconciling Love and Achievement

Upon entering elementary school, a child is confronted with the problem of setting priorities for the use of his time and energy. Given the daily demands of his formal education, he must decide how fully he wishes to meet them. And since the expectations of his educators reflect society's stress on the importance of successful achievement, he is also required to consider how much he wants to devote himself to the pursuit of such success.

Making and sticking to these vital decisions is no simple matter for anyone, much less a child who has not had to face them head-on before. Children have to cope with the basic conflict that will be with them for the rest of their lives, as it is with their parents. If they direct too much of their energy into striving for socially valued accomplishments, they run the danger of seriously frustrating the fulfillment of their need for sexual love. But if they become too involved in fulfilling their need for sexual love, they may jeopardize their development of the skills, competencies, attitudes, and methods of productive work that ensure the achievement of success in school and beyond it.[15]

At this age, the conflict between love and ambition is expressed through a child's approach to masturbation, which is generally the chief means a child has of gratifying his need for sexual love. So he has to decide how much he wants to get involved in masturbation and masturbatory fantasy versus how much he wants to avoid them in favor of activities oriented toward achievement.

Indirect Release: Sports and Games

Given such an ongoing choice, a child may seek to avoid taking personal responsibility for making it. Hoping to have it "all ways," he may refrain from giving himself the love and pleasure of masturbation, while he tries to find socially approved but indirect outlets for it. Many of the ritualistic games that are so popular among children of this age—with their rigid rules and repetitive chants—involve symbolic expressions of their sexual impulses.[16]

Jumping rope, hide-and-seek, folk dancing, and many ball games that require continuous bouncing and leg turning, are often accompanied by rhythmic bodily movements, repetitive rhyming, or constant counting, which build up to climactic peaks of stimulation before giving way to fatigue and lethargy. Such patterned outpourings of energy may provide children with a release similar to actual masturbation, in which the repetitive foreplay mounts to an orgasmic climax, followed by an aftermath of relaxation and exhaustion.[17] Such ritualistic games also serve the purpose of helping children to feel a sense of personal control over the changes and ambiguities that come into their lives at this time, by giving them a common social structure through which they can relate to each other.[18]

A large number of the other physical and athletic activities in which both boys and girls participate may permit them to masturbate in some furtive way. As we have seen with Kris, Vicky, and Maggie, children can rub and stimulate their genitals while climbing trees, sliding down banisters, riding horses, skating, pumping endlessly on swings, working on parallel bars and ropes, or doing body-building exercises and other forms of gymnastics. The movement of thigh and pelvic muscles necessary for these activities exerts pressure on the genitals, sometimes arousing enough sexual excitement to induce a child to continue the action until he has actually reached an orgasm, just as Vicky did.[19]

Some children, like Kris, may not even realize they are

masturbating when they first begin to stimulate themselves in these "recreational" ways. But as their intellectual awareness and their conscience continue to develop, children start to wonder what they are doing, why they are doing it, and what it really means. And inevitably, they begin to ask themselves if sexual self-stimulation is right or wrong, good or bad.

It is natural for children to be troubled by their awareness of the fact that society tends to frown upon masturbation. At this age, they experience a great need to conform to social norms.[20] School brings them into contact with the reactions and ideas that other children have about masturbation and other aspects of sexual functioning. And the sexual misinformation they may get from their peers can intensify rather than diminish whatever anxiety or guilt they may already have.

Unfortunately, many school children still circulate traditional but false tales about the supposed dangers of masturbation, claiming that it causes blindness, mental retardation, pimples, insanity, bodily weakness, and other horrors. However, children who have been well educated by their parents on the normality of masturbation are best protected against the masturbatory fears that they may hear at school or elsewhere.

Compensations and Compulsions

But even children who attach no physical or mental harmfulness to masturbation itself may often be upset by their own particular motivations for masturbating.[21] Some of these children feel they have neither the intellectual capacity to do the school work required of them nor the physical and emotional appeal necessary to attract friends and be accepted by their peers. A few children have real difficulties and deficiencies for which they need special help and attention, but most may be unrealistically worried and nervous about their capacities. Because of unsatisfactory family relationships, they may have developed a negative image of themselves that is unwarranted; and they often try, through their work and relationships at school, to make up for the love and security they did not get at home.

Yet, no matter how high their actual level of attainment may be, these children, like Sue, often feel disappointed with their achievements. Wanting so much to make up for the love they feel they never received, they make inordinate demands on themselves for perfection; and they constantly focus on anything they can interpret as an indication of their lack of personal worth. So when they get a 95 on a test, they may blame themselves for not getting 100. Or they may feel shattered if they are not invited to a party, although they don't even like the child who failed to invite them. Overreacting to their disappointments, such insecure children may feel compulsively drawn to sexual self-stimulation and compensatory fantasy. Then, they may feel very bad about the compulsive need to masturbate, interpreting it as a further sign of their worthlessness.

Insecurities and Inhibitions

While some children feel compelled to masturbate day after day, even when they would like to stop doing it, others feel afraid to begin masturbating, even when they would like to do it. Some of these inhibited children may allow themselves to begin arousing themselves in foreplay with their genitals, but they prevent themselves from reaching an orgasm. Other children, like Irv, may completely suppress their masturbatory urges, refraining from both foreplay and orgasm.[22]

Children are capable of using extremely sophisticated means to suppress the expression of their masturbatory desires. Dr. Berta Bornstein, a child psychoanalyst, reports the case of a boy she saw in psychotherapy from the time he was five and a half until he was eight and a half. This boy had suffered from a severe case of insomnia. He claimed he was unable to fall asleep because he was bored, but in the course of his treatment, it became clear that the insomnia was caused by his fear of giving in to his urge to masturbate. To overcome his boredom, he went to bed surrounded by toys with which he played for hours. When he realized, during his therapy, that he was playing with his toys to avoid touching his penis, he also developed a taboo against touching his toys. Instead, he evolved a complex series of thought operations, centered on the automatic working of imaginary machines. He would imagine a truck going over a bridge and up a hill, very slowly; and very slowly going back down. During these fantasies, the boy's penis went up and down, just as he wanted it to. He could even exert enough control through his purely mental manipulations to keep his penis from going down. And he perfected the skill of directing the descent of his imaginary toys very carefully, so that his erection would not subside too quickly.[23]

Holding back the physical aspects of masturbation may leave such children abjectly dependent upon their fantasies. Since they give the tensions generated by those fantasies no pleasurable release, they may become extremely irritable, excitable, hostile, and aggressive. Dr. Bornstein claims that children who display nagging, quarrelsome, and generally provocative behavior may be relieving the tensions generated by the hostile or compensatory fantasies they might have released in actual masturbation. She attributes a similar masturbatory intent to behavior in which children dramatically exaggerate incidents that occur in their life at school and at home.[24]

When children chronically suppress their desire to masturbate to orgasm, they may express their blocked impulses and fantasies through activities that appear to be entirely unrelated to sexuality. According to William Thomas Moore, a child psychiatrist, this displacement of masturbatory excitement onto nonsexual activities may permanently affect the development of a child's character. In extreme cases, a child's life may become dominated by his repetitive urge to take the gratuitous risks involved in reckless driving, jumping from high places, flying, courting danger, or gambling.[25]

Thus, a child who has never masturbated before reaching middle childhood may be setting himself up for a host of emotional and behavioral problems. At the very least, he is denying himself the healing effects and sensual pleasures he could be enjoying if he felt emotionally free enough to masturbate as a spontaneous expression of his need for sexual love.

Changes before Puberty

Even children who have been masturbating regularly, and with minimal emotional upset, may become distressed by the growing intensity of their solitary orgasms during this period.

As their sexual maturation quickens, children become very acutely aware of their orgasmic sensations. The most repressed of them find it harder and harder to ignore their strengthening sexual needs and impulses.

From about the age of ten, the production and secretion of sex-appropriate hormones—estrogen for girls and androgen and testosterone for boys—increases markedly. These biochemical changes stimulate the development of secondary sex characteristics.[26] The growth of pubic and underarm hair, the budding excitability of their breasts, and the erectile capacity of their nipples highlight this transitional period for girls. These external and observable changes are also accompanied by a corresponding sensitivity to internal sensations and vaginal stimulation.[27] Boys display a similar spurt of growth in their body and facial hair; their voices begin to deepen; and the size and erotic sensitivity of their genitals noticeably increase. Boys may also become sensitive to their internal sexual functioning, which they experience as a need for ejaculation.[28] Several young men have told us that during this period they usually had a vague feeling that something should be "coming out" of them when they masturbated to orgasm. And, like Gregg, many of them looked forward with great enthusiasm to the time when they would be "real men."

Most children usually receive no parental preparation or congratulations for their first experience of orgasm. In our society, children are usually applauded for many other "firsts" of their development—the first tooth, the first step, the first word, the first day at school. And these "firsts" are often recorded and fondly recalled by the child's parents. But how many parents are even aware of their child's first masturbatory orgasm, let alone pleased by it?

Parental ignorance or avoidance of a child's sexual "firsts" tends to cast a shroud of mystery and anxiety over the child's attitude toward his own sexual feelings.[29] Even when they do discuss sexuality openly with their children, parents may tend to emphasize its biological aspects and functions, neglecting its emotional implications and consequences. So most children are left completely in the dark about the psychological experiences connected with their masturbatory orgasms. And it is difficult for them to understand whatever feelings or qualms they may experience in the process of orgasmic release.

Some children worry because they think they are the only ones who have such "mind-blowing" sensations when they masturbate. Several women told us they had picked up the erroneous notion that only boys are supposed to have the ecstatic feelings of an orgasm when they masturbate. Like Constance and Nadine, those women remember feeling they were exceptionally "weird" because they masturbated to orgasm before reaching puberty.

Nick said he was basically relaxed about his childhood masturbation. He felt it was OK as long as he was able to function well in his other activities. But, he admitted, "Sometimes I was concerned about whether I could use up my sexual capacity. I wondered if it could go on and on or if it had limits. I often worried if every masturbatory orgasm I'd had in my youth would mean that I could have one less orgasm in later life."

Preparing Girls for Puberty

As children grow toward puberty, parents have a great responsibility to communicate with them about the meaning of their sexual maturity. A child's physiological changes provide parents with the opportunity to take the initiative to communicate with him about the many psychological changes he will also experience. It is certainly important for parents to prepare their daughters for the onset of menstruation. At the same time, they can discuss the emotional effects of the heightened sexual feelings aroused by puberty, preparing them for the new intensity of their orgasmic sensations and their increased desire to masturbate.

This is a very appropriate time for parents to offer their daughter more accurate information about both the physiological and psychological characteristics of the orgasm. They can also share their own orgasmic experiences of pleasure and apprehension with their child. These personal revelations may alleviate a child's fears about masturbating to orgasm. Knowing that it is natural for everyone, including her parents, to have some anxiety along with the pleasure of an orgasm, a girl will feel better about "letting go" and enjoying her own masturbatory orgasms; and her own increased pleasure will prepare her to respond more fully when she eventually has the opportunity to share an orgasm with a sexual partner.

Preparing Boys for Puberty and Ejaculation

Realizing that a boy's first ejaculation results from his own intentional masturbation or a nocturnal emission, parents may find it more emotionally difficult to prepare their son for his onset of puberty. An honest and detailed discussion of the physical and emotional sensations accompanying a boy's ejaculation would necessarily lead to a discussion of the pleasurable aspects of masturbation and of having an orgasm. And having pleasure is the one aspect of sexuality which parents and educators tend to avoid the most.

Of course, parents may feel generally reluctant to acknowledge the purely pleasurable aspects of sex—as if such an admission might immediately spur their children into endless, uncontrollable orgies of erotic abandon. Still, parents need to be honest with themselves if they want to succeed in having honest communication with their children. The honest truth is that sex is great fun; and for a teen-age boy or a man, an ejaculatory orgasm can be the greatest of all sensual pleasures. So parents can help their sons to anticipate the experience of ejaculation by giving them a clear, but simple, description of the physiological changes that lead to an ejaculation. This information will permit a boy to appreciate how an ejaculation provides physical relief and pleasure at the same time as it serves the purpose of procreation.

A boy whose parents have adequately prepared him for his first ejaculation will not be fearful or guilty when he suddenly finds that strange, sticky fluid spurting forth from his penis as a result of his masturbation. Nor will the first occurrence of a nocturnal emission make him feel that something is wrong with him, or that he is being punished for the lurid content of his erotic dreams. A boy may also feel much better when he knows his parents realize that he masturbates. Such a child will not have to worry about maintaining the constant vigilance that Gregg did to keep his masturbatory behavior secret; he will not have to invent devious ways of concealing the signs of his ejaculations from his parents.

Candid discussions between parents and children about masturbation, orgasm, and ejaculation can lead to a fuller exploration of the entire subject of sexuality and its emotional implications. The sex education children get in school does not necessarily go very deeply into the relationship between sexual functioning, sexual pleasure, and the expression of love. And who could inculcate more positive attitudes about the beauty and wonder of an honest and sincere relationship of sexual love than parents who openly share information with their children about the physical pleasures and emotional rewards of their own experiences with each other?

By communicating such values to their school-age children, parents help them to look forward to the time when they, too, will be able to participate fully in the joys of mature sexual love. A child who acquires that kind of orientation toward his personal future will be in the best possible position to maintain a healthy balance between the release and the containment of his sexual desires. Feeling loved, understood, and respected by his parents, he will not feel compelled to masturbate as a means of rebelling against them or compensating for a lack of their acceptance. Nor will he feel obliged to renounce all masturbatory activity in order to get their love and approval. Rather, he will be inwardly governed by both his spontaneity and his own sense of what is best for him to do, holding himself responsible to fulfill his sexual needs in a way that permits him to feel at peace with himself, to develop his talents, and to find a gratifying place for himself in school and society.

Chapter 6
ADOLESCENCE

The beginning of puberty is the end of childhood. True, a postpubescent child may want to go on being a "kid" for many years; and, for just as long a time, he may not feel completely accepted as a peer by adults. But a child's physiological attainment of sexual maturity is an inescapable event that permanently alters the quality of his existence. Like it or not, he now has a fully ripened capacity to procreate, with all the opportunities, responsibilities, and implications that go with it.

The emotional and social consequences of puberty may not be immediately apparent to a child. But postpubescent children are inevitably struck by the great intensification of their sexual drive, which also increases their potentials for sexual pleasure. So they are freshly motivated to find outlets for their erotic desires, which are instinctively oriented toward union with the opposite sex. Yet cultural conditions and their own pyschological immaturity often discourage them from expressing their needs for sexual love in their interpersonal relationships. As a result, many boys and girls become more involved in masturbation than they ever were at any previous stage in their development.

Some societies actually encourage and permit their children to establish loving sexual relationships shortly after they reach puberty. In those preindustrial cultures, the benefits and responsibilities of both biological and social maturity are simultaneously bestowed on postpubescent children. They are automatically granted—and expected to assume—the status of adults. And their physiological and psychological transition from childhood to adulthood is cemented and celebrated with a formal ritual of initiation.

In technologically advanced societies, the onset of a child's sexual maturity does not signal his attainment of social maturity. He receives no ritualistic welcome by adults, who then accept him as a peer. On the contrary, after reaching puberty, children in modern societies typically face a long interval of years before they can acquire the social criteria of adulthood:

an enduring relationship of heterosexual love and vocational self-sufficiency. In fact, that interval, called "adolescence," is a cultural invention.

During adolescence, a young person has to learn how to transfer the expression of his need for sexual love from solitary masturbation to intercouse with a member of the opposite sex. At the same time, he has to learn how to initiate, evolve, and deepen a loving relationship—both giving and receiving love. He also has to begin thinking in earnest about how he is to become economically self-reliant in a way that sustains his interests, accommodates his limitations, and fulfills his potentials. Finally, after exploring a variety of possibilities for loving and working, he needs to make enduring commitments to a particular partner in love and to a particular occupation.

This is quite a challenging task—especially in the context of Western society, with its rapid rate of change in both technology and social values. It is becoming more and more complicated for adolescents to learn how to prepare themselves for adulthood. And those complications are bound to increase as children reach puberty at an earlier and earlier age. Girls in America and Europe are beginning to menstruate about three years earlier than they did a century ago; and boys show a similar trend in their development of sexual maturity.[1] Now, adolescence may begin at the age of ten or eleven. It may not end until the postpubescent child is in his midtwenties. Meanwhile, he has to cope with the emotional burdens of that lengthy period of ambiguity and irresolution.

Release and Containment

The first burden adolescents have to shoulder is the sheer force of their recharged sexual drive. Often, they are so shaken by eruptions of eroticism that they feel like sex-crazed maniacs who are in danger of losing all the self-control they built up through their years of childhood. To make matters more trying, those eruptions may seize an adolescent when he wants most to be free of them; when they do emerge, he may feel helpless to subdue them.

The sexual changes of puberty also introduce adolescents to

new and exquisite dimensions of erotic pleasure. In particular, they are likely to experience their orgasms as much more powerful and fulfilling than the ones they had before reaching puberty.

Assimilating the Experience of Ejaculation

For boys, the postpubescent orgasm culminates in an ejaculation—something they never had previously. So every boy experiences a definite discontinuity in the physical and psychological characteristics of his masturbation before and after puberty. Sometimes, as in Irv's case, a boy may react to his first ejaculation with acute anxiety and guilt. However, most boys perceive their ejaculations as extremely enjoyable—and so did Irv, once he fully accepted the inevitability of his male gender and took responsibility for it. In fact, boys generally tend to regard their ejaculations as a welcome sign of their manliness.[2]

Tony, an exceptionally insightful and articulate fifteen-year-old, didn't start doing what he called "real masturbation" until he was twelve. "Oh, I'd played with myself a little. I used to touch my penis when I was about ten. I was just curious, and I didn't get any real sexual feelings or a sense of a climax. But when I was twelve, I got my first real hard-on one night and I realized what it was like to have sexual feelings. Then I started to experiment, really rubbing myself back and forth. I didn't have an ejaculation but I did it until I got a tremendous sense of sexual pleasure and I figured that's what a climax was. Later, I started to have wet dreams and I realized what it meant to have an ejaculation. When I masturbated then, I felt so much more relieved, and I realized what I'd been missing out on before."

Tony had heard about ejaculations from other boys, so he wasn't frightened when it happened to him. Although his parents hadn't discussed the subject with him, he felt free enough with them to bring it up. "I told them about my wet dreams. I think it was part of my bragging and trying to show off to them about what a big guy I'd become."

Nick also remembers how wonderful he felt when he had his first ejaculation at the age of twelve. Previously, he had been culminating his masturbatory experiences with a pleasurable sense of climax and completion. But once he could have an ejaculation, he felt that his masturbation became significantly more intense and thrilling.

Intensification of the Orgasm

In contrast to boys, a girl's masturbatory orgasm after puberty tends to be quite continuous with her experience of it before puberty. For the orgasms of postpubescent girls have nothing equivalent in novelty to an ejaculation. If a girl has been actively masturbating before puberty, she already knows how it feels to have vaginal secretions and the contractions that go with a climax. However, the hormonal changes of puberty may lead a girl to experience a great increase in sexual desire, erotic responsiveness, and orgasmic pleasure.[3]

Beth, who is married and in medical school, described how she experienced her first real masturbatory orgasm at the age of twelve. "It happened the first night I ever spent in a foreign country. My parents and I had just arrived in London after five days together on a luxurious ocean liner. The only hotel we could get rooms at was a really old-fashioned, seedy place. It was like something out of an English mystery novel—cold, dark, and dingy. All the pipes and plumbing were exposed along the badly peeling walls. The toilets had those ugly boxes on top with long metal chains that you had to pull to flush them. God, it was really awful!"

Beth had a tiny, cell-like room far removed from the one occupied by her parents. "We all laughed and tried to make a big adventure out of the whole thing. But I remember how scared I was when I walked down that long corridor on my way to bed. I tossed and turned on the lumpy bed. What a letdown that place was from the ship! Suddenly, I realized how much I'd gotten used to being so close to my parents on the boat. And I began to miss all of the great kids I'd met on the trip. I felt so lonely and sorry for myself.

"I tried to think of something pleasant. The first thing that came into my mind was the glamour and excitement of the teen lounge. That's where I met Tom, who had been raised in the Orient. I'd never gone to many parties before our trip, so

I was thrilled when he asked me to go with him to the big dance that was held on the last night of the voyage.

"As I lay there shivering in that creepy room, I began to reminisce about the party. I remembered how it felt when Tom held me and how he looked into my eyes as we danced. I got excited and began to fondle myself. I had masturbated a bit before that. But I didn't do it very much and I don't remember reaching anything like a climax. I'd never discussed my feelings about it with anyone. But that night, I found myself really getting into stimulating my genitals. At first I tried to tell myself that I was just doing it to soothe myself. But the more I did it, the better it began to feel, and I couldn't stop. Soon I was back floating on the Atlantic. In my fantasy, Tom and I sneaked away from the dance and went to watch the wake of foam glistening in the moonlight from the stern of the ship. We turned to face each other at the same instant. He put his arms around me and gave me a passionate soul kiss. Just at that point in my fantasy, I had an experience I had never felt before.

"I shuddered and shook in my bed, and I could barely keep from moaning out loud. I was really frightened by it. I'd had feelings of sexual excitement before. But I never expected anything like that! I couldn't believe what happened to me. But as scary as it was, I couldn't deny how marvelous it felt. I definitely remember how glad I was then that my parents weren't too near my room. I realized that this was something very special and I couldn't help looking forward to it happening again. It's strange, though, because I thought I'd done something wrong. Maybe I believed something that felt so good had to be bad. Why else wouldn't anyone have told me about it?"

Why did Beth find her orgasm alarming? Well, there was the element of surprise in its overwhelming force. But why wasn't the surprise pleasant, since it brought her such profound enjoyment? Questioning her further, we found out that what had really upset her was not knowing how to deal with her newly discovered ecstasies in the future. Since they now were hers to savor at will, Beth worried about how much to give herself over to them. Would it be good for her to masturbate to orgasm every time she felt the slightest bit sexy? If she did that, wouldn't she be wanting to masturbate constantly—day and night? But if she didn't feel spontaneously sexy, couldn't she turn herself on whenever she felt like doing so, just as she did that night in the hotel? And why wouldn't she want to turn herself on all the time, considering how fantastic it felt to have an orgasm?

ACHIEVING A BALANCE BETWEEN RELEASE AND CONTAINMENT

Reflecting on these and similar questions, so prominent in the minds of many adolescents, we felt it might be useful to them to have some guidelines for making decisions about their own masturbatory behavior. In keeping with our orientation, the basic consideration underlying our suggestions is whether an adolescent's approach to masturbation is furthering or impeding his own development. As an adult, such a person would want to contribute economically to the support of a loving relationship and a loving family. In being loving toward himself, he would want to make sure that the work he does also contributes as much as possible to the fulfillment of his own talents and interests.

Accepting these goals for his adulthood, an adolescent can help himself to attain them by the way he chooses to masturbate or not to masturbate. Specifically, he needs to assume complete responsibility for determining whether his capacity for heterosexual love and vocational self-actualization is likely to grow by either releasing or containing a masturbatory impulse. Addressing adolescents directly, we would advise them to search for a gratifying balance between release and containment in the following manner:

First of all, you have to be perfectly honest with yourself about the voluntary nature of masturbation. Of course, your urge to masturbate may sometimes feel so strong that you feel you have no choice but to do it. But you do have other choices available to you; and you know that you have exercised such choices in situations where you felt it would be inconvenient or embarrassing to masturbate. And there are many adolescents—

perhaps yourself included—who have made a deliberate policy of refraining from masturbation altogether, even in their own beds at night, for various periods of time.

OK, so the decision to masturbate is entirely up to you. So what's the point of not masturbating whenever you feel any inclination to do it? What difference does it make what your motivation to masturbate may be? Why not do it when you're angry or disappointed or upset, as well as when you're feeling good about yourself and the world?

Well, the main point is that such an indiscriminate approach tends to separate masturbation from genuine love of yourself. If you don't learn what it feels like to be sexually loving toward yourself, you may have difficulty in learning how to express sexual love toward a potential mate. Or, to say the same thing in positive terms, learning how to combine sex and love with yourself helps you to learn how to be sexually loving with another person.

In sexual terms, being loving to yourself means treating yourself with all the consideration you would give to anyone else for whom you have genuine affection. Would you want to treat that person as a lifeless object rather than as a live and sensitive human being? Would you want to exploit that person just to "get your rocks off" or to "tear off a quick piece"? Would you want to use that person as a mere prop for acting out your ego-trips?

Of course not. If you really liked someone you would want to make love with that person in a way that showed your tender feelings, your respect, and your concern. You wouldn't want to disregard that person's mood or state of mind before making love. You would also want your partner to be emotionally ready to reciprocate your love; to have a flow of love going freely between the two of you. So you would wait for a time when you and that person were in a harmony of loving feelings. And you would do your utmost to make the act of sexual intercourse a celebration of the best that is in you and your partner.

Well, when you masturbate, you are the person with whom you are making love. So it is obviously good and proper for you to make love to yourself as you would wish to love and be loved by someone for whom you really cared. When you were younger, you may have often masturbated when you wanted to blot out unpleasant feelings about yourself or something that upset you. At those times, you may have used your imagination to see yourself as being very different from the way you really were. But now that you are sexually mature and approaching adulthood, it's very important for you to teach yourself how to deal with the problems that bother you in a more realistic way, instead of immediately trying to relieve your tensions by masturbating. By changing in that direction, you'll help yourself to feel more competent, strong, and fully alive. Being realistic about your problems is not a "drag." Instead, it is the best means you can develop for assuring your own happiness, now and in the future.

Assuming you do care deeply for your own life and happiness, you can see to it that you save your masturbation for times when you are feeling truly good about yourself. Similarly, you can decide not to masturbate when you are feeling hostile, wretched, or anxious.

Of course, it is not always immediately clear to you exactly how you feel at the moment you get an urge to masturbate. But you can attain clarity about your emotional state if you let yourself contain it long enough to find out. Rather than beginning to masturbate as soon as you feel the slightest impulse of any kind to do so, you can simply be still and receptive to what your inner promptings are trying to tell you.

Perhaps you'll find out that you felt snubbed by someone you like; and that your sudden desire to masturbate stems from a need to give yourself mental and physical reassurance. In that event, instead of masturbating, you can think of how best to communicate your feelings to that person and put your energy forth to do so. Or, your impulse to masturbate may stem from an attraction to someone you have been afraid to approach. Again, you can resolve to make real social contact with that person rather than imagining it in a fantasy while you're masturbating.

Similarly, you can deal more realistically with tensions that arise from intellectual anxieties rather than sexual or social ones. A guidance counselor in a small college told us that students have come to her for help because, whenever they tried to study for their exams, their anxiety aroused their desire to masturbate. One girl, in particular, said her masturbation was becoming a compulsion; and she was beginning to worry that her behavior might be bizarre. Of course, by masturbating, she did give herself some temporary relief from her nervous tension. But it didn't reduce her basic anxiety about taking tests. In fact, since she wasted so much of her study time in masturbation, she felt even more unprepared in her work. So, as the date for her exam neared and she saw the time running out, her anxiety actually increased.

If that girl had taken more personal responsibility for her behavior, she might have been able to change it on her own. First of all, she could have admitted to herself that it is perfectly natural to experience some anxiety before a test. Having accepted its inevitability, she could have decided to contain her anxiety when it arose while she was studying. Instead of choosing to masturbate as a way of escaping from her anxiety, she could have waited until she calmed down, and then gone on with her work. If she had put the time and energy she devoted to masturbation into study instead, she would have been more prepared for her exams, and she would have felt less apprehensive about taking them.

Then, when her studying rewarded her with high marks, she could have felt good about herself for studying rather than masturbating. By following this procedure in all of her courses, she could build up a realistic sense of her intellectual competence; and her increased confidence in herself would have reduced her inclination to escape from the anxiety of preparing for tests.

By contemplating your own motives, you can determine whether you are trying to avoid coping with some problem in your life by wanting to masturbate. Then, instead of going ahead and masturbating, you can decide on the most effective means of actually resolving the particular problem involved; and you can put that means into practice as soon as it is feasible. By doing that, you will strengthen your ability to fulfill yourself, and you will reduce whatever tendency you may have to masturbate lovelessly and futilely.

Certainly, the many nonsexual tensions that bombard you

may add enormously to your masturbatory inclinations, and you may sometimes decide to masturbate to relieve the tensions of problems that you know can be solved only in social reality. But even when you give yourself such solace, you needn't forget what is best for you in the long run—that is, learning how to overcome whatever problem is making you tense. True, a person could adopt the general policy of trying both to resolve his problems and to masturbate whenever he experiences their tensions. But the temptation to favor the latter "solution" is very great, since you always carry your body around with you. So it is best to focus on figuring out and implementing real solutions to your problems.

In examining your masturbatory motives, you needn't worry about lacking any that give you a really good reason for making love to yourself. There are plenty of times when you will feel sexually aroused by the sheer beauty of being alive and well in the world; when you feel such a sense of exuberance, vitality, and oneness with the world then your masturbation is a love song to life.

Tony says he particularly enjoys concentrating on beautiful thoughts and feelings while he masturbates. "Some of the guys I know suggested using music. But I prefer to have it quiet and be by myself. I like to do it late at night when no one is around. The best experience I ever had was at my grandparents' house in the country. I went out into the woods all by myself. It was so still and wonderful. I felt very alone but I was very peaceful and comfortable about it. So I masturbated and I had a really good time because I could devote my total attention to it."

But you may be one of those few adolescents who steadfastly refrains from masturbation, even when it would be a celebration of your love for life. If you are, it's important for you to realize, as Irv finally did, that there is absolutely no moral, emotional, or physical virtue in such abstinence for its own sake. On the contrary, as you know in the depths of your heart, your inflexible containment of all masturbatory impulses is bound to be frustrating. It is also likely to make you chronically tense and nervous. In fact, complete abstinence from masturbation does violence to your life and your humanity.

So why would you, a presumably noble-minded person, want to inflict violence on yourself? Why wouldn't you want to give yourself the same kind of care and consideration you would be willing to give to others? Why, if you believe in love as a social or spiritual ideal, do you insist on not loving yourself?

You can begin to examine your antimasturbatory motivation with these questions; others may well occur to you. But keep in mind that what you are searching for is an understanding of your reluctance to make love to yourself.

Somewhere in your background, undoubtedly, you felt it was crucial for you to separate masturbation from self-love. Perhaps you were taught that masturbation was vile and sinful, something that no self-respecting or God-fearing child should ever do. Perhaps, as in Irv's case, your reasons for totally avoiding masturbation were more complicated, involving conflicts over your sexual gender or your attractions to your parent of the opposite sex.

At this point, you face the challenge of putting sex and love together for yourself—the way they are, in fact, blended in the fabric of everyone's life. Now you need to learn how to function as a loving sexual being—not only in your thoughts and feelings about yourself but also in your actions toward yourself. It may be neither quick nor easy for you to accomplish such a mental and behavioral integration. But your future happiness in a loving relationship may depend a lot on your getting it together for yourself. For if you don't learn how to feel good about making sexual love to yourself, it may be difficult for you to accept sexual love from someone else.

While you are trying to sort out the origins of your inhibitions, you can begin to overcome them by using the same approach we suggested for adolescents who tend to indulge every one of their masturbatory impulses. That is, you can zero in on any such impulse that crops up in your mind. Then you can decide for yourself whether it would help you to become a more loving person by expressing it. If you feel it would, you can then proceed to release your urge through actual masturbation. Otherwise, you can contain your urge and resolve to overcome the problem that it reflects in the manner we have indicated.

Of course, being a champion in containment, you will probably experience little difficulty in refraining from acting upon masturbatory impulses that do not improve your potentials for giving and receiving heterosexual love. But you are very likely to feel awkward and unnatural about masturbating when you decide it would be good for you to do so. Here, it's best to fall back on the ancient but still useful saying: "If at first you don't succeed, try, try again."

In regard to this seemingly big step from containment to release, it would be most helpful for you to remember that you are completely in charge of yourself. So, just as you once decided not to masturbate at all, now you can change your decision and masturbate as you wish—and under whatever conditions give you the greatest sense of privacy, safety, and comfort. Making all those constructive decisions in your own behalf is an essential part of the whole process of learning how to take responsibility for giving yourself sensual pleasure.

One final point may be helpful for you to admit to yourself: Even if you have avoided so much as touching your genitals, you may have been using mental masturbation as an unrealistic and magical means of trying to solve many of your problems. Like Irv did, you may often sit in class and daydream about being a world-famous scientist, while being terrified, in reality, about the possibility of failing chemistry. Or, as you walk through the halls of your school, you may be mentally going to bed with every member of the opposite sex who attracts your eye. Yet you may have been avoiding dances and other social functions where you could actually meet someone to love.

So you could advance your ability to obtain genuine gratification in your life by becoming aware of how you have been using mental masturbation to mask your fears and to frustrate your needs. Such an awareness could permit you to become more accepting of your actual limitations and to act more effectively on your real intentions.

SELF-ACCEPTANCE AND ACCEPTANCE OF OTHERS
Assimilating Bodily Changes

Seemingly overnight, the physiological changes of puberty shake up the self-image a child has already developed. Confronted by the onslaught of his biolological growth and sensuality, an adolescent can hardly take refuge in his prepubescent conception of himself. For the way he used to see himself no longer squares with the undeniable reality of his bodily changes and their accompanying impact on his erotic feelings and motivation. Rather, he is virtually forced by his own growth to change his image of himself, bringing it more and more into line with what he now is and letting go of his image of what he once was.[4]

These changes in self-concept are difficult for a teen-ager to make, however necessary and desirable they are for the ongoing development of his personality. An early adolescent's difficulty is further increased by the very fact that he has to change his concept of himself while his body is in a state of continual flux. Besides, his bodily growth is likely to be very erratic—rapid in some respects and slow in others.[5] For example, a girl's pubic hair may show a womanly appearance, while her breasts remain the same as they were before she reached puberty—or vice versa. Likewise, a boy's face may remain hairless while his rapidly rising height makes him seem like a fullgrown man in comparision to other boys of his age. In addition, adolescents may inwardly experience marked individual differences in the degree of their increased sexual motivation. So comparing their erotic preoccupations with one another, some adolescents are bound at times to feel either abnormally oversexed or abnormally undersexed.

Luckily, an adolescent can use masturbation as a way of emotionally assimiliating his anatomical and physiological changes, while altering his self-image in accordance with them.[6] While masturbating, a girl can become thoroughly acquainted with her newly protruding breasts, taking pleasure in their shape, texture, and erotic responsiveness. Meanwhile, she can imagine how she now looks with her increased bosom, reinforcing this change in her self-concept with the sensual delight she gives herself in fondling it. Naturally, she can reward herself in a similar way for her other bodily changes. She can build up a favorable image of her changing torso by stroking it fondly; and she can certainly do the same for her pubic hair and genitalia, envisioning their altered size and shape as she stimulates them on her way toward an orgasmic climax.

The same process of incorporating the physical changes of puberty into a new and favorable self-image can be carried out by boys.[7] While masturbating, boys can visualize their rapidly changing bodies, tenderly combing their fingers through the few downy hairs on their faces and chests as they project an affectionate picture of themselves in their imagination. A boy can also pleasurably imagine the increasing musculature of his body as he runs his hands along its length and contours. Finally, he can joyfully explore the freshly charged eroticism of his genitals while he mentally constructs a positive image of them.

Fantasies of Success

Reacting to the beginning of his puberty, Tony had fantasies about being an older man who was completely independent from his parents, relatives, and the rest of society. He saw himself driving around in a sports car, impressing girls and picking them up in bars. Within a few years, his masturbatory daydreams started to reflect his actual interest in music and musical performance. "Now, I see myself as a rock star who's really popular and accepted. I get a feeling that I'm my own person, with lots of individual ability. Then that fantasy gradually builds into a sexual one. Being a star leads to having more sex with more women who are attractive." Tony said that it wasn't just the fantasy of being successful that made him feel sexually excited, but more the idea of "being something you really want to be, like your ideal about life. You can use your imagination when you masturbate to make up what you really want to do."

By using their masturbatory fantasies to portray themselves as sexually attractive, virile, and successful men, adolescent boys can increase their self-esteem and their identification with adult males.[8] All through his adolescence, Gregg also continued to project himself into the role of the strong, handsome, older male. As a freshman in high school at the age of fourteen, he was already eager to try out for the football team. The next year, he succeeded in getting on the team. Then, for the first time in his life, he had a feeling of adequacy, camaraderie, and belonging. Feeling really good about himself, he started to function very well with his teammates, and he was able to get close to the coaches whom he had always respected as outstanding models of adult men. During that time, Gregg often had masturbatory fantasies of being a star player on the team, making love to the prettiest cheerleaders on the squad.

As they imagine themselves in sexual contact wtih members of the opposite sex, adolescent boys can express and reinforce their wish to succeed in finding a heterosexual lover of their own. As a result, they develop the confidence to enact their sexual wishes and motivate themselves to search for a real mate.[9]

In his middle childhood, Nick's masturbatory fantasies were enacted with fictitious women from the sexually titillating stories he had read. By contrast, in his postpubescent fantasies, he imagined making love to girls he actually knew, such as the ones in his junior-high classes. He had not yet started petting or having direct sexual contact with girls, so the nature of his fantasies remained the same—he still saw himself performing the sexual acts that had been described in the books and magazines he read. The difference was that now he imagined doing those things with real people to whom he was attracted, and with whom he really would have liked to make love.

The Effects of Menstruation

Adolescent girls may find that the establishment of their ovulatory cycles is an emotionally stabilizing experience. Some girls respond to menstruation with a mixture of apprehension and physical discomfort. But the feeling of regularity, the awareness of the inner source of their flow, and the need to care for their bodies create a focus around which girls can organize their self-image and sexual functions.[10]

In and of itself, menstruation is not experienced as sexually pleasurable, and it is certainly not induced by sexual self-stimulation. But menstruation does require girls to touch their genitalia much more than they ever did before. Sanitary napkins may stimulate skin irritations or itching; girls may react to those sensations by touching and soothing their vaginal area. The insertion of tampons, which are gaining in popularity with young girls, can arouse erotic feelings and thoughts. The frequent need to change either form of protection creates a need to go to the toilet, where girls must wipe and touch their genitals. Some girls, reacting against their long-suppressed temptations to masturbate, may resist learning how to use either a sanitary napkin or a tampon.[11] But other girls may be tempted to masturbate more frequently than they did before puberty.

Maggie vividly recalls the summer when she was sixteen and had a job as a counselor-in-training at a sleep-away camp. The person she admired most was Jacqueline, the swimming counselor, a lovely, tall, and well-built college student whose swimming form matched the grace of her body. Maggie couldn't help but envy Jacqueline's determination to keep up her routine of swimming across the lake and back even when she had her period. "I had to stay on the dock when I had my period and I felt like a real jerk. One day, while we were supervising the kids together, Jackie suggested that I try using tampons so I could carry on all of my usual athletic activities even when I was flowing hard. And she offered to show me how to use them. At first, I was a bit hesitant. But then I thought that it might be a good idea, since I'd been wanting to try them anyway.

"A few nights later, as soon as my period was over, we got together with a few of the other girls in the counselors' tent. While we focused our flashlights on Jacqueline, she demonstrated how to insert a tampon. I can still see her stretched out on the cot with her legs drawn up and wide apart. As she began to spread open the lips of her vagina I almost freaked. I was torn between wanting to take in every little detail and wanting to run from the entire scene. I was terrified, but I couldn't move because I was ashamed to seem 'chicken' in front of the other girls. So I stayed glued to my spot and I tried not to show my anxiety."

After Jacqueline finished her demonstration, she suggested that Maggie lie down so she could help her to put a tampon into her own vagina. "At first, I was so tense and tight that she couldn't get it in me. 'Relax, relax,' they all said. So I tried my best to just lie back and let her do whatever she had to do. As Jackie kept working on me, I started thinking about how grown-up I'd be and all the mess I'd avoid by not having to use sanitary napkins any more. It was amazing how easily it finally went in. Really, I couldn't believe how good it felt. I didn't even know that anything was inside me."

Later that night, Maggie practiced putting in and taking out the tampon on her own. She was getting herself sexually aroused; she began to feel nervous and confused about the mixture of feelings that had been stirred up in her. Experiencing great difficulty in falling asleep, she finally gave in and began to masturbate, hoping it would help her to relax.

"As I masturbated, I kept seeing Jacqueline's beautiful body. She was making love to Bob, the boys' tennis instructor. I really adored him. While I was watching them from the other side of the tent, she turned into me. Even though I had taken Jackie's place and was the one who was lying next to Bob, I could see myself clearly, as if I was still a bystander. I looked absolutely gorgeous. Bob was kissing me and fondling me all over and it felt absolutely wonderful." As a result of her fantasy, Maggie said she got so worked up that by the time she reached her orgasm, she was thrusting her fingers in and out of her vagina.

Through such masturbatory fantasies, adolescent girls can imagine being sexually penetrated while they actually stimulate and penetrate thmeselves. This self-penetration may help them to gain a more mature understanding of their internal genitalia and how it responds. But the masturbatory fantasies of adolescent girls often go beyond the act of sexual intercourse, portraying the entire romantic matrix of love, marriage, and motherhood. Girls of this age may focus on anticipations of becoming grown-up women, capable of experiencing great sexual pleasure and of giving birth to children. Girls use such masturbatory fantasies to create the incentive for finding mates and to prepare themselves emotionally for their reproductive functions.[12]

Homosexual Explorations

While they are sorting out their future goals and consolidating their identities as men and women, some adolescents may be tempted to explore the possibilities of having sexual relations with members of their own sex.[13] As a life style, homosexuality may appear attractive to adolescents who anticipate only a loss of personal freedom in assuming the responsibilities of a committed heterosexual relationship and a family of their own. In any event, all human beings are potentially bisexual; and people of the same sex are certainly capable of having deep and loving feelings for each other.

Some adolescent boys—like their younger counterparts—may engage in some type of homosexual "play" with a single partner or a group. Their activity may include simultaneous but self-induced masturbation, mutual masturbation, fellatio, or other forms of bodily contact with males.[14] Kris remembers being invited to participate in a "circle jerk" by the boys at school when he was about thirteen. "I never realized I could use my hands like that. Once I stared jerking off with the other guys, I understood what I'd been doing all those years when I shinnied up and down the climbing bars in the schoolyard. But there was so much anxiety connected with that mutual masturbation that, from the ninth or tenth grade on, I never masturbated again, either indirectly or by touching myself—even when I was in the Navy and felt really hard up."

When Tony was twelve and a half, he and a few of his good friends would sometimes start to show off and see if they could get hard-ons. Although he felt accepted by these boys, he felt uncomfortable at first about exposing his penis. Eventually, his gang found an empty room in the apartment-house basement, and they would go down there to have a circle jerk. Typically, they would brag about the size and hardness of their penises, trying to see who could get an erection fastest or ejaculate the farthest. But the main status symbol in Tony's group was to see who could get his penis reddest.

Tony said that his friends were reluctant to touch each other too much; they thought something was wrong with boys who touched each other. But they did "check out" one another to see if each boy really had a full-fledged erection. While they were doing that, they usually joked about girls, saying things like, "Gee, doesn't she have big ones!"

As they got older and more involved with girls, the boys got more up-tight about either masturbating together or confiding in each other about it. When Tony was fourteen, he and some of the boys in his camp started to have intercourse with the girls there; then, they stopped masturbating together completely. Now, whatever sexual contact they have has more of a teasing and joking nature; but they still get into comparing each other's genitals in the shower room after basketball practice. Tony says that he feels sorry for the guys who feel inadequate about their cocks, because they feel they are less of a man than they should be.

In surveys of young women's sexual behavior, very few report group encounters of mutual masturbation.[15] Yet many adolescent girls do get secretly involved in mutual sex play and genital masturbation,[16] as described in the recent autobiographical writings of Ingrid Bengis and Nancy Friday.[17] Of course, it is still more socially acceptable for girls than for boys to touch, embrace, and kiss in public. Perhaps their very freedom to be physically demonstrative in expressing mutual affection permits girls to give each other the sexual reassurances in public that boys feel obliged to seek from each other in private.

Many teen-age girls, like Maggie, develop a crush on a female peer whom they admire, or whose attributes they desire. It is also common for girls to become infatuated with older women, such as their teachers or employers, whose physical or mental qualities they find exciting and would like to emulate.

Girls may not actually masturbate together as much as boys; but, like boys, many adolescent girls do spend a great deal of time in mutual *mental* masturbation. In these verbal equivalents of the circle jerk, girls try to prove their genital adequacy by impressing one another with tantalizing tales of their sexual prowess with men. By bragging about what a turn-on they are to men, girls also derive great sensual and emotional pleasure from being a turn-on to each other. And they may use that turn-on as a stimulus to their own solitary masturbation.

Many adolescents use solitary masturbation and fantasy

as a way of working out whatever conflicts they may have about their sexual preferences. A seventeen-year-old-girl in Sorensen's survey said she was troubled by the fear that she was a homosexual because she lacked interest in men. So she deliberately created images of naked women and girls while she masturbated, testing out their erotic impact for her. Finding that she couldn't have an orgasm in conjunction with such fantasies, she felt assured that she was heterosexual.[18]

Adolescents of both sexes may also expose themselves to actual homosexual relationships as a means of defusing their fear of its attraction to them. Having tried it out, they often conclude, from their own experience, that it is not sufficiently gratifying to them to be a permanent sexual preference. So when they ultimately opt in favor of heterosexual love, they may not feel that they are giving up or fleeing from something they may want.

However, the great majority of adolescents in Sorensen's survey said they never expect to engage in any kind of homosexuality; and only nine percent reported that they ever had had a homosexual experience. Many adolescents appear to be tolerant of homosexual behavior in others, and they do not consider it to be morally wrong, provided no one is being hurt. But, despite their tolerance of homosexuality in others, three-fourths of all the boys and girls in Sorensen's sample agreed with a statement describing homosexuality as unnatural or abnormal. And the same proportion said that they would be upset if their own children turned out to be homosexual.[19]

Possible Explanations of Homosexuality

Still, some adolescents do wind up choosing homosexuality as a permanent life-style. Such a choice has been explained in many ways; experts in the fields of psychology, psychiatry, and human sexuality disagree among themselves about its basic determinants. And none of the proposed explanations seems to fit everyone who prefers homosexuality to heterosexuality.

Thus, homosexuality has been conceived as reflecting some deficiency in either instinctive drive or in social conditioning—or both. On the instinctive side, factors such as constitutional type and hormonal imbalance have been considered as possible causes.[20] On the side of social conditioning, homosexuality has been viewed as a fear of genital contact with the opposite sex,[21] a rejection of sex-role expectations,[22] and an erotic attachment to one's own genitals and to people with the same kind of genitals.[23]

We feel there may also be some children whose ultimate preference for homosexuality is influenced by their perpetual need to create particular kinds of self-glorifying masturbatory fantasies. In those fantasies, a child imagines himself as possessing characteristics he feels he is lacking as a member of his own sex—characteristics without which a boy may regard himself as "not enough of a man," and a girl as "not enough of a woman." Such a child may perceive himself as deficient in looks, stature, or some other aspect of his bodily appearance. Similarly, he may have some self-perceived psychological deficiency or vulnerability, such as a terror of physical danger and injury, or a feeling of being too easily intimidated by people to stand up for his own thoughts and feelings in confrontation with them. Other adolescents may feel they have inadequate artistic talent or intellectual competence.

These fears and feelings of insufficiency need not be grounded in anything real that other people can perceive. Rather, as C. A. Tripp says, the important consideration is the distance a person perceives "between where he is and where he would like to be in terms of accomplishment, image, or whatever. Thus it is the contrast implicit in this distance which determines a person's appetite for same-sex attributes and, consequently, his readiness to admire them, to eroticize them, and to import still more of them."[24]

As long as an adolescent feels inwardly plagued by shortcomings he sees in himself, he may consider himself unworthy of love. And he may feel compelled to compensate for those shortcomings through his masturbatory fantasies, which temporarily give him the feeling of being lovable. When he masturbates with those fantasies in mind, he is reinforcing his tendency to be attracted to the people in them; and often, in his fantasies, he vividly imagines himself as turning into the very person he admires. So an adolescent driven by a chronic need to create fantasies about members of his own sex, whom he perceives to have characteristics he lacks, may start to lean in a homosexual direction.

Eventually, such an adolescent may interact with someone he sees as having one or more of the characteristics he admires. If he has sexual contact with that person, he can psychologically partake of the characteristics he desires, identifying himself with the other person not only in his accompanying fantasies but also through the physical intimacy of the encounter. While actually stroking, fondling, and becoming physically interpenetrated with an admired person, he mentally assimilates the attributes he wishes to acquire; and he feels as if it is he himself who has them. Meanwhile, he may imagine that someone truly loves him, because he has now acquired what he felt himself to be lacking.

Since a person knows that his transformation is imaginatively taken from another, it cannot have a lasting positive effect on his self-concept. He continues to feel as inadequate and imperfect as he did before; and those feelings may keep goading him toward new homosexual encounters, in which he again seeks to absorb vicariously whatever he feels will make him perfect and perfectly lovable. In pursuing his insatiable quest, he tends to search not for any sustained relationship with a single and finite individual but for the infinite acquisition of desired traits that he sees personified in many people. Indeed, in writing about his own homosexuality, Jean Genet has implied that it matters very little to him whether or not an "adored" sexual partner is real or fictional. In either case, what seems most important to Genet are the idealized qualities he first attributes to another man and then tries to incorporate as his own.[25]

An adolescent who uses fantasy to "alter" his "flaws" in such a magical way has to feel convinced that his willful artifice is preferable to reconciliation with his self-perceived imperfections. Unwilling to accept himself as a limited being, he may decisively reject all opportunities for fulfilling the life-creating potentials of his sexual gender. Instead, he may deliberately avoid heterosexual relationships; and he may become a confirmed homosexual, choosing it as a medium through which he endlessly pursues the exciting impossibility of attaining his personal perfection.

In contrast, most adolescents are willing to tolerate their own perceived limitations without feeling compelled to renounce them permanently in favor of a perfection that can be attained only by imagining it. Certainly, they may yearn to be ideal beings; and they may often use their masturbatory fantasies to "improve" on what they feel would make them paragons of their own sex. But they are basically willing to make compromises between what they feel they are and what they would ideally want to be. And those compromises permit them, ultimately, to enter into relationships of heterosexual love, within which they can realize the procreative potentials of their particular gender while experiencing the wholeness of merging with someone from the other half of the human species.

UNDERSTANDING AND COMPETENCE

The most important new behavior an adolescent needs to learn is how to make love with someone of the opposite sex. Just as he must acquire the social skills required for obtaining dates, he needs to learn the specific sexual skills that will make him a satisfied and satisfying lover. The way an adolescent masturbates may either increase or decrease his potentials for being a competent lover.[26] It is very important for adolescents to understand how their particular approach to masturbation may affect their sexual actions and reactions with another person. Various masturbatory techniques and attitudes have interpersonal implications; and they may either facilitate or impede an adolescent's ability to share the joys of sexual love with a partner. In addition, the enjoyment of sexual relationships may, in turn, have a positive impact on an adolescent's masturbation.

The Effects of Heterosexual Experience on Masturbation

At the age of fourteen, Nick started to have his first sexual relationship with a girl. Engaging in serious petting, they stimulated each other to have orgasms. "I would put my penis between her thighs and move back and forth until I came. After my experience with her, I didn't feel so much of a need to masturbate. But when I did it, I was able to enjoy touching myself much more. It wasn't so all-important just to ejaculate. I began to indulge myself during the process, drawing it out while I fantasied a replay of my experience with my girlfriend. Sometimes, I would even see myself as having intercourse with her."

Tony said that he started to masturbate a lot more after he had sex with girls. He felt more comfortable with masturbation than he did before; and he let himself get into it more fully. In the past, he had masturbated simply by rubbing his penis with his hands. But after having had intercourse, he started to masturbate by lying on his stomach in his bed, pumping up and down and getting into it with his whole body. Previously, he used to have an orgasm very quickly; but now he tries to prolong his masturbation as much as possible, making the pleasure of his foreplay last longer before he has an ejaculation. Tony also has more erotic material for his masturbatory fantasies, recalling his actual experiences with girls.

In his fantasies, Tony mentally tries out all sorts of sexual positions he has heard or read about. He often sees himself with older girls, who are very experienced and who introduce him to things he has never tried in reality. In that way, he has developed a desire to have oral sex with a real partner. "I guess I was just turned on by the idea that it was 'different' from ordinary sex. I had felt nervous about the idea before. But after a while, after I'd imagined doing it, I was actually able to start doing it."

A fifteen-year-old girl in Sorensen's survey reported that she used masturbation and masturbatory fantasy in a similar way. In addition to creating fantasies about her boyfriend and other good-looking men, she also imagined other, "more useful" things. "I could find out a lot about my fears that way. . . . I tried masturbating to some thoughts that I didn't dig. Such as oral sex. . . . I've finally come to that thought. Anal sex I tried masturbating to, but I couldn't come to that. I'm not really free about that." This girl felt that her ability to have a masturbatory orgasm while imagining oral sex was a sign that she had conquered her fear of it.[27]

The Effects of Masturbation on Heterosexual Intercourse

Kinsey found that women who had masturbated to orgasm before experiencing intercourse were better able to respond orgasmically in their sexual relationships.[28] For many girls, in fact, masturbation may provide an excellent way of testing and triggering their orgasmic ability.[29] Their solitary orgasms may give them confidence that they are capable of having a shared orgasm if the situation and their feelings about their partner are right. Through masturbation, many girls may also discover their ability to have multiple orgasms. In particular, girls who have learned to stimulate their entire external and internal vaginal area, with emphasis on their vaginas, seem to make a very good adjustment to intercourse.[30]

However, some girls may get into habits of masturbation that hinder their ability to enjoy sexual intercourse. Girls who have used indirect methods of self-stimulation, such as thigh-pressing and breast-rubbing, may find it difficult to "get off" on the direct clitoral and vaginal stimulation they receive from a male partner in intercourse. Because they have avoided touching and fondling their own genitals, they may also resist similar stimulation from their sexual partners, limiting their potential level of physical arousal.[31]

Sometimes, a girl who has had no difficulty reaching a climax from her own sexual stimulation may find that the particular position she has become accustomed to using during masturbation inhibits her response during intercourse. One girl consulted a counselor at her college because she was unable to experience an orgasm when she and her boyfriend had intercourse. Although she was very turned on to him, and he was extremely patient and affectionate, nothing they did seemed to work for her. She revealed that she had been masturbating since the age of five or six and never had trouble reaching orgasm through masturbation. When she masturbated, she would always lie face down and move her whole body back and forth, rubbing her genitals against her hand.

The counselor advised this girl to try other positions when she masturbated, suggesting that she flip over and explore her responses to various ways of arousing herself while on her back—the position she typically assumed when she had intercourse. At first, she had difficulty reaching a masturbatory climax lying on her back; but, with practice, she became comfortable with the new position and stimulated herself to orgasm. Now she can let go during sexual intercourse and achieve a satisfying climax with her partner.

For boys, overly quick methods of masturbation may undermine their ability to share sexual enjoyment with a female partner. If boys become accustomed to reaching a masturbatory climax as quickly as they can, they may be inclined to have premature ejaculations during intercourse. Wardell Pomeroy, a sex counselor, advises boys to masturbate slowly, just as Tony and Nick began to do intuitively, drawing it out as long as they can before having an ejaculation. In that way, their masturbation can provide very good training in sexual endurance and prepare them for their future roles as desirable sexual mates.[32]

Many adolescent boys do not yet realize that girls are capable of having orgasms, too. And they are even less aware of the kind of stimulation that facilitates a girl's sexual arousal. Boys and girls who are in a sexual relationship could help each other by openly sharing their histories of masturbation and their particular preferences for sexual arousal. Tony said that he felt very good about being able to talk about masturbation with some of his girlfriends. When he learned that girls could also have an orgasm, he felt even better, knowing they had feelings similar to his own. He added that he would have been more uncomfortable about having sex with girls if he hadn't masturbated in the presence of other guys. Since he knew the feeling of coming in front of someone else, he felt more natural when he had an orgasm with a girl.

Tony feels that masturbation is very helpful to him when he is sexually involved with a girl but things aren't working out right. If he isn't sure about his own feelings toward her, he focuses on them while he masturbates. "Sometimes you love a girl, but certain things annoy you and get on your nerves. By masturbating you can sexually think things over. Like you can think about your past activities with the girl and try to see if it's worthwhile or not. If you don't want intercourse with that person and you're not sure what you want to do, masturbation helps you to make up your mind about what to do."

INDIVIDUALITY AND RELATEDNESS
Shifting from Masturbation to Intercourse

Because most adolescents have to postpone marriage for years after reaching puberty, their relationships with members of the opposite sex are bound to be fraught with uncertainty, ambiguity, and complications. These difficulties cannot help but affect the quality of their sexual interactions; and it may take considerable time and experience before adolescents feel comfortably "settled in" to intercourse in preference to masturbation. Meanwhile, they may shift back and forth between masturbation and intercourse. Indeed, according to Sorensen, a very large percentage of teen-agers are actively and simultaneously involved in both sexual intercourse and solitary masturbation.[33]

There does appear to be some difference, however, in the way boys and girls deal with masturbation while they are having sexual relations with others. Thus, Sorensen found that boys tend to forgo masturbation when they are regularly engaging in heterosexual intercourse. In contrast, girls reported masturbating just as often whether they were actively involved in sexual intercourse or not.

This discrepancy between boys and girls may reflect a lower level of gratification that the girls derive from their sexual relationships. Although the risk of pregnancy may make both partners anxious, its consequences are clearly more personal and serious for the girl than for the boy. In fact, more girls than boys report feelings of fear, guilt, and worry connected with sexual intercourse. By contrast, more boys than girls tend to perceive intercourse as providing them with excitement, satisfaction, and increased self-esteem.[34]

Girls may also be more adversely affected than boys by tensions related to both the physical setting and the social context of their sexual relationships. While many adolescent couples are now having sexual relations in their own homes, they may not take enough time for the girl to attain the fullest pleasure in it. Or, they may select a place for lovemaking that the girl finds uncomfortable or too public.

For girls, the ability to have an orgasm during intercourse may be particularly affected by the quality of their relationship with their sexual partners. In his research on the female orgasm, Seymour Fisher, a psychologist, found that women who experienced difficulty in having orgasms during intercourse were often concerned about the uncertain and undependable character of their relationships.[35] Since adolescent girls often experience such uncertainty with their sexual partners, they may find it difficult to attain an orgasm whenever they have intercourse. Consequently, many adolescent girls may rely on masturbation for the kind of orgasmic release that they fail to obtain in their sexual relations with boys.

Still, adolescent girls, like boys, generally feel it imperative for their personal growth and future well-being to overcome their previous reliance on masturbation for sexual satisfaction. Given that feeling, they struggle to find ways of making their relations with sexual partners as emotionally fulfilling as possible.

Regina said she set no sexual limits on herself as a teen-ager. Yet she was very romantic and she liked to feel she was "in love" whenever she was sexually involved with a boy. "High school was a very eroticized period in my life. I had intercourse for the first time when I was fifteen. And I had moved away from home by the time I was sixteen. My mother was very negative about sex. But she was also very contradictory and she didn't set any limits on me either. But I usually stayed with one partner for a fairly long time."

For Tony, the shift from masturbation to sexual intercourse was relatively easy to make. Like many other adolescent boys, he saw in that transition a large step forward toward acquiring adult status. But apart from that consideration, Tony enjoyed the subtle nuances of feeling and sensation that he derived from sexual intercourse, finding them preferable to those he experienced in solitary masturbation. "It's hard to explain exactly what the two different things feel like. When I masturbate, it feels kind of like it builds up and it's not really expected. Then all of a sudden it's like a rush . . . a feeling all over my body . . . many different feelings in a split second. Sorrow, happiness, excitement. It's different from any other feeling. Afterwards, it's sort of like a let-down . . . I feel a little tired out or that it was too short."

"How does it feel when I'm with a girl? Well, I guess it feels like masturbation . . . but much more multiplied. A couple of times I was lucky enough to have a climax at the same time as my girlfriend and then I felt it in every inch of my body, from my little pinky down to my little toe. It was very magnified and much more intense. It was less lonely than masturbation . . . a feeling of being very, very close . . . like being united with someone." Tony went on to say that "even though some of the feelings are the same, when you masturbate it's with one person. It's very enjoyable, but with two people it's more enjoyable. You're not only getting your own climax, but you're feeling the other person's, too."

We asked Tony if there was any difference in his fantasies when he was having sexual contact with a girl. "With intercourse it's sort of a fantasy and sort of not. I'm with another real person so I can't fantasize about being with someone else. I try to feel as close as possible to the girl I'm with, and I put as much emotion into it as I can. When I'm very emotional—you know, when I feel *real* emotion for the girl—I can't fantasize as much. I don't even want to. Maybe I'll fantasize when we first get started, like during the foreplay. But not during the actual intercourse. Sometimes the girl I'm with becomes part of my fantasies then." Tony summed it up by saying, "I guess when you're with someone it's more of a *feeling* than a thought. Thoughts don't go through my mind. Or if they do, I just don't pay any attention to them."

Oedipal Conflict Revived: Separation Anxiety

While many adolescents may begin to share Tony's preference for sexual intercourse over masturbation, they also feel no more ready than he does to leave the protection of their parents and to start an independent life on their own. For all his precocity and sophistication, Tony is still entirely dependent on his family for his basic emotional and financial support; while he and many other adolescents of both sexes may put on a great display of "hip" and "cool" mannerisms, which, they feel, indicate psychological autonomy and maturity, they remain inwardly fearful of actually doing what they still have to do to attain genuine adulthood. Even as they ardently pursue lovers among their peers, adolescents may privately tremble at the thought of becoming really committed to any relationship of sexual love; even as they ask their parents for the clothes or cars they think will make them seem like adults, they often avoid making the necessary educational preparations and vocational commitments that could lead them to real economic self-sufficiency.[36]

Reacting to their fears of sexual, emotional, and economic independence, many adolescents experience a resurgence of the anxiety they felt in early childhood about separating themselves from their parents. That separation anxiety, in turn, may reactivate their old childish desires to cling to their parents and to become sexually involved with them. But adolescents are likely to find the reactivation of such desires morally repellent and threatening to their emotional security. So they are inclined to react defensively against them, with a rebelliousness that belies their underlying yearning to remain as attached to their parents as they were in their childhood days.

Of course, most adolescents would not want to become childishly dependent on or have incestuous relations with their parents. Rather, they are motivated to escape from or to defer what they perceive to be the fearful pressures and challenges of adulthood. But when they feel particularly seized by those fears, they may regress to magical means of dispelling them, reaching out in fantasy for the powers they feel their parents—tested and proven in the crucible of adulthood—already possess.

Despite her outward attempts at appearing very self-sufficient, Regina's masturbatory fantasies revealed the depth of the attraction that her parents still had for her. Through those fantasies, she tried to maintain her emotional connection with them, although she was actively involved in sexual relationships with her adolescent peers.

"I masturbated constantly, even when I was having intercourse. The two things served very different functions. I was heavily involved in fantasy during both activities. But I was very split up, so my fantasies were very different. Sex was for acting out 'as if grown-up.' I was the sex-kitten working hard at being a real woman. I saw myself as someone like Bette Davis. Actually, I had a reputation at school of being very sexy in a good way. But when I was having intercourse, I always felt that I was a spectator, watching myself play a part. And I needed to get validation from a man."

Regina reserved masturbation for creating her own "private romances," in which she could remain emotionally attached to her parents—even though she publicly appeared to rebel against them. "My masturbatory fantasies were very elaborate. They were pretty much variations on a theme—always my family. There would be lots of people in them. I was playing all of the parts and I would appear in several different forms at the same time. Often, the settings were very 'monied' and the clothes were expensive and lavish. Usually, I enacted sexual scenes with members of my own family. I saw myself having sex with my father and I saw my brother having sex with my mother. But, of course, they were all me. Sometimes, I also had sex with the family butler."

In Regina's fantasies, she was always the one who took the initiative to have sexual contact with her father, showing how much she wanted to remain emotionally tied to him. The fact that she portrayed her parents as being so elegantly dressed, in luxurious surroundings, and rich enough to have servants also reflected Regina's deep need to see her family as much more affluent than they really were. Thus, she could feel they had more economic security for her to rely on and to bolster her image of herself.

Oedipal Conflict Revived: Defensive Reactions

In their efforts to overcome their rearoused Oedipal yearnings, adolescents like Regina may suddenly become very distant from or rigidly rebellious against their parents. Some adolescents may also begin to act the same way toward other adults and toward all people who have authority over them, convinced that they are asserting their independence rather than reacting to their fear of it.

These defensive reactions may sometimes help adolescents to pull themselves away from their parents and to force themselves into tests of their ability to function on their own. But bravado and a mindless rejection of all authority may also get adolescents into trouble, or into situations and relationships they are emotionally unprepared to handle. In such cases, they may wind up feeling more personally inadequate, and even more emotionally dependent on their parents, than they did before their false show of independence.

Adolescents typically fail to realize that, no matter what they eventually do or become as adults, they cannot help but be enduringly influenced by their parents. After all, they have lived with their parents and have been dependent on them during the most impressionable years of their lives. Consequently, they have deeply and permanently identified with many of their parents' personal characteristics, even though they may adamantly insist on trying to be totally different from them.

Regina, for example, remembers that during her adolescence she rebelled against her mother, a psychiatric social worker. By contrast, she looked up to her father, an artist and film-maker. Regina demonstrated her admitted admiration for her father by studying art at a special high school and by getting married at eighteen to a man who was hoping to become a film-maker. Nevertheless, she subsequently also showed her deep-seated identification with her mother by choosing psychiatric social work for her own career. Now, Regina shows signs of having integrated her identification with both her parents—for while she earns a living as a social worker, she maintains a strong avocational involvement in making videotapes.

Unlike Regina, many adolescents work very hard to censor their rearoused fantasies of incest, since such fantasies overwhelm them with anxiety and guilt.[37] Adolescents who masturbate to such fantasies may feel trapped by a dangerous and uncontrollable compulsion. Such feelings may even be more frightening than the prospects of adulthood. Intensely troubled by incestuous fantasies, those adolescents may react by trying to renounce masturbation altogether, hoping to rid themselves of the preoccupation with their taboo desires.[38]

Irv's extreme avoidance of masturbation, even throughout his adolescent years, indicates the sexually inhibiting effects of his incestuous motives. For the same reasons, Kris felt unable to take real responsibility for his indirect form of masturbation during his middle childhood. He was even afraid to engage in masturbatory fantasy; he used his indirect self-stimulation simply as a mechanical form of tension reduction. Kris's father, a traveling salesman, was gone from home four or five days a week; when his father was away, he frequently slept with his mother until he was almost fourteen years old.

"My mother was the one who initiated the idea of our sleeping together. She was only seventeen years older than me, and all during my youth she carried on a pseudo-romance with me. But she alternated between being very seductive and very rejecting. I remember how anxious I used to get when I was so close to her—wanting to look and wanting to touch. And I was absolutely furious when I heard that my parents actually fucked."

For years after his adolescence, Kris remained very anxious about sex. In his mind, he had what he called "a madonna-whore model of sex"—going from one extreme to the other in his attitude toward women. He tended to be sexually attracted to older women; and when he eventually had actual sexual relationships, he always needed a woman to give him an immense amount of permission and support for his sexual initiatives and reactions.

Oedipal Conflict Revived: Parental Reactions

The relationship between Kris and his mother shows that parents may also experience a rearousal of the reverse Oedipus complex—a replay of the one they had previously experienced during their offspring's early childhood. But, unlike Kris's mother, many parents are entering middle age just when their children are going through adolescence. Instead of worrying about what their first menstrual period will feel like, mothers are becoming apprehensive about the onset of their menopause. Instead of fearing the embarrassment of uncontrollable erections and ejaculations, fathers may fear being unable to have them. So when parents see the exuberant energy, the increased attractiveness, and the overflowing sexuality of their teen-agers, they are very likely to feel a rearoused sexual interest in them.

However, an adolescent's sexual development also tends to stimulate parental resentment. This resentment stems largely from the parents' fear of losing their own youth. While they may identify with their teen-agers as a substitute for staying young, they also cannot help but realize that they are growing old. This realization motivates parents to take stock of their past. As they examine the realities of their personal, marital, and vocational limitations, they may envy the open possibilities that still lie ahead for their children. Many parents may actually feel jealous and competitive, contrasting what they feel are their own failures with what they imagine their children will accomplish in the future.

Of course, if parents lack sexual gratification in their own relationship, as Kris felt that his parents did, they are likely to be even more threatened by the budding sexuality of their children. They may want to delay their child's development, keeping him immature and overly dependent, and preventing him from establishing loving and gratifying sexual relationships of his own. This kind of overprotection could make adolescents feel extremely inadequate and, in some cases, increase their motivation to rely on masturbation as an outlet for all of their tensions.

In contrasting cases, some parents may overreact to their personal lack of sexual gratification by pushing their children into premature sexual liaisons. Such parents may try to achieve a sense of youth, attractiveness, and sexual promiscuity by living vicariously through their children's sexual escapades. But by pushing adolescents beyond what they feel emotionally ready to handle, parents may encourage them to get involved in relationships that they pursue simply to prove their adequacy. The ultimate failure of these relationships, and the negative experience associated with them, may lead adolescents away from interpersonal sex and back into solitary masturbation. So the net effect is to keep such children even more dependent upon their parents.

Interestingly, in Sorensen's survey, many an adolescent felt that his parents would be happier if his sexual intercourse before marriage occurred in loveless relationships. One boy described this hypocritical parental attitude in his way: "They don't want their little boy to have loving sex, only dirty sex. They think if I have dirty sex that somehow it's less dirty than if I have loving sex. Yet they go around talking as though sex were dirty. What do they want, anyway?" [39]

Undoubtedly, such parents are not letting themselves realize what they really want for their children. But these irrational attitudes do reflect a parental desire to prevent their children from forming truly loving sexual relationships. Parents may fear losing their children to loving mates with whom they could develop a permanent relationship. Or, on an even deeper and more repressed level, parents who have never known real sexual love themselves may be jealous of their own child's possibilities for finding it.

Talking about Oedipal Feelings

Given these mixed emotions, it is understandable that parents may experience particular difficulty in talking about sexual matters with their adolescent children. Their difficulties are compounded by the guilt they feel as a result of the re-arousal of their reverse Oedipal feelings—which are felt even by parents who have a good sexual and emotional relationship themselves. Still, what better help can parents give themselves than to discuss all of these matters with each other and to share them with their children? By openly discussing the reasons for their mutual attraction, parents and children do not seduce each other. Rather, such discussions serve to defuse their shared sexual feelings. Parents can help their children and themselves to become more aware of the impossibility of their reciprocal incestuous fantasies. By talking candidly about the pleasures and the problems of their own marital relationship —while showing their deep love and loyalty for each other— parents can serve as appropriate role models for their teen-age children.

After all, parents *do* want their children to become adult, to be able to face all of life's emotional, social, and economic demands without feeling too fearful to cope with them. Didn't they have to deal with all of those demands themselves? And wasn't it their very willingness and commitment to deal with such problems that gave them the strength and perspective to be able to function as parents at all? Certainly, most parents do not want masturbation to be their child's ultimate form of sexual expression. They would not have become parents themselves if they had limited their own sexual development solely to masturbation.

According to Dr. Anne Welbourne, co-founder of the Community Sex Information service, many parents who call her agency for advice are worried because their adolescent children masturbate. Mothers seem particularly disturbed by the masturbatory behavior of their sons, saying, "He spends an awful lot of time in the bathroom," or "He has a lot of dirty magazines. Is he OK? Is it harmful?" Parents worry about what an adolescent's masturbation will lead to. Does it mean he's having sex already? An even more frequently expressed concern is: "If a boy masturbates frequently and spends a lot of time alone, is he, or will he, become a homosexual?"

Yet most parents say they are reluctant to discuss their child's masturbation with him. The main thing they want to know is how they can *stop* him from masturbating. True, they may also want their teen-agers to abstain from sexual intercourse. However, Dr. Welbourne feels that most parents would much rather their children be involved in a sexual relationship than be overly involved in masturbation.[40]

Talking about Masturbation and Related Issues

Only 17 percent of the adolescents interviewed in Sorensen's survey had ever been told anything about masturbation by their parents. According to Sorensen, "This is a small proportion . . . even in light of the low incidence of full and free discussion of sex."[41] But in her recent research on parent-child communication about sex, Dr. Welbourne found that adolescents really want to talk to their parents. All the teen-agers she interviewed expressed a desire for more parental information and discussion about masturbation. They also want to know how their parents make decisions about their own sexual behavior, and they are eager to learn what their parents think about love, relationships, and homosexuality.

Dr. Welbourne emphasized that adolescents want parental guidance in order to gain a better sense of what will be helpful to themselves—but they also want to make their own decisions. She feels that the proper parental attitude should be one of ready accessibility: "It's OK to talk, and I'm here to listen." She also advises parents to be sincere and honest in expressing where they stand on all issues. She feels that adolescents have a right to know what their parents *really* think. They are very sensitive to nonverbal messages, and they often get upset by the hypocrisy and contradictions between what their parents say and what they really mean or actually do.

Although parents who have a great deal of relevant information tend to talk more to their children about sexual matters than less informed parents, Dr. Welbourne found that parental *attitudes* are more important than the facts they impart. Parents who are most pleased with their own sexual relationship also have the most accepting attitudes about masturbation, premarital intercourse, and homosexuality. In addition, those parents have personally engaged in a wide range of sexual behavior and they tend to talk to their mates more frequently about sex and their sexual feelings. Parents who have these positive and accepting attitudes are the ones who communicate most frequently with their children in regard to masturbation and other sexual activities.[42]

Although the competitiveness of our society certainly does not make it easy for adolescents to feel that they have proven their ability to fend for themselves—let alone for a spouse and children—most adolescents really do desire to relate lovingly to another individual. Many of them see their sexual contacts with each other as a way of expressing these feelings. Moreover, for those adolescents in Sorensen's survey who had engaged in interpersonal sex, emotionally meaningful and monogamous relationships were preferable to promiscuous "adventuring." The solitariness of their masturbatory activities is in direct conflict with their desire to love and be loved. As Sorensen says about masturbation, "the adventure, the feeling of conquest or being possessed, and, above all, the love relationship are absent." [43]

Adolescents who are deliberately masturbating in place of having, or trying to have, a sexual relationship with another person often feel very bad about themselves. They may react defensively to their masturbation, seeing it as a threat to their self-esteem. Many of the adolescents who telephone Dr. Welborne's agency make such comments as: "I don't want to masturbate. I want to fuck. Masturbation is only second best." Besides, many adolescents feel that, by masturbating, they are actually admitting their deep need and desire to be recognized, loved, and sought out sexually by another person.

An adolescent who feels he is escaping from the problems of his life and the challenges of adulthood by becoming immersed in masturbation and masturbatory fantasy may usefully apply the relevant techniques for self-help that we present in this book. Still, such a child may also be grateful for parental help, even while he is taking responsibility to help himself.

By sharing their personal values and sexual insights with their children, and by encouraging their children to share such feelings with them, parents do not rob their children of their capacity for autonomous choice and self-direction. On the contrary, we feel that this kind of sharing actually frees an adolescent to regulate his own masturbatory behavior more effectively, because he becomes capable of making wiser choices and decisions for himself. If a teen-ager sees that his own parents have enough faith in him to take him into their confidence—revealing their own sexual needs, experiences, conflicts, and vulnerabilities—their very trust shows him that they feel he has the strength and maturity to deal with his own sexual problems. Sorensen makes a similar point: "What a young person thinks he is hearing from his parents about sex has much to do with that child's judgment of his parents' attitudes toward him. There are few other subjects of discussion as powerful in forming the young person's perception of how his parents view him." [44]

Through such discussions, parents do not *solve* their child's difficulties for him. However, they do provide the emotional support and honest concern that can help an adolescent to develop the self-confidence he needs to confront his sexual conflicts and his motivations for enacting them in masturbation and fantasy.

Talking about Vocational Choices

An adolescent also needs to have some kind of economic base to maintain a loving relationship and to rear a loving family. To enjoy his economic activity, he needs to earn his living at an occupation that is commensurate with his talents and interests. In this respect, an adolescent's history of imagined achievement via masturbatory fantasy may no more realistically prepare him for a real vocation than it does for an actual relationship of sexual love.

Of course, an adolescent may use masturbatory fantasy as a means of mentally sampling and rehearsing future occupations, as we have shown. Often, however, their imaginary successes far exceed what they are actually capable of doing; in their fantasies, they may endow themselves with qualities of perfection that go beyond the limits of any human being. Yet real worldly accomplishments require a person to recognize and accept his imperfections and to work within the limitations of his actual abilities.

As they speak to their child about his sexual problems, parents can further help him by broaching the issue of his occupational future. Naturally, an adolescent may be unready to commit himself to a particular field of work. However, by bringing up the desirability of making an occupational choice soon after leaving high school, parents can assist their adolescent in freeing himself from whatever unrealistic and inappropriate fantasies he may have nurtured through years of solitary masturbation.

Despite their mutual ambivalence, both parents and children who honestly share their feelings about these important matters can grow emotionally in the very process of weaning themselves away from one another. Parents who are mindful of their true mission in child-rearing can derive their greatest emotional rewards from knowing they have succeeded so well that their children have finally learned how to fulfill themselves in the world without them. "A good parent very skillfully and wisely works himself out of a job," says Sidney Callahan in *Parenting*. "Good parenthood has a built-in disappearing dynamic; in the language of ecology, good parenting is biodegradable." [45]

Eventually, most adolescents come to realize that individual freedom is an empty and meaningless potential unless it is exercised in behalf of one's heartfelt desires. So they bring their own adolescence to an end when, having searched their hearts, they freely choose a mate, an occupation, and a way of living among other adults—the world of those who have made psychological peace with the responsibilities of biological maturity.

PART III
Masturbation and Adult Fulfillment

While growing up, everyone accumulates some unresolved conflicts about masturbation that crimp his ability to be a loving and productive adult. Sometimes, his development has been impeded mainly in one of the four areas of personality we have discussed. Generally, however, his impediments are likely to affect all four areas, since they are closely interrelated.

Naturally, the negative residue of an adult's masturbatory history may not basically impair his ability to form loving relationships, to enjoy sexual intercourse, or to do productive work. But personality development is, fortunately, a lifelong process. So all adults, both married and single, can increase their pleasure and fulfillment in life by understanding their masturbatory behavior and by working through the unresolved conflicts over masturbation that they acquired during their childhood.

Addressing couples, we explain how people in a committed relationship could foster the lifelong development of their individual personalities and increase their marital satisfactions by communicating about their secret involvements in masturbation. Similarly, we describe how they could use various techniques of masturbation to free themselves from sexual dysfunctions and to heighten the erotic gratifications of their lovemaking.

Then, we speak to the unmarried adults—including the divorced and the widowed—who are seeking to build a viable and fulfilling life on their own. We suggest how single people could examine their histories and current patterns of masturbation with a view toward continuing their personal growth and deepening their sexual enjoyment. As we show, they could also use their masturbatory fantasies to resolve whatever ambivalence they may have about establishing an enduring relationship of sexual love.

Chapter 7
COUPLES

From time to time throughout their lives, even the most happily married adults share the universal human tendency to yearn for the impossible; and they may get an urge to masturbate when they feel hemmed in by the inherent limitations of their marital commitments—when they want to be completely free to follow their own desires, without any consideration of their mates.

The tendency for married adults to continue using masturbation is shown in Morton Hunt's national survey of sexual behavior in the 1970s.[1] Of married people in their late twenties and early thirties, seventy-two percent of the husbands and sixty-eight percent of the wives said they were masturbating.

Of course, these figures deal only with reports of physical masturbation. But masturbation can also be purely mental, consisting of self-aggrandizing and unrealistic pipe dreams, which may or may not be explicitly sexual. Since every adult is bound to spend some of his time in such mental masturbation, we can say that all married adults induge in masturbation, even if they do not actually touch their genitals.

While the involvement of marital partners in separate masturbatory excursions is inevitable, it just as inevitably contradicts the essence of their relationship, which is the fullest possible sharing of their lives. That sharing includes their sexual love as well as the contents of their consciousness. So whenever they resist such sharing, they are working against the very goal they have committed themselves to fulfill; and they are undermining their enjoyment of being with each other.

Seen in this perspective, it can only benefit a loving couple to learn how to share more and more of their impulses of sexual love as well as their thoughts and feelings. Indeed, only through such endless learning can a couple continue to deepen their mutual love and the intensity of the fulfillments it gives them. In that way, they reduce the amount of energy that they siphon off into solitary masturbation, while increasing the amount they give to each other.

Growing Together

Each partner in a loving relationship needs to realize that growing with another person is a process very different from the one through which he formerly developed his personality. From birth until he chose a partner in love, he was learning how to separate himself from his parents, and masturbation was a vehicle for his individuation. Masturbation helped him to become physically and emotionally independent from his parents. That kind of learning was essential to give him the confidence and competence to survive without their aid and protection.

By the time he reaches adulthood, a person is likely to place an extremely high psychological value on being entirely self-sufficient, associating it with the skills and attitudes he needs to fend for himself and to maintain his separate existence. Basically, he has acquired ways of interacting with others without committing himself to an emotional merger with them. In fact, the prospect of such a merger is likely to arouse his fear. For it evokes his previous and long-standing dependency on his parents, which was so difficult for him to give up. Of course, he may have learned to be polite, courteous, and cooperative in conducting social transactions that guarantee his survival and the success of his pursuits. Inwardly, however, he feels primarily committed solely to himself—and people do not expect him to feel otherwise in his relationships with them.

Having become convinced of his ability to rely on himself alone, a person begins to sense an emotional emptiness within himself, a need to complete his biological and psychological wholeness, which he can fulfill only by sharing his life in a loving relationship with someone of the opposite sex. The overwhelming majority of people then decide to get married or to live with a lover.

In making that decision, a person drastically changes the path of his personal development. Previously, his growth depended largely upon his learning how to give up his attachment to his parents and to feel good about being on his own and gratifying himself. But, having chosen a partner in love, he has implicitly decided to continue his growth and fulfillment through their relationship. Now, both he and his partner continue developing all aspects of their personalities primarily by learning how to love each other more and more completely, and by working through their individual and mutual problems together. Often, people are not aware of these implications of their decision to form a loving relationship; even if they are intellectually appreciated and accepted, the fundamental change in the focus of their development—from individual-centered to relationship-centered—is very difficult to put into practice.

Some unmarried couples maintain and deepen their commitments to a loving relationship more genuinely than many couples who are legally married. It is often true that people who are living together resist making their relationship "legal," fearing the responsibility for the complete and lasting commitments of a genuine marriage; they may also fear falling into the ruts and miseries they have seen in the marriages of their parents or other people they have known. But being married or unmarried, by itself, is no sure sign of the quality of the relationship experienced by the people involved. Thus, when we speak of "marriage" in this book, we are not referring to a legally defined arangement between two people. Rather, we have in mind the kind of loving relationship in which both partners share the same primary commitment to fulfill themselves through their mutual love.

Motivated by their need for sexual love, married adults desire to become one with their mates; they sense that they can derive the greatest joy from their relationship by merging as lovingly as possible—both psychologically and sexually—with each other. But the process of merging also arouses a person's deepest fears, for it seems to threaten him with a loss of individuality. People are often afraid they will lose control of their own lives or become overly dependent on their mates if they become too loving toward them.

All lovers have to deal with the conflicts between their desires to merge and their desires to preserve their individuality. The acutely troubling mixture of emotions that many brides and grooms experience on their wedding day dramatically illustrates such motivational conflicts. However, by getting married, a couple begins to resolve them by opting in favor of merging.

Because they both continue to reexperience those conflicts

throughout their married life, spouses are often tempted to withdraw their love from each other when their fears of merging are aroused. They often express such fears in their inclinations to engage in solitary masturbation or to become individually immersed in masturbatory fantasies that exclude their mates. One woman in Leah Shaefer's study of female sexual behavior "found it difficult to have a feeling of closeness without feelings of compulsive dependence." She felt she was using masturbation as a way of keeping herself independent and detached from her husband. "I don't feel great about doing it because I feel I'd much rather have sex with him. . . . Part of the reason I feel badly is that I know that masturbation keeps me in a self-sufficient system, which is my problem. It's always been my problem." [2]

Another woman in the study could experience an orgasm with ease, either through masturbation or intercourse. Still, she chose to masturbate periodically as a way of maintaining a sense of control over her own life. "I guess it was my way of not having to feel that any man could just have me at his mercy because of my sex needs." This woman was troubled by her attitude, feeling that she was trying to take her husband's powers away from him. "I felt guilty because I was delighted that I still had control over me." At the same time, she loved to feel that she was her husband's woman "and all that implies . . . that he is the man that could satisfy me, and that I do need him" [3]

Obviously, partners in a marriage have chosen to be completely interdependent, recognizing that they need each other for the fulfillment of their mutual love. By sharing their lives as fully as possible, they do not weaken themselves as persons in their own right, as these women feared they would. On the contrary, learning how to love, cooperate, and communicate with ever-growing fullness, spontaneity, and freedom from fear is the best way for a person to strengthen his own individuality. Genuine emotional strength grows in someone who knows that he has had the courage to reveal himself without disguise to the very person he has chosen to entrust with his life; who knows that he has given all it takes to permit his mate to be as trusting in return; and who has faced up to the recognition of his needs, fallibilities, and limits, permitting him to make compromises that are satisfying to both himself and his mate.

RECIPROCITY AND COMPLICITY

As human beings, spouses share the same basic capacity to sense and to feel—to pick up and derive meaning from emotional "vibrations." When they interact, they cannot help but affect each other equally and reciprocally. Of course, they may differ greatly in their outward expressions of the feelings that pass between them. But each one inwardly experiences the emotional messages sent out by the other.

When they are in each other's presence, mates reciprocate all their feelings, both positive and negative. Sexual intercourse offers them the most intimate and pleasurable means of reciprocating their positive feelings. A husband's love for his wife is expressed as he responds to her by having an erection. In a complementary way, his wife reciprocates her love for him as she responds with the relaxation and lubrication of her vagina. Interpenetrated during intercourse, they reach the ultimate consummation of their merger in orgasms.

But as loving as any husband and wife may be, they all harbor some feelings of inadequacy that block their ability to give each other sexual love. Reacting to these feelings, either partner may often prefer masturbation or masturbatory fantasy to having intercourse. When one spouse follows such a preference, the other is also affected by it. Naturally, a person may not know that his mate is masturbating or fantasizing. But he can certainly sense his partner's state of detachment, defensiveness, or tension; and he can begin to inquire what is amiss with his mate. Some husbands and wives regularly make such helpful inquiries. But people often pretend not to notice what is going on with their mates, because they do not want to risk exposing their own inclinations toward emotional withdrawal.

Even when they feel totally committed to each other, spouses are very reluctant to let each other know just how inadequate they feel about various areas of their being, such as aspects of their physical appearance, or of their functioning, such as their sexual or occupational performance. Not wanting to face their own negative feelings about themselves, they seek to avoid revealing them to one another. For if they did reveal them, they would have to confront them fully within themselves, and they imagine the emotional pain of such a complete self-confrontation would be too difficult to bear.

Consequently, when people first form a relationship, they enter into many unspoken agreements about how they will refrain from "blowing each other's cover," which would force them to reveal the truths they are afraid to face about themselves. We refer to such unspoken agreements as "complicities." These complicities may be very complex, even though a couple never exchanges a word about them; and they also tend to be very persistent, since each spouse tends to feel a tremendous vested interest in maintaining them. It is amazing how many agreements of this kind can be made in total silence. Spouses are much better at reading each other's minds than they want to admit, for such an admission would make it harder to pretend not to know what the other is thinking. So, through their common pretensions of inscrutability, spouses agree to spare one another from the recognition of their mutual deception.

Irv: How long did it take us to talk about masturbation after we were married?
Sue: It was over a year, I'm sure. I know I was terrified to even bring up the subject—especially since I was still doing it so much.
Irv: What about me? I couldn't even see that my being a chronic nonmasturbator was a problem.
Sue: And we thought we were being so open with each other.
Irv: Right. You didn't hesitate to tell me about how you carried on with so many different guys while you were still single.
Sue: And what about your "war stories"? It's true you were six years older than me, but you really got one-up on me, bragging about being such a big whoremaster in the army. But I was glad to let you get away with it. I played the in-

nocent bobby-soxer because I didn't want you to see how sexually driven I'd always been.

Irv: Well, you didn't exactly strike me as uninhibited when you described how you did everything but fuck all the guys you dated the summer before you made up your mind to marry me.

Sue: But I wouldn't dare to mention my own masturbation.

Irv: I was just as messed up as you were. But I had no idea it was related to my fear of masturbation. You knew I had a couple of relationships that lasted more than a one-night stand. But I had my affection pretty well sealed off from my sexual kicks. Of course, I exaggerated my sexual conquests. I felt really powerful having you see me as someone who could get any woman I wanted. And I could kid myself that I wasn't worried about being as sexually up-tight as I really felt. Christ, at the time we were married, I still was afraid to touch my own cock and balls—except to wash them.

Sue: Well, I was certainly never afraid to touch my genitals. And I was still doing it a lot after we were married—even though our sex together was so great. But I was sure afraid to let you in on the fact that I was doing it.

Irv: We were just like a lot of other middle-class couples in the late 1940s. You tried to cover up your fear of being overly involved in sex by acting like a demure little lady. And I played the part of the strong male to cover up my fear of being sexually inadequate. But we were very turned on to each other. I had no doubts about that from the start.

Sue: I'd never gone all the way with a guy before. But I just let myself get into it like I did when I masturbated—and it felt great. I'd always been afraid that if a man saw how hot I could get, he'd know what a masturbator I was, and he'd think I was abnormal. But seeing your response to the wild animal side of me turned me on to you even more. You seemed pretty crazy too, groaning and screaming so loud when you came.

Irv: Knowing we loved each other made our sex fantastic for me. I didn't have to feel guilty, the way I always did when I felt I was using women just to get my rocks off. And you were always available, so I could finally start to express all the pent-up horniness I never let myself satisfy through masturbation. But sometimes, I felt childishly dependent on you for that. And possessive, too. I constantly needed physical expressions of your love to feel that I was desirable and lovable. Part of it came from reacting to you like a mother-figure. And you know how possessive I was of my mother.

Sue: I sure do. If it wasn't for that big fight I had with your mother after we got married, we'd probably still be living in your parents' house. I was only too glad to let you rely on me so much and be so sexually possessive. That was my way of feeling needed when I actually felt so insecure myself. But I was scared to be too emotionally intimate with you. I often held back my real thoughts and feelings. It's ironic—the main reason I fell in love with you was because I felt you understood me more than anyone else I'd ever known. But then when I had someone I could open up to, I clutched up and felt I just had to keep my masturbation and my fantasies to myself.

Irv: I felt exactly the same conflict about revealing my deepest fears to you. I had my own secret fantasies. Of course, I wouldn't admit to myself that I was mentally masturbating. But I definitely felt there was something wrong about being so involved in daydreams of glory. Otherwise, I wouldn't have been so careful to keep them from you.

Sue: I know. But our secrecy was more than just a fear of facing our weaknesses. It was also a way of holding out on our commitments to each other. I know I was terrified by the responsibilities of being married. After all, I was only eighteen. The more we had to come through for each other, the more frightened I became and the more I tried to overcome my anxiety in my usual way—by masturbating. After the way my parents carried on when I wanted to marry you, I had to prove how great our marriage would turn out. Remember how my father accused you of robbing the cradle? And my mother was convinced we'd end up living in a garret. I still needed their approval so badly. How could I face the possibility that things weren't perfect between us?

Irv: But in some ways, your parents' reactions, and the fight we had with mine, brought us closer together. We had a romantic image of ourselves as being two against the world. That feeling of being a close-knit team gave me a lot of reassurance. But I often felt you were hard to reach emotionally, and I sensed your withholding. I was afraid to challenge you enough to find out what was behind it. I often had the feeling that I couldn't rely on you to stick by me if I didn't meet your parents' expectations. After we got married, you never stood up to them the way you did to my parents. When I got mad at you, I could feel myself becoming very cold and detached. At those times, I would drift off into fantasy-land, imagining myself with gorgeous women who appreciated my self-styled perfection. I was really trying to prove to myself that I didn't need you to feel good about myself.

Sue: I could space out into my masturbatory fantasies easily, even while we were having a conversation. But it was a lot harder for me to do the physical part when you were around. Sometimes, even when we had really good sex, if I felt tense about something that wasn't going well, I'd wait for you to fall asleep and then I'd roll over on the far side of the bed and masturbate. Of course, I was very careful not to wake you up. But when I was alone, I hardly controlled myself at all. As time went on, it got worse and worse. I became more and more guilty about being so secretive. God, how many times I deluded myself that I would stop masturbating. I kept thinking, just one more week and I'll get over it on my own. Why bother to aggravate you? I'd always heard my mother say, "What your husband doesn't know won't hurt him." I thought I disagreed, but I guess I absorbed a lot of that fear and mistrust about being totally honest with you. And I was desperately afraid you'd reject me if you knew what I was doing.

Irv: But I distrusted you just as much. I was so preoccupied with my own problems in graduate school that I didn't want to know anything about yours. After I refused to become a salesman like my father, I had to be a success in psychology. I was determined to outdo my father and my two brothers.

So I spent as much time as you did in fantasizing totally unrealistic achievements. I usually hid my anxieties by acting very sure of myself. But I was also convinced that revealing my biggest worries to you would lead you to reject me. In those days, I didn't understand how uncovering my imperfections might have reduced your fear of being honest with me and let you feel strong enough to give me more love and support. It never occurred to me that we were each using masturbation in different ways to deal with the tensions we felt in our relationship. That was the furthest thing from my mind.

Having vowed to give all their sexual love to each other, spouses are naturally inclined to perceive their separate and secret involvements in masturbation as violations of their common pledge. Feeling guilty about those violations, they are motivated to confess them to each other, since confession is a means of expiating guilt. However, the prospect of confessing arouses their fears of rejection and retaliation, which are likely to be very intense, considering the depth of the interdependency that is involved in their marital relationship. Because of those negative anticipations, spouses tend to succumb, as we did, to the temptation to continue keeping their masturbation and fantasies secret from one another.

As a consequence, they begin to feel hostile to each other. For if their mates are the ones they perceive as making them feel both guilty and fearful, how can they help but be angry at them? Yet this hostility, like the fear that inspired it, is not the kind of emotion a person is "supposed" to feel toward someone he loves. So it becomes a further barrier toward opening up honest communication with one's mate.

Over time, husbands and wives, as in our case, may get so caught up in such a reciprocal and vicious cycle that they believe it would be catastrophic for them to let each other know about their secret masturbatory preoccupations. Acting on that belief, they engage in a complicity aimed at perpetuating their secrecy;

and they may sustain such a complicity for years—perhaps, in some cases, even over the entire span of their marriage.

Sources of Tension
Career Strivings

The pursuit of vocational and financial goals can arouse so much anxiety in one or both marital partners that they may forget the importance of their relationship. Such anxiety, as we found in the early days of our marriage, is often experienced as an exceptionally strong and irresistible impulse to masturbate or to indulge in compensatory fantasies. In fact, over one-third of Hunt's sample of male adults and nearly one-third of all the female adults said that their urge to masturbate did not result from sexual desires; they often attributed their masturbatory urges to the tensions created by their vocational and personal problems.[4]

Paradoxically, when a person gets too caught up in pursuing his own preoccupations, he is unlikely to succeed in truly enhancing either his image of himself or his mate's esteem for him. Instead, because of the anxiety his excessive strivings create, he tends to feel less competent to achieve the very success with which he hoped to prove his adequacy to himself and his partner. So he often gets involved in a vicious cycle of self-defeat, which leads him to withdraw even more from his mate into increased solitary masturbation and fantasy.

Beth and Fred have been married for three years. Beth is now finishing her first year of medical school, and Fred has been studying law since they've been married. After her experience in London, when she had her first really exciting orgasm, Beth continued to masturbate occasionally throughout her adolescence. Fred had masturbated all during his childhood years; and while it was never a source of concern for him, he told Beth that during his high school years he had often done it when he was nervous about exams.

"When we got married, we talked a little about masturbation. But our sex has been so wonderful that neither of us ever felt like doing it once we started living together. But this year, Fred's gotten quite up-tight about preparing for the bar exam. We still make love as usual. But for a while now, I've gotten so engrossed in my work that I haven't been enjoying sex so much."

Hesitating, Beth went on: "One night, Fred shocked both of us by going off to the bathroom and masturbating soon after we'd had intercourse. He even admitted he had a fantasy of making love to his old girlfriend when he did it. I felt he was letting me down, and we had a big fight about it. It was really awful. He began to complain about my neglecting him and the apartment. I started screaming that he wasn't living up to his end of the bargain to help with the housework. I could see he was really upset about what he'd done, but I was totally freaked out. I accused him of being an immature momma's boy. But I didn't want to admit that I'd been letting him down, too. It all ended up with Fred shouting that I'd have to go a long way to get as good a fuck as he'd been giving me."

The next morning, after they had calmed down, Beth felt much more sympathetic about what Fred had been going through. She realized what a strain it had been for him to try for the highest grades he could get his last year in law school, just when she had become so involved in starting her own stressful career. She was very eager to get close to him again and talk about what had happened. As they discussed the incident, they tried to get insight into what it meant. Fred said he'd felt the impulse to run to the bathroom and masturbate several times before, when Beth seemed to ignore him completely because of her work. And they both admitted that their pleasure in making love had gone way down. As they talked, they could see how worried Fred was about finishing school and going out to find a job as a lawyer; and how upset Beth was about the long haul she still had to make before she got her M.D. As a result, they were able to give each other more reassurance. "We both saw that we had become unnecessarily worried about our work. We've proven that we can do very well in our studies. So why kill ourselves to keep on proving what we already know? Now, we've decided to take more time out to be with each other and have fun."

Temporary Separations

Because of their occupations, some people have to learn how to tolerate forced separations from their mates. Traveling salesmen, and others who work far from where they live, must be away from home for long periods of time. But aside from such occupational separations, all spouses are bound to experience some periods of physical separation that do not arise from any emotional estrangement in their loving relationship—for example, temporary separations caused by unexpected demands of their work, illnesses, or emergencies among relatives or friends.

Relying on masturbation as a substitute for intercourse under such exceptional and unavoidable circumstances is often viewed by mates as an expression of their commitment to be sexually faithful to each other. One twenty-nine-year-old woman said that, although she enjoyed sex with her lover much more than masturbation, she did rely on it as a substitute when he was away. She said that masturbation provided her with satisfaction and peace—and kept her from wanting to look around for someone else.[5]

Couples who have to abstain from sexual intercourse during periods of forced separation should certainly feel free enough to give themselves the emotional solace and physical release that they are unable to give each other. But even in such situations, it would be best for their relationship if each mate told the other about having masturbated during the absence, sharing his masturbatory fantasies and his emotional reactions to his masturbatory experiences.

In many cases, such couples could change their jobs or their work schedules in ways that would permit them to spend more time with each other. With more time together, they could have more chance to talk about and resolve their personal and marital problems. They would also have more time for making love. Of course, such changes are difficult for many people to make; and they may even require some sacrifice of status or money. But if a couple can accept whatever losses may be involved for both of them, they are likely to find that their sacrifice is well worth the price in terms of increased pleasure, intimacy, and harmony in their relationship.

Pregnancy

Paradoxically, one of the stresses that may temporarily separate spouses, and put a crimp on their sexual fulfillment, stems from the fruition of their sexual love—the conception of a child. During and after a woman's pregnancy, there are times when sexual intercouse may be medically inadvisable and less enjoyable than usual for either partner. At those times, both spouses may feel the acute desire for some kind of sexual release. Of course, there are people who prefer to contain their desires, feeling content to abstain entirely from any form of sexual gratification. But many husbands masturbate during their wives' pregnancies; and some pregnant wives do the same.

One woman told us that her husband had not masturbated very much in his youth. From the time they married, he masturbated only when she was pregnant, saying he needed a "substitute." Dr. Barbach describes a woman who experienced considerable discomfort from intercourse during her fourth and fifth months of pregnancy, so she temporarily lost interest in having sexual relations with her mate. But she found her desire for solitary masturbation markedly increased; and she masturbated frequently.[6]

Doctors no longer believe that it is necessary to abstain from sexual intercourse during pregnancy. The medical consensus is that a woman whose preganacy is normal can continue to have intercourse as long as she feels comfortable in doing it.[7] In cases where there *is* the danger of a miscarriage due to uterine contractions during an orgasm, it is advisable for a woman to refrain from both intercourse and masturbation. But apart from those special situations, couples can go on having intercourse, using their patience and ingenuity to find mutually gratifying positions as the wife's pregnancy advances. They can also use alternative ways of making love, such as oral-genital stimulation or mutual manual masturbation.[8]

Both partners may adjust much better to the stress of becoming parents if they continue giving each other sexual pleasure and relief during the wife's pregnancy. According to Dr. Barbach, "Having a couple refrain totally from sexual activity during a period in which both are going through considerable changes and may really desire and require the intimacy that sex provides may put an unnecessary strain on the partners and the relationship."[9]

During pregnancy, both men and women may naturally experience many new nonsexual tensions, which stem from anxieties about their ability to cope with all the responsibilities of having a child; women may also feel anxious about the physical risks involved in pregancy and delivery. Those worries may also contribute to a spouse's motivation to withdraw into private masturbation and fantasy as a way of gaining reassurance and temporary relief from nervous tension. But couples could benefit more by containing their masturbatory impulses and using them as an impetus to discussing their concerns with each other. In that way, they can give each other the emotional support they both need, while they also develop more individual strength and self-acceptance. By developing a common understanding of the anxious anticipations they have about their future roles and responsibilities, spouses can prepare themselves to cope effectively and realistically with the challenges of parenthood.

SECRET ESCAPES

It is inevitable for every couple to go through periods of the doldrums, during which they may be motivated to escape from the humdrum, day-to-day strains of maintaining the commitments they have made to each other and to their children. It is equally natural for married people to be occasionally turned on by other people they meet. Nevertheless, spouses ordinarily go on keeping their marital commitments, even as they are tempted to get out of them. They know that the uniquely fulfilling gratifications of their marriage depends on their very willingness to endure its demands and frustrations.

Still, even the most happily married and conscientious of mates may occasionally feel the need to escape from the inevitable limitations of monogamy. In such a mood, spouses may indulge in masturbatory fantasies of having extramarital liaisons, in which they magically remedy whatever shortcomings they perceive in their mate or in the quality of their marriage.[10] By sharing their fantasies with each other, spouses can identify specific areas of their discontent, some of which can actually be overcome. Like Beth and Fred, they can also help each other to release their pent-up and mutual resentments, rather than continue to nurture them in private. While they might not be able to undo many sources of tension between them, such as the unremitting pressures of their work, they may at least succeed in accepting them more fully and compassionately. Thus, they can transform their inclinations to blame one another into a more genuine mutual acceptance of the life they have decided to share together.

The habitual use of secret masturbation, with extramarital fantasies, merely glosses over rather than resolves the tensions that arise from the discrepancy between what mates wish for in their relationship and what actually exists in it. Meanwhile, those tensions continue to build up inside each partner and between them. Thus, as Hunt observes, masturbation and masturbatory fantasy can be "misused to fend off one's mate when intercourse has become blighted by emotional conflict. Here the analogy to the use of alcohol is particularly appropriate. It deadens discomfort, serves as an avoidance device and allows the underlying problem to go uncorrected and thus to worsen." [11]

One woman described to us by her psychotherapist, used masturbation in this way because she was unhappily married. As soon as her husband got out of bed in the morning and went into the bathroom to shave, she would masturbate and create fantasies of having sex with another man, whom she portrayed as being much more loving than her husband. This woman regarded her masturbation as a kind of "nourishment" that was essential to give her whatever motivation she needed to get out of bed and get going before she could face the day.

In their survey of over 100,000 women, Carol Tavris and Susan Sadd, authors of *The Redbook Report on Female Sexuality*, found that wives who masturbate often "are compensating for bad sex with their husbands, and they don't find masturbation especially gratifying." Rather, these wives use it "as a weapon or a release from frustrations." As one such wife remarked: "I masturbate only when I quarrel with my husband, and I don't know why, exactly—maybe it's to get back at him. Only he doesn't know it." [12]

Kris, who always needed women to give him an immense amount of permission and acceptance before he could feel the self-confidence to enjoy intercouse, felt that his wife was never loving and supportive enough. "I started to masturbate again *after* I got married because our relationship was no good and our sex was so bad. I used it mainly for tension reduction—as a substitute for sex. But I never felt I was entitled to give myself any real pleasure. I always had an implicit sense of shame and disapproval for doing it. And there has always been a lot of anger and defiance connected with my masturbation. I guess I had the feeling that 'I'm going to do my own thing, no matter what.' So I used to jerk off on the bathroom floor while I had fantasies of screwing all sorts of other women in a wide variety of settings. I can remember my wife inquiring about all the time I spent in the bathroom. I did quite a lot of masturbating when I was in my middle-to-late thirties, before I got divorced. Even though I didn't find it all that pleasurable, I felt it was OK compared to actually screwing around with other people."

According to Dr. George Bach, a therapist who conducts groups for married couples, "a commonly used strategy of underground sex fighters is the practice of infidelity by fantasy. The weapon is masturbation. It is often used when one partner feels it is too much trouble to 'turn on' the other. It is an easy practice to slip into because it is usually kept secret . . . it allows the straying partner to remain ostensibly faithful . . . and is therefore less conflictual than extramarital involvement." So, Dr. Bach concludes, "In marriage, masturbation is a poor idea. It violates our rule of sharing intimate concerns." [13]

When the professionals he trains ask Dr. Bach why they should risk starting trouble by disturbing the status quo of a reasonably stable marriage in which one partner is engaging in secret masturbation, he points out that "to disturb such an arrangement is not to start trouble; the trouble is already there." Dr. Bach feels it is important to direct a couple's attention to the fact that the invisibility of either partner's private masturbation is deterring them from facing their problems honestly and working out a joint resolution of them.[14]

There I was in Irv's arms, pretending to be so much into our lovemaking. And I was having the same kind of fantasies I usually had when I masturbated, seeing myself married to an attractive guy in Irv's program who was already a famous psychologist, making lots of money. And my parents were visiting me in my big colonial house, praising me for the wonderful marriage I'd made.

Oh, I'd become pretty good at faking it—at least at first, before I started having real trouble coming. Sometimes, Irv seemed so eager to get his own pleasure that he didn't notice the subtle signs of my withdrawal from him. But when it became obvious to me that I wasn't having orgasms anymore, I got very concerned that he'd realize it, too.

Finally, he couldn't help asking me about it one night, after he kept pumping and pumping, waiting for me to come. I admitted it right away, but I felt awful about not bringing it up myself. I was so guilty, feeling I was the only one who was holding out in our relationship. But I often felt Irv was just as distant from me. Sometimes, I thought his head must be swarming with fantasies as far-fetched as mine. But I never asked him about his fantasies any more than I let him in on mine. And it never occurred to me to wonder if he ever masturbated.

I was still having orgasms from masturbating—but they weren't that satisfying any more. They certainly couldn't compare to the ones I'd had with Irv. In fact, I was beginning to feel like a nymphomaniac. I'd finish masturbating and then I'd feel just as tense right afterward as I did before. I'd try to relieve that tension by having one orgasm after another. But they never satisfied me. And the nights when Irv was out of town working at the VA hospital were unbearable. I began to get very scared that something was terribly wrong with me.

One time when Irv was away, friends of mine asked me for dinner. But I gave them some excuse because I had vowed to myself that I was going to stay home alone and try to control my impulse to masturbate. My experiment was a total flop. I got so anxious that I went speeding around from one room to the other in a fugue state. Finally, I ran out of the house so I'd *have* to control myself. But walking on the deserted streets wasn't enough. I had to talk to someone else or I felt I'd go out of my mind. In desperation, I dropped in on my friends. It was eleven-thirty and they were shocked to see me. They must have sensed my distress because they were very nice. I remember feeling embarrassed about how disheveled I looked and how weird I was acting. But I didn't care any more. I just needed someone to comfort me.

That night, as I walked home, I knew I couldn't hold back from Irv any longer. When he returned the next day, I blurted out the whole story from the time I was three. Then I started crying and begging him to forgive me. He was bitter and resentful. But I was relieved because I'd finally opened up. I hoped that now we'd be able to deal with my problem about not having orgasms. I'd begun to feel hopeless about ever coming again. We'd even stopped talking about it because we'd reached such a dead-end. Every day I'd felt deader and deader inside; and Irv was getting more and more turned off from me. But we kept trying, hoping I'd finally come. But I didn't and I began to feel I was just going through the motions to service Irv. So I saw my confession about masturbation as the beginning of some possible solution. But, just as I had feared, Irv saw it as something abnormal.

Naturally, we both focused on *my* problem. In my own mind, I tried to blame Irv's appearance of control and detachment for my fear of talking about it sooner. But maybe he wouldn't have been so distant if I had been more honest right from the start. Despite how psychologically sophisticated we thought we were, neither of us could even imagine that Irv might have a problem because he *didn't* masturbate. And we couldn't see that both my masturbation and my inability to have an orgasm were related to the problems *we* were having together.

Concentrating exclusively on my problem deflected our attention completely away from our mutual problems. Irv put on a good show, patting me on the head condescendingly. But I sensed how immature he thought I was. I couldn't help but feel like an ailing neurotic who needed treatment.

But I couldn't blame it all on Irv. I was a real bitch. My deception was a sneaky way of expressing the hostility I'd stored up and was afraid to show to him directly. It's true that I leaned on him and was willing to take the back seat in terms of having a career of my own. But even though I'd renounced my own ambitions in favor of fostering his, I was really very jealous of his status and achievements. Underneath, I felt very competitive with him. But I pulled the same tricks as I did with my father—I was just plain, sweet, unassuming Sue, not a nasty thought or a shoddy motive in my head. And he was the Big Daddy I idolized. So how could he possibly help loving me?

We didn't have much insight into what was going on then. Maybe if we did, I never would have gone for therapy. Who knows what would have happened if Irv had been a real masturbator, too? I sometimes wonder what it would have been like to live with a man who had masturbated as much as I had. But I evidently wanted someone like him to give me a sense of the control I never felt I had. And he wanted someone like me to help him loosen up and feel free.

Admitting I had problems, and taking responsibility for doing something about them, was a large part of my therapy. Relating to another adult male, who took me seriously and accepted me, was also a tremendous boost to my self-esteem. I was finally able to feel in my guts how much I really wanted to grow up and make it with Irv. I saw that I couldn't be an irresponsible, self-centered child *and* a mature, responsible wife, all at the same time. I could also admit how unreal my fantasy was about my relationship with my father—thinking we were so close and that I was so special for him. Actually, he was frequently more concerned with his own problems than with his children, and he often promised us more than he could deliver. I could see, too, how I'd put my mother down. In reality, she'd given me much more love, attention, and worthwhile guidance than I ever gave her credit for. Gradually, as I developed a more realistic perspective about my parents, I was able to stop blaming them for all my problems. As I got those insights, I no longer felt so compelled to masturbate whenever the slightest thing went wrong.

Being an outsider to a wife who was in therapy was hard for Irv to take. For a while, I was sharing more of my inner life with my therapist than with him. Naturally, he couldn't help but be jealous of my intimacy with my therapist. He had needs of his own to be taken care of, too. But he was really patient and stuck by me. It was better when I began to improve and have orgasms again. After that, we started to talk more openly about the things that were really important.

Little by little, we both got a new sense of security in our relationship. And we felt we could really count on ourselves to come through for each other. The more I felt the reliability of Irv's love, the better I was able to respond sexually. And the more I turned on to him with real love, the more secure and loving he became.

Dr. Barbara Waxenberg, a family therapist, told us that most couples who come to her for help with their marital problems or sexual dysfunctions have not been honest with each other about their involvements in masturbation. One of the first things she asks them in front of each other is whether or not—and how much—they have been masturbating. It is often a shocker to wives when they find out how much their husbands have been masturbating. Women frequently blurt out: "What's the matter, aren't I enough for you?" Husbands often reveal their long-smoldering hostility toward their wives by replying: "You don't give me what I want." Men become just as upset when they hear how much their wives have been indulging in masturbation. And wives who have been masturbating in secret often express the hostility they have been feeling for their husband's inability to satisfy them sexually. "Men don't know what to do," is a frequent way wives blame their husbands.[15]

As Dr. Waxenberg says, these attempts to place blame are neither accurate nor helpful to a couple's understanding and resolution of the problems that bother them. She tries to get spouses to understand that their individual masturbatory inclinations and dysfunctions are problems they really share in common, since they take place within the context of their relationship; and she orients a couple toward getting insights into how each spouse may negatively affect the other, even though only one of them may have a sexual symptom.

OVERCOMING CONFLICTS AND SEXUAL DYSFUNCTIONS

Unresolved conflicts in a marriage may show up in a variety of sexual dysfunctions, such as a wife's inability to have an orgasm, a husband's inability to have an erection, or his tendency to ejaculate prematurely. Consequently, spouses may continue to use masturbation because it provides them with the sexual release they are unable to attain with each other. At the same time, they may be too embarrassed to face up to their difficulties and take the necessary steps to overcome them. But the continued use of secret masturbation by either partner cannot possibly solve their problems. Fortunately, however, in addition to talking about their solitary tendencies to masturbate, couples can deliberately use various physical methods of masturbation as a therapeutic technique in helping each other to overcome their difficulties.

Sexual Dysfunctions: Women

When a wife has difficulty having orgasms during intercourse, her husband can help her to learn how to attain them. As the first step, a wife masturbates herself to orgasm while her husband watches. Observing her, he finds out exactly what kinds of stimulation are most pleasing and arousing for her. Next, she can practice attaining orgasms while her husband masturbates her, stimulating her in the ways she used in her own masturbation. She and her husband are then ready to build the final "bridge" that permits her to have an orgasm while having sexual intercourse with him.

Taking her husband's hand, she can guide it in following hers as she stimulates her clitoris and vaginal area. When she feels ready to have an orgasm, she and her husband remove their hands and he puts his penis inside her, permitting her to experience her climactic release while their genitals are joined. After going through that experience, she and her husband may decide to include their "bridging" techniques as a regular feature of their intercourse, and either of them can feel free to stimulate her clitoris—or any other part of her body whose stimulation gives her pleasure.

Despite their attempts to apply such methods, some women continue to resist the experience of having an orgasm during intercourse with their husbands. Yet those same women can readily bring themselves to orgasm through solitary masturbation. One of Dr. Waxenberg's patients felt an enormous fear of sexual union with her mate, anticipating a dreaded sense of loss afterward. Other patients reported that they held back from having an orgasm during intercourse because they did not want to acknowledge their intense need for a sexual partner.

Judy Kuriansky, a psychologist who has done research on the effects of sex therapy, told us that some women resist having orgasms during intercourse because they feel that those orgasms are not really theirs. Such a woman tends to feel that, since her mate participated in the attainment of her orgasm, it "belongs" to him. For those women, having an orgasm with their husbands is equivalent to losing out in a power struggle they are carrying on with them.

Most married women, however, do not want to rely on solitary self-stimulation as their only path to orgasmic release and gratification. Commenting on the findings of her research, Dr. Leah Shaefer says, "No woman in the sample nor, for that matter, among all the women I have counseled ever stated a preference for autoeroticism over heterosexual relations no matter how successful she was at masturbating to orgasm." Dr. Shaefer found that, for most women, the idea of "sex for release" or "sex without love" was unacceptable.[16]

Sexual Dysfunctions: Men

Just as husbands can help their wives in overcoming specific sexual dysfunctions, wives can do the same for their husbands. Again, various methods of masturbation play a crucial role in permitting wives to help their husbands learn how to enjoy sexual intercourse.

One of the most common problems that men experience is the tendency to have a premature ejaculation. According to Carole Altman, a sex therapist, a man may be able to maintain an erection for a few seconds or several minutes, but if he ejaculates before he really wants to, or is unaware of the fact that he is about to ejaculate, he is a premature ejaculator.[17] Such a man may feel that he is not getting enough love and acceptance from his mate; so he expresses his hostility to her by ejaculating too soon. But he spoils his own pleasure as well as his wife's. Such a couple may get caught up in various patterns of mutual blame; the husband frequently begins to feel inadequate and depressed, feeling he is not virile enough to satisfy his wife.

Regardless of the psychological and interpersonal factors involved in the man's problem, he and his mate can help themselves by using specific behavioral techniques that have been developed for overcoming premature ejaculation. Of course, at the same time, it is essential that they begin to talk honestly to each other and share whatever individual feelings, concerns, conflicts, and desires they may have.

In treating premature ejaculation, many sex therapists believe it is important for couples to use masturbation within their relationship. Other sex therapists also advise supplemental and similar masturbatory exercises that a man can do on his own. By having both husband and wife cooperate, the husband sees that his wife is very willing to offer him love and acceptance. Thus, he can begin to feel less fearful of rejection from her and less hostile toward her. Besides, while letting her manually stimulate him, he can concentrate totally on his own bodily sensations and learn how to tune in to them.

It is important for the husband to avoid any kind of fantasy or mental distraction that might reduce his awareness of the physiological cues that signal the premonitory stage of his orgasm. Most men who suffer from this problem have generally failed to sense their impending ejaculation before the point of no return.[18] But it is too late by then, and their semen is already being released. So, as his wife stimulates his penis, a man can concentrate all of his attention on the feelings in his genitals and on the exact sensations he experiences just before he is about to have an ejaculation.

To further improve his awareness of the sequence of feelings that precede ejaculation, it is helpful for a man to focus on the sensations in his testicles—before ejaculation, the testicles tend to tighten and rise, feeling as if they are going up into the body. Also, the vein along the outside of the penis begins to swell. As he inwardly experiences these changes, the man tells his wife to stop masturbating him. When his arousal subsides, his wife resumes stimulating him, until he can maintain his heightened arousal longer and longer without ejaculating. Some wives also become so attuned to their husband's reactions that they sense exactly when to stop stimulating his penis. However, as Carole Altman says, it is essential for the husband to take responsibility for telling his wife when to stop, so that he can develop his own awareness and self-control.

A couple continues to use this stop-start technique of masturbation until the man feels he has enough control to attempt intercourse. It often helps to begin with the wife on top of her husband, where she can best control her bodily and vaginal movements. The same stop-start procedure is then continued during intercourse—when the husband feels he is about to ejaculate, he tells her to pull away from his penis. When he is ready to continue, she resumes her position astride him, stopping her movements each time he is about to have an ejaculation. This method is continued until the man can hold back for longer and longer periods of time. Couples can develop their control to whatever extent they wish by following this step-by-step procedure for *gradually* increasing the amount of time that the husband can thrust and maintain his erection before ejaculating.[19]

Adapting variations of these therapeutic approaches to the use of masturbation, sex therapists have developed methods with which couples can work together in similar ways to overcome other sexual dysfunctions that either a man or a woman may have. For men, these include impotence and retarded ejaculation; for women, vaginismus and the inability to be sexually aroused at all.

Removing Blocks to Honest Communication

Whether or not couples go for outside help, they need to communicate cooperatively and openly if they are to succeed in repairing the rifts in their relationship and in learning how to work through their problems of sexual loving on their own. Even if they are in therapy, they have to rely on each other through all the hours and days between sessions, and they have to learn how to relate to each other successfully when their professional therapy is over.

Viewing their relationship in this way, married people can make honest communication between them their therapy of daily life. Telling the truth to each other is the most effective of all therapies. In fact, most professional psychotherapists work with the prime obective of helping their patients to assume personal responsibility for finding and revealing the truth of their thoughts, feelings, desires, and behavior.

It is crucial for mates to realize, however, that the search for the truth about themselves and each other is a constant, lifelong, and demanding struggle. In carrying out that struggle, they need to confront themselves and each other whenever they sense they are giving in to their fear of being honest and loving by withdrawing into private masturbation or fantasy. Of course, as we found, the tendency to fear being honest and loving arises again and again throughout a couple's life together; as people face and overcome one particular instance of their fear of open communication, they will inevitably encounter another.

To prevent and get over harmful retreats from each other, spouses can learn to benefit from their fear of personal disclosure instead of being victimized by it. For the fear of disclosure—and the negative emotions of guilt and hostility that follow—are the clearest signals they have that there is a disturbance in the flow of love between them.

Sharing Fantasies

Couples can also learn to use their masturbatory fantasies as a way of preventing and overcoming emotional retreats. If you feel afraid of revealing a masturbatory fantasy, your fear indicates that you consider its content to be highly problematic. So you could benefit most from disclosing precisely such fantasies to your mate. Only by revealing them can you help yourself to overcome your fear of them. Your reluctance to communicate those fantasies also shows your resistance to becoming more loving and to merging more fully with your mate. When you share your most idiosyncratic fantasies, you free yourself of their inherent futility and the oppression of keeping them a secret; you get rid of your tendency to indulge in them as a way of withdrawing emotionally from your partner; you open your consciousness more fully to the one you love; and you give your mate a chance to help you resolve the conflicts that originally motivated you to spin those fantasies.

When you and your mate talk about your own masturbation, both of you are confronting what is happening between you—and why. In the first place, you are actually admitting that you've been involved in masturbation. As you talk, you will naturally reveal how frequently you feel the impulse to masturbate. Then, both you and your mate will want to figure out *when* and *in what kinds of situations* you feel the desire to masturbate and have masturbatory fantasies.

As you examine those facts about your masturbatory inclinations or behavior, along with the contents of your fantasies, you can try to make connections between what you are doing and the factors that you feel are causing you to do it. Such causal generalizations can help you to gain insight and awareness into your needs and motives. It is then possible for you and your spouse to decide on ways to change—to improve the concrete circumstances of your life, to remove unnecessary tensions and strains, and to try to fulfill your individual desires and potentials as best as you possibly can—instead of turning to masturbatory fantasy as a substitute fulfillment.

Of course, since it is impossible for anyone to completely give up the tendency to indulge in masturbatory fantasy, you can practice using your capacity for fantasy in ways that could help you to become more loving and more effective in dealing with your problems. When you want to make yourself feel good by having an erotic fantasy, think of your spouse; use your imagination to think of possible solutions to your mutual problems; or work out alternative solutions in your mind for the unresolved personal conflicts of your own, which, if solved, would release more of your energy for sexual love with your partner.

Spouses who maintain this kind of self-accountability and communication, can gradually break their old patterns of behavior and set up a new and positive cycle of understanding and change, which will enhance the growth of both of them. Naturally, it is risky and time-consuming for people to break their old habits of mutual and self-deception. But if husbands and wives cannot risk being honest with each other, with whom can they take the chance? And if their marriage cannot embrace the truth about themselves—if it has to be maintained by lies— what is the point of it?

Irv: When you finished your psychotherapy, we both thought you were "cured" of masturbation forever.

Sue: Yes. I felt I had it completely under control. But I was kidding myself. After my therapy, I was so afraid of giving in to my old habit that I became overcontrolled. I kept watch on myself all the time to avoid situations that would make me feel inadequate and tempt me to masturbate again. I did stop touching myself. But I focused too much on my outward behavior. Even in therapy I never talked about the nitty-gritty details of my masturbatory fantasies. And I still wasn't leveling wtih you about how much time I continued to spend spinning them.

Irv: Of course, I could use my busy work schedule to hide my own involvement in mental masturbation. I became very skilled at giving you the impression that I was pondering over some important issue in my research, when I was really tripping out in totally unrealistic daydreams.

Sue: So what happened to us? We thought my giving up masturbation was a milestone in our lives. But our problems seemed to go on and on, even though we were basically so lucky. We'd had our kids just when we wanted them— a boy first and then a girl. And everyone else thought we were Mr. and Mrs. Healthy-and-Wholesome. Why didn't it ever seem to be enough for us?

Irv: Well, for me, our success meant getting into a fixed routine of being an absolutely reliable husband, father, and provider. I began to see myself as stuck with the role of giving and giving and being counted on to come through for you and the children. Of course, I wanted that—just as I wanted the professorship and tenure that I finally got. But I never expected to feel so boxed in and restricted by having to maintain what I had achieved. I kept hungering for the kind of freedom and spontaneity that both of us had lost along the way.

Sue: We tried to keep the romance going. We took every opportunity we had to jump into bed together and make love. I remember what a kick we got out of doing it when the kids were out playing or in school. But it wasn't easy for me to keep the spark going when I felt so bogged down by the job of keeping everything and everyone in our house running smoothly. I was beginning to feel like a martyr, too. There had to be more to life than that. But I wasn't really giving as much as I thought. Actually, I was taking just as much as I was giving—trying to get my kicks vicariously by identifying with your status and prestige. I also pictured myself as the great earth-mother. Naturally, I thought my children performed so successfully solely because of my endless devotion. But no matter how much I tried to blame my frustrations on my role as a wife and a mother, I knew I wasn't putting forth the energy to express what was really in me. I was still scared stiff to face the responsibility of pursuing a real career of my own.

Irv: I didn't help you to resolve that conflict, either. In fact, I put you in the impossible position of having to satisfy my own contradictory needs. I wanted all the support I could get from you to cope with the anxieties I felt in competing to become an academic success. I wanted you to be around all the time to nurture me and be my haven of solace from that competition. But I also tried to lay my own frustrated creative trips on you; I tried to push you into becoming a successful artist, so I could identify with what you did without having to take the chance to do it myself. And I could always blame you for the failures I saw in myself.

Sue: Look, your prodding wasn't so bad. You did inspire me to go back to my painting. And that was very good for me. I was able to prove that I could get involved in working creatively on my own again without turning to masturbation as a balm for my frustrations. And I did accomplish a lot. I sold some of my pictures and I was in a few exhibits. But we made too many perfectionistic demands on ourselves. And we were still too afraid to open up to each other about what was really troubling us.

Irv: I had already published many scholarly articles and a well-received textbook. My students praised my teaching—and I enjoyed it enormously, too. But nothing I did seemed to come close enough to the greatness I demanded of myself—and that I associated with being a "creative" writer. My mental masturbation grew more and more extravagant —so much so that I couldn't think of sharing it with you, because you knew me too well to take my fantasies as the realities I wanted them to be.

Sue: God, how many years did I spend spaced-out in front of the kids? While they begged me to push them on the swings in the playground, in my mind I was pushing myself up and down Madison Avenue trying to arrange the exhibit of all exhibits. Or, as I read them their bedtime stories, I was mentally proofreading the children's book we had tried to do together, marveling at the poetic imagery of your well-turned phrases and the enchanting colors of my captivating illustrations. And how often did we sit in the living room together, engaged in conversation, while our heads were miles apart? You were probably seeing yourself autographing your latest novel. I know I was imagining how I'd look at the glamorous opening of my own art show.

Irv: We were both ripe for an affair. But I didn't have to go looking for one. Typing manuscripts of my poems and stories gave Wanda plenty of opportunity to praise and flatter me as an unrecognized literary star. For years, she had been thirsting for publication of her own poetry. And she had already pretty well made up her mind to leave her husband. Our frustrations happened to mesh, which gave us a lot of empathy for each other. But the fact that she was much younger than me was what tempted me to accept her offer of total compliance. She made no demands on me and gave me the feeling that I could do no wrong. In her dreamy eyes, my cop-outs and limitations seemed like the faults of an insensitive world. When we strolled hand-in-hand through the park as the trees were blossoming, she made me feel that anything was still possible for me—even my deluded wish to live my life all over again.

Sue: Yeah, you were certainly an easy mark for her. And don't forget—you started up with her just when I'd finally decided to go back to graduate school. I thought I could cope with it easily and still keep our relationship going well. But all of my suppressed ambitions got unleashed. I had to get all A's. I know I neglected you and made demands that you take more care of the kids. But we never talked those things through. And I think you got so involved with Wanda because you were really threatened by the fact that I'd gotten so preoccupied with my own academic strivings.

Irv: I knew it was unreal from the beginning. It was one big masturbatory fantasy, but that was its appeal for me. It wasn't much of an affair, at least not sexually. The one and only time we tried to have intercourse, I felt so false and guilty I was totally impotent. But even after I broke off the affair and told you about it, I had a tremendous need to continue it in my secret fantasies. Whenever I felt trapped by problems in our relationship, I would imagine getting involved with her again. Even though I wouldn't, and didn't really want to, I didn't want to give up the possibility of fantasizing about it. That's why I went for years without telling you about those fantasies.

Sue: God, I remember how upset I was when you told me about what was going on between you. I had been beginning to wonder when you suddenly began to go to the office every day instead of working at home as usual. But as threatened and angry as I felt, I was too guilty to be completely self-righteous. While you were seeing Wanda on the sly, I was having a passionate affair inside my own head. In my typical way, I didn't even try to act it out. But I devoted as much of my time to fantasizing about my philosophy professor as you did about Wanda. He was very tall and handsome—and also a lot younger than me. How I knocked myself out on the term paper for his course, so he'd notice me. I even used to park my car next to his, hoping I'd bump into him. While I sat in class, admiring his brilliant lectures, I was imagining how we'd meet in the parking lot later that night. He'd ask me to go with him for coffee. And after I turned him on with my sensuality and my sensitive appreciation for his viewpoints, we'd end up going to his apartment and making love.

Irv: I guess we both had to go through those fantasies of being with other people to test out how much we really wanted to be with each other.

Sue: Yes, we could finally accept how much happier we'd be by being completely honest and helping each other to give up our reliance on masturbatory fantasy. We opened up about all of the mental escape hatches we'd been hiding over the years and we decided to drop whatever fantasies of promiscuity we'd been using to titillate ourselves.

Irv: That's when I also saw how much I had been afraid of truly loving myself. Because of my lifelong fear of masturbation, I had always been abjectly dependent on other people to comfort me, when I could have been comforting myself. I realized how much my frustrated need for that kind of solace had made me vulnerable to getting it entirely from other people. I could see how much that made me susceptible to my secret affair. And I saw how much I had become dependent on grandiose fantasies to give me the affection I could have been giving myself. Once I started getting these insights, I began to feel that I had to do something about them. That "something" hit me one day when I was looking at myself in the mirror. I was almost overcome with tears of pity for myself for all the years of self-denial that I saw etched into the lines of my face. Right then and there, I vowed that I would become kinder and more considerate to myself. I started in little ways. I began to let myself rest when I really didn't feel like working. Then I became bolder, learning how to get stoned and just watch a beautiful day in the country go by. But I kept feeling that something more was needed. Finally, I understood that I needed to learn how to masturbate with love and pleasure.

Sue: I remember how freaked I was when you expressed your need to understand more about how your inability to masturbate had been affecting you and our relationship.

Irv: But that didn't discourage me—even though my first attempts were pathetic failures. I aroused myself easily enough, but I couldn't bring myself to orgasm. And I felt weird and anxious about doing it without you around. I finally had to ask you to masturbate along with me before I could succeed in stimulating myself all the way to orgasm. After that, I felt I'd be able to do it when I was all by myself. But I didn't even try that until the time you were in the hospital.

Sue: At first, I felt crazy trying to masturbate after all the years I'd spent blocking my desires to do it—especially right in front of you. But once we actually did it together, and I let myself get into it, I could see how the tyranny of my self-imposed discipline against masturbation had affected me, too. I guess I had to go cold turkey because I'd always felt so hooked by masturbation. But I could see that I'd been much too hard on myself. What would have been such a catastrophe if I had done it occasionally? The main thing was not to keep it secret from you. Maybe if I had masturbated and used it as an impetus to revealing my fantasies to you, we would have gotten a lot more understanding much sooner about what was bothering us. Once I got those realizations, I was able to use the energy I had tied up in my masturbatory fantasies to imagine projects that I had the ability to accomplish and really intended to do.

Irv: After I masturbated with complete joy and without any guilt, I started to feel released from my fantasies of becoming a creative giant. Those impossible ambitions had actually been crushing my creativity, rather than helping me to express it. When I decided to ease up on myself, I could also give you the support you needed to get going on fulfilling your realistic aspirations.

Sue: Together, we gradually began to drop the stereotyped sex roles we'd been playing in our marriage. It was a frightening process. But by sticking it out we were able to help each other concentrate on doing the things that would fulfill both of our potentials, rather than fighting over who does what for whom. That's how we could get the idea of collaborating on this book.

Irv: Overcoming our conflicts about masturbation has helped us to get more pleasure from our lovemaking, too. Now, we feel free to stimulate our own bodies as a natural part of our sexual relations. And we know that it's good for us to share our masturbatory fantasies as soon as we spin them. Telling the truth has become our best aphrodisiac. Besides, it has the extra benefit of giving us a lot of laughs. What could be funnier than our own mental antics in trying to imagine ego trips that we know are wildly absurd?

Aging

Just when a mature couple may think they have their marriage completely "together," they tend to encounter fresh challenges to their capacity for adaptive change. Their children grow up and out of their household, leaving them feeling less essential than before. As retirement from their work looms ahead, an aging couple may feel even less useful to anyone else in the world. The previously unfilled goals of their lives now return to the forefront of their consciousness, creating uneasiness and a feeling that time is running out on them. Simultaneously, they begin to notice the unmistakable signs of their physical aging. The threat and actuality of menopause casts its shadow over both husbands and wives. And lifelong mates may become ill, or even die.

But all through the inevitable social and physical changes that accompany aging, the need for love and sexual fulfillment, which plays such an important part in everyone's life, remains alive. In the past, people have suffered from misconceptions about human sexual desires and behavior during middle age and the later years of life. And, according to Dr. Martin Berezin, older people often have felt either embarrassed or guilty for having any erotic urges at all. "What is considered virility at twenty-five becomes lechery at sixty-five. . . . The stereotype of sexless older years it not only a myth, but it is deleterious as well, for it interferes with the health and welfare of millions of old people." [20]

A number of studies indicate that the sexuality of aging adults, even those in their seventies and eighties, reflects their sexual behavior during their younger years. If a person has been sexually active throughout his adult life, he is likely to maintain his sexual spark when he is going through old age. Age itself does not seem to be such a significant variable in determining change in a person's sex life. What is more important is how a person feels about himself, the success of his life, and the quality of his relationship with his mate.[21]

Confronted by the loss of their former occupational and parental statuses—and the reduction in their physical energies—aging couples may often go through phases of deep alienation from each other. Nursing their individual responses to their common losses, spouses may often seek to withdraw into separate worlds of rumination. During these periods of mutual withdrawal, they may temporarily lose their previous motivation to engage in sexual intercourse, deliberately turning off from each other sexually and immersing themselves in their individual struggles to cope with the changes that life has forced on them. In fact, they may even become downright hostile toward one another, each seeking to blame the other for their inescapable human fate, or for how they might have been better off now, if only it hadn't been for some stupid mistake made by their mates.

Thus, people in middle and old age may continue to use masturbation and fantasy as a way of vicariously satisfying their needs for emotional comfort. And a married person may turn again to solitary and secret masturbation as a means of venting anger against his spouse. "Oh, she's no good any more," a sixty-eight-year-old husband told Irv, referring to his wife. "She just wants to take care of her flowers and push me around to do things for her. All she thinks about is how our kids and grandchildren are doing. She doesn't give a damn about me." This former electrician, Archie, and his wife have been married for forty years. Their three children live with their own families, far away from the country village where this couple has retired. Now, they both putter around their little house and involve themselves in local politics and social events. But their individual wallowing in self-pity keeps them from loving each other the way they used to.

"Yes," Archie admitted, "I masturbate—a whole lot. What else can I do but pull on my dick? My wife isn't very interested in sex anymore. You know what," he went on, a devilish gleam in his eye, "it's better than fucking. By doing it myself, I can get it any way I want—loose, tight, or in-between. I can make it last long or short. And I don't have to worry about pleasing her at all. I don't have to take her out to dinner just to get a piece. Besides, I like to think about hot young girls when I do it."

As Archie talked, it became obvious that he was projecting on to his wife much of the fearful preoccupation he had about losing his own youth and sex appeal. To cope with it, he turned back his own mental clock as he constructed his masturbatory fantasies. "I have a lot of trouble getting to sleep at night. Sometimes, I keep picking up my watch from the table near my bed to check on the time. Masturbation has helped me to get through many a night. What I like most to do is remember some girl I knew as a youngster—somebody I liked a lot but never got to lay. I see myself talking with her, the way we did in those days, maybe sitting near a stream under a birch tree. 'Course I was very shy as a kid. But I give her a big line about how good I was in high-school sports. Pretty soon, she's just waiting for me to put it to her. But I don't rush it, know what I mean? I keep on talking while I put my arm around her and pull her close. I start feeling her tits—and, boy, she just about crawls into my pants!"

Like Archie, many elderly married men, as Simone de Beauvoir says, "prefer their fantasies to their wife's age-worn body." [22] For their part, many wives, like Archie's, become self-conscious with aging and withdraw sexually from their husbands. One man in his late fifties admitted that he masturbated because his wife put him off, claiming that intercourse made her sore since her menopause. So, when he got horny, he decided it was better to "take care of myself" than to get bad-tempered.[23]

Other married men are drawn back to masturbation because of their own feelings of sexual inadequacy. If a man becomes indifferent to his mate, and if the success of his performance during the sex act worries him, he may feel relieved when his age allows him to take refuge in continence. Rather than be embarrassed by their impotence or difficulties in ejaculating, such men may hide behind the presumed sexlessness of old age as a face-saving device.[24] And they may either avoid sex altogether or else turn to solitary masturbation for gratification.

As Archie's fantasy shows, elderly people tend to change the direction and quality of their masturbatory fantasies. When they were younger, they imagined themselves doing all kinds of marvelously unrealistic things in the future. But in old age, they tend to reach backward into their "good old days." In conjuring up the illusion, an elderly person can deceive himself into believing he is actually younger than his age.

But old people also seek to temper their daydreams with their accumulated wisdom. "If I knew then what I know now" represents the kind of attitude they are inclined to bring to their fantasizing about their past lives. Thus, they are likely to have masturbatory fantasies in which they rerun actual events of their past, editing them in the light of their present knowledge. In such fantasies, a sexy senior citizen may begin by recalling the event accurately, as Archie did. But then he begins to alter it, bit by bit, rewriting his own history to make him appear more masterful, successful, and erotically fulfilled than he was at the time.

It is also natural for older married women to turn to masturbation as a way of satisfying their sexual frustrations; they, too, may use fantasies to try to compensate for their lost desirability, beauty, and youth. According to Kinsey, there may be several reasons why older married women masturbate: The erotic responsiveness of women may actually increase with age; there may often be a reduction of inhibitions among older women; and, through years of interpersonal sexual experience, women may have learned that similar erotic satisfactions are obtainable from their own self-stimulation.[25]

According to Masters and Johnson, every healthy aging woman has sex drives that need to be satisfied: "There is no time limit drawn by the advancing years to female sexuality." [26] They found no physiological reason why the frequency of sexual relations that was satisfactory during a woman's younger years should not be continued after her menopause. Yet research shows that women have a less active interpersonal sex life than men do during their later years. Women have been traditionally dependent upon the sexual desires and capabilities of men for their sexual fulfillment. And it has been more difficult for women to engage in extramarital sex if they have found relations with their husbands to be unsatisfactory.

"A book on masturbation?" exclaimed Selma, a seventy-one-year-old immigrant woman, in response to Sue's request for an interview. "To tell you the truth, I do it. You know, it's not easy for old ladies like me. Since Joe's prostate operation, things aren't like they used to be. I never told this to anyone before. But at my age, who cares? I'm entitled to a little pleasure, isn't that right?" After Sue gave her a little reassurance, Selma was delighted to talk about herself. "Joe gets very upset if things don't work out right. So what, is sex everything? Anyway, we play cards till late at night. Then there's the TV. And I love to read a good romance. That's when I feel like doing it. You know, when they make love. Who can stand it? When I get that way, it feels like I have to go to the toilet. I do have a weak bladder. But in the bathroom, I still feel excited, so I do it."

When Sue asked Selma what she thought about when she masturbated, she replied laughingly, "'So, what *should* I think about? I was a beautiful girl. They were all after me. But I was very particular. There was one boy, Maxie, I liked the best. He was crazy about me. Oh, was he handsome—so strong! He didn't have much education. But, believe me, he was very smart. In those days money and a future is what counted most. So my parents were against him and I gave in to them. Then Joe came along. He had a high-school diploma and a good job. He treated me like a queen. 'This is the man for you,' my mother said. Don't get me wrong—I love my Joe. But it hasn't been all peaches and cream with him, either."

She paused and sighed heavily before going on. "So what did you ask? Oh, yes, what I think about when I do it. Well, sometimes . . . Joe is in the hospital for treatments. One day, while I'm visiting him, I bump into Maxie. There he is, a doctor. Can you imagine it? He's so glad to see me and he insists on taking me out to dinner. He still looks so handsome—only a little gray. And I'm glad I kept myself so slim. We go out to an expensive restaurant with music. Then he tells me how much he's been thinking about me since his wife died. When he takes me home, we kiss and he holds me very close. It feels even better than it did when we were young kids . . . So then I finish myself up and go back to bed."

As in Selma's case, many aging women turn to solitary masturbation because their husbands become physically unable to continue having sexual intercourse (naturally, the reverse is also true). However, even in such cases, the healthy spouse need not withdraw sexually from the ailing one. Rather, they can still do together whatever they can to express their sexual love directly to each other. Even if only the wife is capable of having a full sexual response culminating in orgasm, she can let her mate give her the erotic stimulation she requires, instead of doing it furtively herself, as Selma did. Of course, the mate who provided the stimulation may feel frustrated by not being able to enjoy it reciprocally, with his own complete sexual response. But he can at least give himself the psychological satisfaction of knowing that he is continuing to give his mate pleasure, that he is remaining in the most intimate contact with her, and that she is not rejecting him. In this way, spouses can also alleviate each other's guilt. The ailing partner does not have to feel that he is causing his spouse to suffer from sexual deprivation, and the more potent partner does not have to feel guilty for withdrawing into secret and solitary masturbation.

Fortunately, many older couples are not afflicted with specific ailments that interfere with their sexual fulfillment. It is true that aging people do slow down sexually. For both men and women, sexual arousal takes longer. The amount of seminal fluid which a man ejaculates is gradually reduced and the force with which it is expelled also diminishes. The duration of the orgasm for both men and women shortens; they have fewer contractions. And it takes longer after one orgasm before a man can become aroused again.[27]

However, these physiological factors of aging do not have to impair a couple's enjoyment of intercourse. Because their slower rate of arousal requires husbands and wives to spend much more time in the sensual pleasures of caressing and fondling each other as they build up their level of excitement, they may actually experience new and heightened pleasure from their lovemaking. Since the aging male does not tend to ejaculate so quickly, he is much better able to prolong his wife's enjoyment by engaging in longer periods of foreplay. "Many aging males say that they enjoy foreplay far more than previously, for they do not feel as compulsively driven toward the big O, or moment of ejaculation."[28]

Even if elderly partners have not been highly involved in sexual intercourse earlier, it is never too late for them to find out about what they have been missing. Some research studies have found that a change in emotional state or motivation can inspire sexual responses and pleasures that an aged person may never have experienced before. For example, a woman in her eighties, who had been sexually unresponsive for twenty-two years, was again able to become erotically aroused to such an extent that she recovered her ability to have an orgasm.[29] Masters and Johnson have reported similar findings for elderly men who have not engaged in sexual activity for long periods of time. Thus, such men—even in their late seventies and eighties—can learn to enjoy sexual relations if they permit themselves to be interested and properly stimulated, and if they like their sexual partner.[30] Many sex therapists have been able to help aging couples to experience renewed pleasure by using the various techniques we have described.

In truth, many elderly couples are more free to live completely in the here and now than they ever were at any previous stage of their marriage. They have more freedom to love each other—sexually and in every other conceivable way. After all, their energies are no longer drained off from each other by either the cares of child-rearing or those of their former jobs—so they can devote themselves totally to caring for themselves and one another.

In their new-found leisure and privacy, elderly couples can realistically resume and extend the courtship period of their lives—the time before their romance was burdened by the internal and external pressures of striving to make their marriage a success. Now, having made it through all the challenges they faced and met together, they can relax and savor the joys of their fully ripened and fruitful relationship.

Although their sexual powers are not as great as they used to be, older spouses do not have to withdraw from each other into solitary masturbation and fantasy. Rather, they can benefit by incorporating their own masturbation directly into their lovemaking. For example, they can stimulate themselves as part of their foreplay, before having an orgasm through sexual intercourse. Or they may decide to masturbate themselves to orgasm in each other's presence. Such open display of their masturbatory behavior can break down many emotional barriers between them. The ability to be "out front" about this formerly secret and taboo activity can deepen their emotional intimacy, enhance their erotic pleasure, and give them a tremendous and much-needed sense of personal validation and reassurance.

Chapter 8
SINGLES

Many millions of adult Americans live as singles, uninvolved in a relationship of sexual love. Some have never married or lived with a lover; others have been involved in loving relationships that ended because of separation, divorce, or death. So some singles have chosen to be on their own, while others are single by force of circumstance. But what they all have in common is the fact that they have no regular partner with whom they feel committed to share their lives and their love.

A single adult is deprived of the opportunity of developing his personality in the ways we have described as unique to a loving relationship. However, this does not necessarily mean that people who are single cannot function and go on developing as loving people. In fact, many people who have chosen a life of celibacy have given of themselves lovingly to others through good works in religion, social service, and other humanitarian endeavors.

But most single people do not completely renounce the possibilities of giving and accepting love through sexual relations with others. Nor do they give up the erotic and emotional gratifications of masturbation. Of course, single adults can use masturbation as an expression of some of their need for sexual love, as well as for the release of some of their nonsexual tensions. And they can also approach masturbation as an aid to the growth of their personalities.

By using masturbation in the insightful ways we have described, single people can increase their understanding of whatever psychological blocks and conflicts may be preventing them from becoming more loving. A single person can also use his masturbatory experiences as an aid to determining whether or not he really wants to have a mate; if he decides to form a loving relationship, he can apply the self-awareness he gets from his masturbation to help himself change successfully from being a single to being a partner in a couple.

The Widowed

For those adults, young or old, who have known the joys of a fulfilling marriage, masturbation may be a pale substitute for the gratifying sexual love they shared with their mates. However, once they are widowed, they may find that masturbation provides them with a great deal of pleasure and solace. Of course, as they establish new loving relationships, their desire to masturbate is likely to diminish. But finding new partners may be difficult or impossible for many widows and widowers. Often, they may prefer to masturbate rather than to force themselves prematurely into new relationships or into loveless promiscuity.

Compared with men who have lost their wives, widows have a much harder time in attracting new spouses. A widowed mother with little children may have a lot of trouble finding a man who is willing to become both her husband and the father of her children. Elderly widows are severely restricted by prevailing cultural stereotypes that regard them as less attractive to younger men than widowers of their age are to younger women. As Simone de Beauvoir writes, "A young man may desire a woman old enough to be his mother but not his grandmother. A woman of seventy is no longer regarded by anyone as an erotic object."[1] In addition, elderly widows are handicapped by the simple fact that they far outnumber the single men of their age.

Since the trend in our society is toward an increasing population of aging women without men, fewer and fewer women will have the opportunitiy to remarry, even if they very much want to. Thus, more and more older widowed women will feel the need to resort to masturbation. But despite their sexual frustrations, many widows try to resist masturbation because of the negative attitudes they developed toward it in the sexually repressive days of their youth. Reacting to their long-internalized prohibitions, these women may experience acute guilt, increased anxiety about becoming ill, and a loss of self-esteem when they masturbate—even though they may have no other sexual alternative. Nevertheless, many widows continue to masturbate while feeling very disturbed about it.

Lester Dearborn, a psychotherapist, reports the case of a seventy-three-year-old woman, widowed for five years after a very happy marriage, who sought his help because she was upset about masturbating two or three times a week. She wanted to know if there was any medicine to prevent her from masturbating. She was extremely embarrassed and felt that something was wrong with a woman masturbating at her age. The counselor tried to calm this woman's fears by reassuring her that self-stimulation was a valid outlet of her needs for sexual gratification in the absence of any other means of satisfaction. He told her that she had no need to worry about it, as long as she was otherwise leading a normally active life, taking care of herself and her home, working outside, and engaging in fulfilling social commitments with other people.[2]

Naturally, men and women who have lost their mates and cannot possibly find suitable new partners should feel free to masturbate with as much pleasure as they can give themselves. But they can also express their loving energy through nonsexual interactions with other people. Rather than withdrawing from others into solitary masturbation and fantasy, they could share their blocked or untapped reservoirs of affection. By letting their loving feelings flow in helping people, they could enliven their own existence and also get from others the social expressions of love they so much need and desire. Numerous opportunities for such voluntary service are now available to aging widows and widowers—for example, companionship to the sick and the handicapped, or helping young children who need academic tutoring or emotional support. Apart from such avenues of fulfillment, elderly widows and widowers can express their creative and sensual impulses in artistic, musical, or intellectual forms that they may not have had the chance to pursue during their younger and busier years.

However, many people who lose their mates are still young enough to view the establishment of a new loving relationship as a very realistic possibility. Sylvia is a pretty and intelligent woman whose husband died from leukemia when she was only thirty-nine, leaving her with two teen-age children. Their marriage had been an extremely happy one; they were emotionally compatible and sexually in tune with each other. Fortunately, Sylvia was left quite secure financially, but shortly after her husband's death she went back to work as a secretary—not so much for the money as for the social and intellectual stimulation. "For a long time after Jack died, I was just going through the motions. I felt absolutely numb. I couldn't even think of the possibility of getting involved with another man. Actually, lots of men in the office wanted to get friendly with me, but I just couldn't respond. I was also very busy with my kids. They needed emotional support very badly after Jack's death, and my son was very worried about starting college. I guess I was a bit suspicious, too, about men being after me for my money." Sylvia paused and smiled at herself before going on. "I certainly never felt the urge to masturbate. I hadn't done that since I was in adolescence. It seemed awful to have to resort to *that* again."

For ten years, Sylvia remained very dedicated to her children, who went through a lot of emotional turmoil after the death of their father. "After both of my kids dropped out of college, I had a devil of a time getting them back again. I feel I did a great job with them . . . I'm not really worried about them any more. Now it's mainly me I have to take care of," Sylvia laughed. "After I was on my own for a while, my friends tried to fix me up. I knew I wouldn't meet another Jack, and I hated the dating game. I had sex with some of my dates but it was awful. That's when I started to masturbate again. It seemed better than having intercouse with men I didn't like."

Sylvia described how she got very involved in her own masturbation, giving up her guilt and inhibitions about it. "It was around the time my daughter started going steady with her boyfriend. I knew they were having sex together. We've always been very open about those things. I finally couldn't stand it any longer, thinking about my little baby making love and me feeling so hard up. So I began to get into masturbating. I'd read a few articles about how good it is for you, so I decided, why not? Soon I began to look forward to it. Instead of preparing to make love to Jack the way I did—you know, putting in my diaphragm and all—I prepared myself for my own lovemaking. After my shower, I'd rub powder and perfume all over myself and brush my hair slowly in front of the mirror. Then, I'd fondle myself, softly and gently at first, drawing out the pleasure. When I got into bed, I really let myself go. Sometimes, I'd spend an hour or more giving myself one orgasm after another."

Sylvia told us how she recently refused to go out on a date even after her best friend had urged her to try "just once more" with a man who had lost his wife, describing him as "just right" for Sylvia. "Even though he sounded pretty nice when he called me up, I still wouldn't say yes. But that night, when I started to masturbate, I found my mind wandering off, wondering what this man might look like. My friend has very good taste and excellent judgment about people. As I touched myself, I began to have a fantasy of making love with a man who was warm and understanding. It was the first time in years that I let myself get completely into imagining how wonderful it would feel with a real flesh-and-blood man again, with a real penis. God, how I missed being taken into the arms of a man I loved and who loved me! It suddenly hit me that I was being such a big snob—for what? I saw how much I wanted a relationship . . . how much I needed it. Well, the next day I called Bob and said I'd be willing to go out with him. I guess it was my good fortune, but I was also ready to let it happen. Anyway, Bob turned out to be not exactly what I had fantasized . . . but very nice. We've become very, very close, and it feels so good."

As Sylvia's case shows, involvement in a loving relationship depends very much on a person's willingness to have it. For someone who is doubtful about how much he wants to reestablish a loving relationship, masturbation can help him to make up his mind. Letting himself enjoy it to the fullest, as Sylvia did, he can see how much his need for sexual love with a real partner is not being fulfilled by his solitary masturbation. If he finds that he does experience that need for interpersonal love, a person can decide what he wants to do about it. He can make a very conscious choice either to learn to live without it and make the best of it, or else to do his utmost to find someone with whom he can share his love. Naturally, we believe it would be desirable for people to form new relationships of sexual love with suitable mates, if they possibly can. We fully realize how difficult it is to find a new partner, especially for women; and we're aware that everyone is not as fortunate as Sylvia. But if a person is willing to make compromises, he vastly increases his chances of finding somebody with whom he can be happy. Compromising does not mean to settle for a relationship that is not based on mutual love. But it does mean facing the facts that no one is exactly like your former mate or as good as your expectations of perfection.

THE NEVER-MARRIED

Unlike people who have been widowed, some adults have chosen to remain single for life; many of these confirmed singles have taken full responsibility for their choice, seeing it as more personally fulfilling than marriage. For example, some people have decided that they want to cultivate their own talents and creative potentials without being distracted in the slightest by commitments to a spouse and children; others may renounce marriage in favor of devoting their lives wholeheartedly to a religious order; still others may not get married because they prefer a homosexual life-style.

Ambivalance about Remaining Single

Most singles, however, have not completely renounced the possibility of forming a lasting and loving relationship with someone of the opposite sex; they continue either to look actively for suitable mates or to hope for them to appear. But such singles can do more for themselves than just look and hope. They can also help themselves in two ways: First, they can recognize their ambivalence; they have remained single, while thinking and saying that they want a loving relationship. Then, having realized their basic conflict, they can resolve it decisively one way or the other.

As long as they remain ambivalent, single people are bound to find it difficult to open themselves up with sufficient love and trust to form a marriage. They may find it hard to see how sharing themselves both mentally and physically with a heterosexual partner could fulfill their potentials as human beings. Or they may be reluctant to face the fears that have led them into developing fixed patterns of withdrawing from others into the compensations of masturbatory fantasy. Because of their unacknowledged and unresolved ambivalence, many single people let themselves become attracted again and again to people of the opposite sex who are unavailable, unattainable, or unsuitable for them, and they wind up being rejected by such people. Conversely, the same ambivalent singles may habitually avoid or reject those who sincerely like them and offer them the possibility of genuine love.

As a result, there are many single people who may repeatedly pass up the gratifications of a loving relationship rather than tamper with the seeming emotional safety of their indecisiveness. Thus, some ambivalent singles may drift into being "loners" all of their adult lives. Of course, their social and economic needs impel them to relate to others, to make friends, and to maintain interpersonal relationships over extended periods of time. But they may remain basically self-enclosed; and they may eventually rely on masturbation as their only means of satisfying their need for sexual love.

Donald is a rather handsome, assertive, and well-groomed man of forty-two, who is an executive in a large travel agency. "I love my work and it loves me—I think I have a damn good chance of becoming head of the agency within a couple of years." Donald has responsibility for arranging tours for organizations and professional groups, and his business activities require him to travel regularly to various parts of the world. "It's very exciting, and the stewardesses aren't bad either. A lot of the women on the tours are also looking for a little quick action. Oh, it does get lonely sometimes," he admitted. "None of us are getting any younger, right?"

During his childhood, Donald felt dominated by women— his mother and his two older sisters. He had the sense of being hounded by their demands. "I couldn't even jerk off in peace. When I was in the bathroom masturbating, my sisters would bang on the door for me to get out. They were always worried about getting ready for their goddamn dates. And they were a regular chorus for my mother—whenever she nagged me about the way I dressed or ate or kept my room, they chimed in with their bitching. My father was the only one who ever took my side. He really loved me . . . what a man he was! But he died when I was eleven." Donald paused for a moment. "My mother loves me, too. But she was always after me to improve myself.

My father . . . well, he made me feel I was OK without having to prove anything."

Donald's father had been a struggling insurance agent. After his death from a heart attack, Donald became the man of the family. He started working in a grocery after school to help his mother meet the household expenses. She had to get a job for the first time in her life; and she would come home at night and try to get sympathy from Donald for her sufferings as a saleslady. Donald's sisters also took part-time jobs while they still lived at home, but they both got married before Donald finished high school. After that, he and his mother shared the apartment for eight years, while he completed high school, took a full-time job as an office boy in his present agency, and went to college at night. "It was terrible—the roughest period in my life. I remember I used to masturbate a lot during that time. I wanted to get the hell out of the apartment but I couldn't until I had the money to afford it. With my sisters away, things got better between me and my mother. She had to depend on me more, so she stopped being so bossy. But then she started asking me what she should do about every little thing she had to decide. It drove me crazy, but I had to take it. Luckily, they liked me at the agency. When I got my degree in business administration, they promoted me to a regular travel agent. After that, I made damn sure to work my way up."

Once he had a high enough salary, Donald moved into his own apartment. "It upset my mother, but she knew I had to do it. Anyway, I began to give her some money every week. Now I give her a lot more. So I've turned out to be the 'good' child. Really, she appreciates me a lot and she shows it. It's my sisters she complains about now. They're well off, but they don't give her a penny." Donald brightened. "It was an amazing feeling to have my own apartment and do whatever I felt like doing without any monitors. I finally had the money to take out girls— and I could take them back to my place after a date. I tell you, I really made up for lost time."

Donald has often thought of getting married. But he feels that marriage would have a bad effect on his career. "What kind of a woman would want to put up with my being away so much of the time?" But he is very ambivalent about the issue of marriage; his best friends, Marc and Betty, are a married couple. "I like to hang out with them and their children. They give me a feeling of how beautiful family life could be—not the way it was in my home. My parents used to fight all the time, especially over what I should do. Oh, I'd hate to get bogged down. Sure, Marc and Betty seem very happy. But they have their troubles, too. I haven't seen them fight, but Betty let out a few hints one night when I dropped in on them and Marc was still at work. She seemed to want to confide in me. Look, I don't even want to know their problems. To me, they're both great people. But I don't need the hassels of married life."

Donald said that his pattern of masturbation has been changing recently. In past years of touring, he would masturbate in his hotel room if he had failed to find a sexual partner for the night. Now, he doesn't masturbate very much when he's abroad. "I'm usually so knocked out after a day on tour that I just flop into bed and fall asleep—if I don't have anyone to sleep with. If I do, I manage to save some energy for having sex with her. It's the return trip that gets to me. I start to think about how lonely it feels to come back to my empty apartment after all the excitement of the trip. Lately, on the night flights back to the city, I get very tense, very nervous. When the lights go out and people fall asleep, I start playing with myself under the blankets. That's not so abnormal, right? What bothers me though, is who I think about while I'm doing it—Marc and Betty. I start out imagining how we're going to go out to hear some jazz when I come home. We're a great threesome . . . we have such wonderful times together . . . I feel so comfortable with both of them. Then my fantasy changes and I see Marc and Betty in bed, making love. It's like I'm right there with them, only invisible. Sometimes . . . it gets a lot heavier . . . I see myself swinging with them, giving it to Betty while Marc is hugging both of us. That's the most scary part."

Donald's fantasies about the couple make him feel guilty when he sees them afterward. "It's crazy sitting there talking and laughing with them and me remembering all the details of my fantasy. We've always been very physical with each other— hugging and touching. But now, that's beginning to upset me, too. I wonder if they can guess what I've been imagining about them. And I sometimes feel I might lose control of myself and start pawing Betty. I know I can't go on like this. I'll have to do something to straighten myself out."

We gave Donald some immediate reassurance, telling him that many people had similar masturbatory fantasies about their friends or having sex with several people at once; and we added that such fantasies could help a person to identify his unfilled needs, permitting him to take realistic action toward filling them. "Yes," he agreed, "I have to get some real love into my life. I sure can't expect Marc and Betty to take me into their bed. But . . . that thing about Marc is what has me really worried . . . his hugging me while I'm screwing Betty—does that make me gay?" Again we assured Donald that it was natural to have sexual fantasies about a man he liked so much. Then we commented that a person doesn't *have* to act on any of his fantasies, sexual or otherwise; and that it was entirely up to him to decide what he wants to do about any of his thoughts and feelings.

"I know, I know. But I'm so damn busy I don't even have time to think about my personal life. I'm flying back and forth across the ocean every few weeks. And when I'm in New York, I work my ass off at the agency. There are a few other vice-presidents slugging it out with me for the top spot. It's no sure thing for me, I can tell you that. Ah, fantasies, schmantasies . . . I've got to keep plugging away. What the hell have I been killing myself for, if not to become president? After that, I'll see. Maybe, then, I'll be able to think about my love-life."

Donald's reluctance to understand the psychological meaning of his masturbatory fantasy clearly indicates his ambivalence about deciding whether or not to get involved in a loving relationship with a woman. He uses the pressing demands of his upwardly mobile career as the rationalization for his failure to confront his emotional problems honestly and to resolve them conclusively. Naturally, he can go on living with the inevitable tensions of his ambivalance. However, if he wants to free himself of his frustrations, Donald can help himself in two basic ways: by making the intellectual effort necessary to get genuine insight into the motivational conflicts behind his ambivalence; and, as a consequence of that self-awareness, by choosing to throw the full weight of his being toward one side of his ambivalence or the other—toward remaining single or toward finding a real mate.

Fantasy—Key to Understanding Ambivalence

First, to gain a full appreciation of his present mode of functioning, Donald needs to give himself a chance to focus all of his attention on some aspect of his inner life that can inform him of the nature and origin of his ambivalence. His masturbatory fantasy about Marc and Betty would be an ideal focal point, since he not only created that fantasy but was obviously very upset about it. And, as we have pointed out, the very masturbatory fantasies that trouble people the most are the ones they could profit the most from understanding.

So let us suggest the kinds of things Donald could learn about himself by dwelling on his fantasy with patience and undistracted contemplation. The most outstanding part of his fantasy was the sexual threesome he was having with his friends; specifically, he was having intercourse with Betty while Marc was hugging both of them. This fantasy reflects Donald's need to have a good sexual relationship with a woman he loves, while he also gets love and approval from a man he loves and admires. The fact that Donald imagines himself in such a situation—where he is simultaneously in the loving embrace of both a man and a woman—vividly portrays his reluctance to make a definitive choice to have an exclusive relationship with a woman. In addition, by seeing himself making love to Betty, a happily married woman, he is also showing his resistance toward getting together with a woman who *is* available.

If Donald had no need to have a basically good relationship with a woman, he could have created a fantasy of having sexual release with one of the stewardesses or other women with whom he had experienced casual and loveless affairs. But by picturing himself as making love to Betty, a woman for whom he does have strong affection and respect, he is expressing his desire for the kind of relationship that Betty and Marc have with each other.

Donald could learn about the origins of his ambivalence by viewing his fantasied threesome in the light of his developmental history. Because of his closeness with Marc and Betty, it is easy to see how he might regard them as symbolic parent figures. Viewed in this perspective, Donald's fantasy indicates that he has not yet separated himself emotionally and sexually from *both* of his parents. He continues to long for his dead father's love and unconditional acceptance. As for his relationship with his mother, Donald tends to protest too much about wanting to be independent from her and feeling that she is such a burden to him. It is understandable for him to have adopted such a defense, given the fact that his father's untimely death put him in a position of being a quasi-husband to her. Donald's willingness to be the man of the family shows that he always felt a need to get his mother's love and approval. Now, he takes great pride in the fact that he has turned out to be the "good" child, beating his sisters in the competition for her highest esteem. By continuing to cling tenaciously to the role of a child in his family of birth, Donald can delude himself into believing he is younger than his age and that he has all the years of adulthood still stretching out before him. That's why he may see no urgency about making a definitive choice about either marrying or remaining single.

Donald's defensiveness about showing truly affectionate feelings to women was increased because he lived alone with his mother for many years and felt he had to be particularly careful to control his sexual impulses in relating to her. Before his sisters went off on their own, he also felt sexually inhibited by their presence. Donald harbored a great deal of hostility and resentment toward his mother and sisters because of the ways they tried to dominate him. Projecting his hostile attitude onto *all* women, he has very mixed feelings toward them. So he vacillates between really wanting to relate to a woman like Betty, whom he feels good about, and wanting to have exploitative and superficial sexual relationships with women for whom he has no real feelings, as he does while he is on tour abroad. Thus, Donald has developed a fixed formula for compartmentalizing his feeling for women: he directs his affection toward women like Betty, who are unattainable sexually; and he expresses his hostility by having entirely self-centered sexual relations with women from whom he withholds love. And as long as Donald maintains his attachment to his parents, including his yearning for the lost love of his dead father, he will have an additional source of motivation to resist getting involved in a genuine relationship of sexual love with a woman he can marry.

Essentially, therefore, Donald uses his masturbatory fantasy about Marc and Betty as a safety device for avoiding the resolution of his ambivalence. And the more he relies on his fantasy while he gives himself the sexual gratification of a masturbatory orgasm, the more he is reinforcing his unrewarding indecisiveness.

Career vs. Commitment

But does Donald really gain in safety by not resolving his ambivalence? The answer is clearly no, even by his own admission. First of all, he repeatedly indicated how anxious he was about all the areas of his life. Second, he expressed the fear that his long-suppressed feelings of sexual love might come out in some uncontrollable form that would get him into serious trouble. Third, his deep unhappiness was evident in the fact that he couldn't see his life as having been worthwhile *unless* he succeeded in becoming president of his company. Yet his very anxiety and potential impulsiveness may turn out to prevent him from getting the very thing he says he wants the most.

Obviously, Donald is using his career as a rationalization for his inability to resolve his ambivalance about forming a relationship. In terms of his values, he has been putting ambition above love; and anyone who does that to such an extreme is bound to suffer in some way from all the tensions and lack of love that Donald is experiencing.

Many single people, like Donald, attribute their lack of commitment to a loving relationship to their career strivings, claiming they do not want to be tied down by any emotional involvements that might require them to limit the amount of time and energy they can devote to their work. A recent national survey found that, compared to married people, proportionately more never-married single men and women consider a fulfilling career to be their most important life goal.[3] Peter Stein, a professor of sociology and author of a book on singles, told us that one of the major positive reasons that people give for remaining single is their belief that they can advance better in their work without the encumbrances of a spouse and children.

Contrary to such a belief, however, many employers give preference to married or divorced men and women, even when the available singles have the same qualifications and experience. In addition, singles are often subject to both the envy and the contempt of their married colleagues. On one hand, their married coworkers may be envious of them, imagining them as living a free and loose sexual life; on the other hand, the same married people may be condescendingly sorry for singles, perceiving them as being lonely and having many emotional problems. According to Stein, "singles don't quite fit the pattern" at company parties and social events. In general, people who have family responsibilities, whether married or divorced, are regarded as much better bets for promotion than singles who have never married.

Of course, such prejudiced attitudes toward single people are grossly inaccurate and unfair; "they neither help us to understand the lives of singles, nor . . . help singles themselves to deal realistically with their lives." As Stein says of single men and women: "Their lives are filled with exciting experiences and lonely times, with personal growth and with moments of depression, with feelings of belonging and of isolation, with both a clear sense of who they are and with times of confusion." Yet, Stein adds, "single men and women report many more positive experiences than negative ones."[4]

Still, the idea that a loving sexual relationship and fulfillment in work are incompatible is an unfortunate misconception, which many single people may share with Donald. Rather, according to Wilhelm Reich, it is only when people derive the fullest physical and emotional satisfaction from their relationships of sexual love that they can express their creative and intellectual talents most productively in their work.[5]

The Toll of Loneliness

It is easy to see why Donald has always felt inwardly resentful about having to come through for a woman. Because he had to assume so much responsibility for helping his mother at the age of eleven and all through the rest of his youth, he now tries to avoid what he thinks are the hassles of married life. But it is not as if Donald is escaping hassles by not being married. His style of singlehood has hassles of its own; the most obviously frustrating of them stem from his lack of regular and loving sexual gratification. Lacking such pleasure and orgasmic release, Donald is hassled by his pent-up needs for sexual love. Since the tensions of these basic human needs do not disappear simply because they are not expressed, their continual pressure for expression burdens Donald with chronic tensions, which he would not have if he were in a loving and sexually fulfilling relationship—and that tension takes its toll physically as well as emotionally.

Understandably, Donald becomes most acutely aware of his loneliness and feels the urge to masturbate on his return trip to New York. For him, being on tour in Europe is equivalent to arranging a passing fantasy for himself and other people; its very appeal lies in its transient escape from the ordinary cares and responsibilities of daily life. When he is abroad, Donald can use his talent and energy to make arrangements for everyone's enjoyment—expressing his creativity in a form that gives him great intrinsic pleasure and social rewards. But New York represents the real world, where he must directly contend with his competitors at the agency. For Donald, New York is also *home*, the place where he grew up, where all his current emotional involvements are centered, and where he, too, could have a family waiting for his return.

It is not unusual for adults to use masturbation as a way of trying to overcome their feelings of loneliness. In Morton Hunt's survey, over a fourth of the males and over a third of the females said that their urge to masturbate was aroused when they felt lonely; "significantly, too, this response was far more often made by single people than by married people of like ages." [6]

Dr. Anne Welbourne told us that many lonely single men have phoned the Community Sex Information service for advice and reassurance because of their worries about masturbation. Most of them say they have never talked to anyone before about their concerns and they have nobody else with whom they can communicate about their anxiety, guilt, and confusion. Many of them say they feel like "abnormal freaks" because of their masturbatory thoughts and behavior. When the Community Sex Information service first started and advertised on disk-jockey radio programs, many single young men called but wanted to talk only to a woman. If a man answered, they would hang up. The professionally trained listeners usually knew which males telephoned because they wanted to be sexually turned on by a conversation with a woman. Some of the men would even say: "I don't know how to masturbate; could you tell me how to do it?" Often, there were long pauses in the conversation—the callers had become temporarily speechless because they were so involved with their own masturbation.

Other counselors have told us similar stories of men calling "Help Phone" services for the sole purpose of using the conversation as a stimulant for their masturbation and erotic fantasies. Such calls from women are relatively rare. Dr. Welbourne says that many of the masturbating callers eventually disclose tremendous feelings of guilt, loneliness, and unhappiness about having absolutely no other outlets for the expression of their sexual and emotional needs.

No matter what their motivation may be in calling, the people who telephone the Community Sex Information service tend to feel helped by hearing counselors tell them that they are not alone or unique; that many other people are also upset by the same masturbatory behavior, fantasies, and anxieties. The thing callers find most helpful is *talking* to someone who really cares; many of them say, "It feels so good just to be able to talk about it. I feel so much better already."

Anxiety—a Warning Signal

Both single men and women could benefit from communicating with friends or professional counselors about the anxieties aroused by their masturbation and masturbatory fantasies. But they can also help themselves by using both their anxiety and their fantasies as unequaled sources of information. As we have said before, anxiety is an adaptive mechanism that is telling you that you are trying to run from facing and resolving a conflict about whether you want to pursue a particular objective or renounce it.

For example, you may find yourself in situations where you feel anxious because you are sexually turned on by someone; but you aren't exactly sure what you want to do with your attraction, just as Donald felt when he became aware of his sexual feelings for Betty. As an immediate emotional reaction, you may be tempted to have sexual contact with the person you like. But as you consider the implications of that course of action, you realize that you really don't want a sexual relationship with that person. Still, you do want to be friends and you don't want to stop seeing the person. So, as Donald did with Betty, you use your masturbatory fantasies to act out your sexual feelings. But your reluctance to decide one way or the other in reality— either to become sexually involved or totally renounce the possibility—makes you feel so anxious that you don't know how to behave in the actual presence of that person.

Donald experiences just that kind of anxiety when he is with Betty and Marc; and he leaves them with all his stirred-up and unexpressed sexual feelings inside him, pressing for some release. So he masturbates and creates masturbatory fantasies that enable him to feel that he can do the impossible—fantasies in which he can have sexual intercourse with Betty while Marc lovingly approves. His masturbatory fantasy gives him the illusion that he can transcend the limits he is, in reality, putting on his behavior with his friends. Because his fantasies enable him to think he still can have a sexual threesome with Marc and Betty, they reduce Donald's motivation to pin himself down and resolve himself definitively—not only about his conflictual relationship with his friends, but also about his general ambivalence about having a loving relationship of his own. Thus, whenever he is with Betty and Marc, he feels the anxiety that indicates his wish to escape from resolving his conflicts; he again takes temporary refuge in his masturbatory fantasy when he leaves them; and his futile cycle of irresolution goes on and on.

To break such cycles *once and for all,* you need to take a different attitude toward your anxiety, recognizing it as a friend rather than an enemy. If you feel anxious when you are in a situation with a person about whom you have ambivalent feelings, you can take that anxiety as a signal that you want to escape from resolving a conflict you have about how you want to relate to that person. So, like Donald, you may subsequently masturbate while fantasizing the expression of all the sexual feelings you were undecided about expressing toward that person. Fortunately, however, you can effectively free yourself from your anxiety by deciding to resolve the conflict that gives rise to it. For example, you can decide that you are not going to have sexual relations with that person; and that you are going to have a loving but nonsexual relationship with him. Having made that definitive choice, you are now free to express your affectionate feelings openly toward your friend; and you don't have to worry that you will become seductive, go too far, or do anything that you do not want to do. Then, having shown your affection during your ongoing interaction with the person you like, you will not feel driven afterward by any unresolved tensions that motivate you to express them in solitary masturbation and fantasy.

In this way, you can feel much more relaxed and get more enjoyment from social relationships with people you like, but with whom you really do not want to become sexually involved. Conversely, if you do decide to have both a sexual and affectionate relationship with someone you know is available and suitable, you can go all-out in taking whatever steps are necessary and appropriate to form such a relationship with that person.

Everyone uses the magic of masturbatory fantasy to give himself the feeling that he can do the impossible, have it all ways, and not be bound by his actual limitations or those of the people he imagines as sexual partners. Yet, in reality, everyone makes himself anxious by wanting to escape from accepting what *is* possible: to make the kinds of choices that permit him to fulfill some of his motives while letting go of other, conflicting ones that he is unable or does not truly intend to gratify in reality. So all people—single or married—can benefit from learning how to resolve their conflicting feelings toward others. It might be temporarily enjoyable and self-flattering to indulge in erotic masturbatory fantasies about people with whom you don't really want to have a genuine relationship. In the long run, however, such fantasizing tends to keep you stuck where you are. By definitively deciding whether or not you really want to form a committed relationship of sexual love with someone—rather than just going on giving yourself a masturbatory fantasy about it—you free yourself to do something constructive about your life, regardless of what choice you make.

Unrewarding Perfectionism

Since leaving her home in the Midwest, Harriet, now thirty-six, has been living alone in New York, where she teaches English in the City University. "'After I finished graduate school, I had an excellent job offer in a college near home. But I had to leave that area; I felt too constricted. My kid sister was already married—very successfully, as they say. The pressure on me to do the same was just too much.

"Somehow, I haven't been able to find the right one for me. Believe me, it isn't that I haven't tried. I know I have high standards. But I can't help it. My father was a prominent doctor, and my mother was a professional musician. At my age, everyone who's at all attractive and well-adjusted seems to be married. If not, they have so many problems they're not worth bothering with." Harriet hesitated before going on. "'Yes, I masturbate. I don't feel all that good about doing it. But it's better than having to go to bed with every man the first time you go out with him."

As the first of two daughters, Harriet didn't quite fulfill the expectations of either of her parents. Her father loved her for her intelligence and sensitivity, but he didn't think she was very pretty, certainly not as beautiful as her mother. "My father might have been somewhat disappointed with me, but as far as my mother was concerned—forget it. I think she only had children because she wanted a son who would dote over her. I did my share of idolizing her, but she wanted it from a man. She never felt my father appreciated her talent enough. My sister was much prettier than I was. But that wasn't good enough for my mother, either. She was always away on concert tours while we were growing up. My father was very busy, too. But since his

260

office was in our house, I spent more time with him than I did with my mother. Sometimes, when she was out of town, he would come into my room at night to tuck me in and he'd tell me all about how wonderful it was to be a doctor . . . how much he loved working with people and helping them."

Although Harriet felt her father wanted her to follow in his footsteps, she wanted to do something different from either of her parents. "I felt a need to do something in my own right. My sister was the beautiful performer, like my mother. She'd been into modern dance since she could walk. I spent a lot of time alone before she was born. I loved playing make-believe and using my imagination. In school, I took naturally to literature. So I eventually decided to make a career in that field."

When Harriet first came to New York, it was difficult for her to get as good a job as she'd turned down at home. "I was very busy in those days running to professional meetings, delivering papers, and trying to advance my career. But don't worry. I also used those occasions as a way of meeting men. At first, I just got into the sexual thing. You know what it's like at those conventions. I guess I was happy that men were attracted to me, and I didn't care too much about getting heavily involved. But after a while, I felt a need for a more meaningful relationship. I was beginning to get tired of going back to my apartment and having fantasies of my ideal man while I masturbated."

One summer, when she had a share in a house on Fire Island, Harriet thought her ideal man had finally come along. He was urbane, witty, extremely talented, and handsome, too. She was struck by him the first time she saw him sauntering along the beach. Gossiping with the women, she learned that he was an up-and-coming young painter. "They all gave me fair warning. Apparently, Ron was known for loving them and leaving them. It all registered on my mind, but I had the powerful feeling that it would be different with me. I might not have been as pretty as some of the other women on the beach, but he loved my body and he appreciated my depth and understanding. I loved his work and he gave me the feeling that I could help him to develop what he wanted to express. When he asked me to model for him, I was hooked. We had quite an intense and torrid summer. The girls couldn't get over me. I was a new woman—I absolutely glowed."

That fall, Harriet spent most of her spare time in Ron's studio. He was working day and night getting ready for a one-man exhibit of his work. After that, she hoped she and Ron would be able to make plans for living together or maybe even getting married. Watching his expressive face while he worked, she often thought of what a beautiful child they could have together. But after the success of his show, Ron was busier than ever. He started breaking dates and making excuses for not getting together. "When we did see each other, our sex wasn't the way it had been. I just couldn't confront him about what was happening between us. I found myself going home and masturbating again, only then I was having elaborate fantasies of how I could hold on to Ron. I saw myself as the voluptuous woman in all of his paintings. But I was in much more suggestive poses than he had actually done of me. I imagined my presence in his paintings as a big factor in his success. When Ron heard that another artist asked me to model for him, he became very jealous and wanted to be with me all the time, the way we were that summer. But all of that was just fantasy. In reality, I came back from class one day and found a note from him saying it was all over and he was on his way to the West Coast. After that experience with Ron, I was very shaken up . . . to think that my judgment had been so bad. For a long time, I gave up on men and threw myself into my work."

One of Harriet's colleagues finally got her to go to a party. It was a wild affair, and Harriet wasn't in the mood to let herself get into it. There was a very nice-looking man also sitting on the sidelines; and when they started to talk, Harriet found herself relaxing and responding well to him. Stan was a professor of classics at an Ivy League college, and they shared many interests and tastes. He'd been divorced for about a year. "Stan and his wife hadn't been married long before they realized that they just didn't have enough in common. She was a Greek girl he'd met in Athens on a sabbatical, and she felt it had been a mistake for her to come to America. Before the night was over, I could see Stan was very taken with me. In a few months, we became serious lovers. He was a little older than me, and I know he was very anxious to settle down and remarry. At first, I was very pleased about the idea. Our relationship was basically good in many ways. I could respond to him quite well sexually. It wasn't the passion I had felt with Ron, but it was fine. When we went home to meet my family, everyone seemed to like him. I can't believe it, but we actually talked about who to invite to our wedding. Then . . . I don't know what happened. I just couldn't bring myself to go ahead and marry him. There were many things I liked about Stan. He was so steady and reliable. He wanted to have a family. I know he would have been an excellent father. And I knew he loved me. But he had certain tendencies that frightened me. He still seemed too attached to his mother. I was afraid he'd be too passive. He was also very involved in doing translations and writing books. I thought I might have to subordinate my career to his. Somehow, I felt we'd have too many problems and I just wasn't ready to risk it."

Since she gave up the chance to marry Stan over a year ago, Harriet has had a few fleeting sexual relationships with other men, but none of them have been satisfying to her. While she hasn't given up the idea of meeting a man she can really love, she finds it more and more difficult to make a connection. "I wonder if I did the right thing with Stan. He wasn't my idea of an emotionally mature man. But when I meet someone who is, he's got a wife and kids. And I don't need that load of guilt . . . breaking up a family. Recently, I've begun to rely on masturbation an awful lot. I usually do it to help me relax at night after I've been up late and working hard. Sometimes, I even feel the urge to do it when I'm in the middle of my work—you know, when I get bored marking students' papers. But lately, I seem to get especially tense when I'm frustrated or upset about my own writing coming out just right. And then I often feel I can't control my urge to stop right then and there, and masturbate." Harriet paused. "This may seem out of character for me . . . what I find terribly exciting when I do it now is imagining a scene at a professional meeting. Several of the men there tell me how much they admire my publications. They're all eager to have sex with me. But just the thought of turning them down gets me very aroused. The more they beg me, the more I spurn them and the more aroused I get. Finally, one of them talks me into having a drink in his room. As soon as we get inside the door, he grabs me and pulls me onto the bed. No matter what I do to resist, he forces me onto it. I can never recognize exactly who he is. His face is a blank but he's very strong and muscular. He even gets a little violent . . . keeping me spread out on the bed by pressing his body against mine. I squirm and squirm, and when I feel completely helpless and overpowered, I have a marvelous orgasm."

Why is it that so many women like Harriet, who are highly educated, articulate, attractive, and perceptive, still fail to implement their professed desires to form a committed relationship of sexual love? Like Donald and similarly ambivalent men, these women also feel blocked in functioning as the loving people they could be. Dr. Waxenberg told us that most of the single women she sees in psychotherapy feel as free as Harriet to have casual sexual relations with men; and many of them have as much trouble as Harriet in establishing a good and lasting emotional relationship with a man. While they do not rely solely on masturbation for their sexual release, many of them often find their superficial sexual relations as lonely as masturbation. Eventually, they may prefer, as Harriet does, to masturbate rather than go through the motions of having loveless sexual affairs. But for these women, as for Harriet, masturbation provides only temporary release, after which they tend to feel acutely lonely again. In fact, according to Dr. Waxenberg, such masturbation may only intensify their sense of loneliness.

Fantasy—Key to Understanding Conflicts

Because Harriet has not yet resolved conflicts stemming from her childhood development, she fails to make correct judgments in evaluating potential mates; and she presently feels caught up in a negative cycle of masturbation and fantasy, which is keeping her in a state of suspended animation and emotional withdrawal from men. Harriet's masturbatory fantasies, particularly her most recent ones, reflect the kind of motivational conflicts that have impeded the development of her personality in all four areas of functioning that permit an adult to merge happily in a relationship of sexual love.

First, Harriet's fantasies indicate her attempts to compensate for the negative self-image she acquired as a child; and she still sees herself as not being pretty enough to attract a lover who meets her high standards. By portraying herself as a voluptuous sexpot in Ron's paintings, Harriet was trying to enhance her sense of attractiveness to him. In her latest fantasies, she seeks to compensate for the inadequacy she feels because she has no lover, imagining that several men, who in reality never showed any particular interest in her, are begging for her sexual favors and admiring her professional accomplishments.

As a child, Harriet felt that both her mother and her sister were better looking and more creative than she was. And, despite her keen intelligence, she felt inadequate compared to her father and unsure of his love. Besides, she felt bad that she wasn't a boy, who could please her mother and follow in her father's footsteps. So she didn't accept herself fully as a woman. As a result, she rebelled at the prospect of being emotionally dependent on any man, as she might have been if she married Stan. Her lack of self-acceptance as a woman also made her jealous and hostile toward men, preventing her from truly accepting them. However, because she admired her beautiful mother, Harriet also wanted to be sexually attractive. Thus, she flourished when she could play the part of a desirable model in her relationship with Ron.

While Harriet's father accepted her more than her mother did, her uncertainty about how completely he loved her led her to doubt how lovable she could be to any man. Trying to overcome that doubt, she felt particularly attracted to self-centered men, like Ron, who were inclined to withhold genuine love from any woman. And, when Ron rejected her, she felt even more doubt than ever about whether she could get a desirable man to love her wholeheartedly. On the other hand, she is suspicious of the intentions—and even the emotional state—of men like Stan, who offer her genuine love without her having to do anything in particular to get it from them. Having love offered by a man like Stan has the paradoxical effect of making it seem worthless to her. For since she secretly considers herself so imperfect, she begins to wonder what is wrong with him: How could he really love her if he saw her as she sees herself? So she begins to look for shoddy motives in him and winds up using the fallibilities she projects onto him as the reason for rejecting him.

Indeed, Harriet gets great erotic pleasure from her recent fantasies of spurning men who eagerly desire her. In such fantasies, she reveals the deep hostility she feels toward men, her basic distrust of them, her disbelief that any man could possibly love her, and her attempt to deny her need for them. Even when she thought she wanted a committed relationship with Ron, she portrayed herself in fantasy as being instrumental for his success, indicating her desire to be superior to him and to assert her independence from men.

Harriet's bad feelings about herself prevented her from developing a realistic image of her very substantial assets and competencies; but they also led her to resist accepting the inevitability of her own limitations and inadequacies. As a result, she never developed the understanding that all people have similar limitations and anxieties about their adequacies. Failing to realize that no one is—or can ever be—free of emotional hang-ups, she refused to accept whatever inadequacies Stan actually did possess. Because of her perfectionistic expectations, Harriet has also been unable to develop the understanding that every relationship, as loving as it may be, has its inevitable problems and conflicts. This lack of understanding led her to believe that being married to Stan would involve her in more hassles than she had to cope with by remaining single. Yet, like Donald, she was denying how hassled she was by the frustrations and tensions of being single; and she also was overlooking the gratifications that she could be getting from being married to someone who loved her, as Stan did, and with whom she could share both the joys and the challenges of loving. Harriet had no appreciation of the fact that, in the process of resolving the conflicts one has with a mate, a person can continue his own development as a stronger and more fulfilled individual.

By spurning the men in her fantasy, Harriet expresses her basic fear of merging with a mate in a relationship of real love and equality. For she still does not sufficiently trust her ability to maintain her sense of individuality in such an equalitarian merger. Allowing herself to get sexual release only when she feels totally overpowered by the unidentifiable and sadistic man in her fantasy, Harriet shows how much she is abdicating personal responsibility for making her own choice about the kind of man with whom she really does want to have a loving relationship. Despite her assertion about not marrying Stan because she wanted to maintain her autonomy, her masturbatory fantasy of submitting sexually to a man who dominates her totally indicates the lack of respect she actually has for her own individuality. And the "marvelous" orgasm she experiences in fantasizing such an unequal relationship only tends to reinforce the negative image she has of her individual worth.

Harriet, like Donald, has impeded the growth of her own individuality by remaining emotionally attached to her parents. Because of her overdependence on her parents' approval, she felt a strong need to live at a distance from her family; and she even gave up a promising academic position near their home because she didn't feel strong enough in her own right to stand up to them and to tolerate the competitiveness she felt toward her mother and sister. But her rebelliousness was a cover for the basic attachment she still felt for her parents, particularly her father, who was the only one she felt close to when she was young. Yet when her parents approved of Stan as her potential husband, Harriet did not view their blessings as an acceptance of the maturity and wisdom of her choice. Rather, in rejecting Stan, she was also striking back at her parents; and her apparent defiance actually resulted in her continuing to be much more their child than she would have been if she had gotten married. So, whereas Donald kept himself in a childlike emotional state by playing the role of the "good" child, Harriet did exactly the same thing by playing the role of a "bad" one.

Individual Development vs. Commitment

Many single people, like Harriet, say they have never married because they have a greater opportunity to develop their talents and abilities by remaining single. Compared with married men and women, almost four times as many never-married men and women say that their most important goal in life is to develop as an individual.[7] They often see marriage as emotionally suffocating, as an obstacle to self-development, and as a restriction on their personal growth. By contrast, they perceive in singlehood the opportunity for change, mobility, self-sufficiency, and psychological as well as social autonomy.

It is true that people who have made a definitive choice to live alone can pour all of their energies into their own personal growth and development. But, if people still feel ambivalent about their single status, as Harriet does, they are often hampered in their ability to develop themselves because of the lack of love in their lives. Because Harriet has not shared her loving energies with a mate, her self-containment has made her feel self-pitying and misunderstood. In the past, she tended to blame her unhappiness on parental pressures and their unwillingness to love her unconditionally, or on the emotional problems of potential husbands.

Lately, because she is not experiencing any fulfillment of sexual love, she is finding it harder and harder to contain her nonsexual tensions. When she becomes frustrated in her efforts at professional achievement, for which she has denied herself all the gratifications of a loving relationship, she tends to seek the immediate physical release and emotional solace of masturbation. However, by not allowing herself to contain her anxieties long enough to face them squarely and use them constructively, she is only compounding her frustrations; and she is preventing herself from feeling the full force of her unhappiness, which might finally motivate her to confront her unresolved developmental conflicts and overcome them enough to get into the kind of loving relationship she has been yearning for but avoiding.

Like Harriet, many single people may have similar problems in finding a balance between their ability to release and contain their need for sexual love. Naturally, a loving relationship with a real person involves both the giving and receiving of love. But many singles who use masturbation as their main expression of sexual love may be unwilling to give love—although they may desperately desire to get it. What such people have trouble appreciating is how much they are hurting themselves by not letting their love flow freely to another. It is the "rush" of energy that goes outward from a person to a lover that gives him so much of the "high" that is involved in loving. For if a person does keep his love too much to himself, he is not only depriving someone else of it; he is also depriving himself of the ecstatic pleasures involved in its interpersonal release.

Breaking the Shackles of the Past

How could people like Harriet and Donald shed the developmental shackles of their past and break out of their negative and vicious cycles of masturbation and fantasy? First of all, before a person can go beyond the influences of his past, he must face them squarely. The choice of singlehood gives a person the fullest possible opportunity to enjoy his masturbatory inclinations and to use them in furthering his development as a loving person. Being on your own, you can get totally immersed in the search to understand yourself and the meaning of your life. When you masturbate, you can let yourself completely revel in the pleasures and sensations of every bit of erotic self-stimulation you may wish to explore. At the same time, you can let yourself be open to all the feelings and fantasies you have, with a view toward deriving insight into your emotional conflicts and the best means of resolving them. You can review your masturbatory fantasies, as we have done with Donald's and Harriet's, to gain an understanding of how your own childhood development affected your functioning in the four basic areas of personality that we have discussed; and you can use that understanding to remove the blocks that may be preventing you from being more loving to others and from living up to your potentials.

Once you have gotten insight into how your personality has been affected by your past, and how your reactions to your childhood experiences are affecting your present approach to sexual love, what can you do about it? First and foremost, you can face and accept the fact that *there is absolutely nothing you can do to alter the past*. It is dead and gone; and no matter what negative effects it may have had on you, you have *no* choice but to work with what you are *right now*—if you really want to change and resolve your ambivalence about being single.

The best way for you to leave the past behind you is to forgive your parents (and siblings and everyone else) for whatever they may have done to hamper your development. As long as you continue to blame them for not loving you more or better, you maintain your emotional attachment to them, and you keep yourself from assuming a fully adult responsibility for yourself. So instead of focusing on how they might have treated you—or should treat you now—you can focus on all the things you can do to treat *yourself* with the kind of loving consideration you have felt your parents didn't give you and still owe you.

Having forgiven all the other people you had been blaming, you can then proceed to forgive yourself for whatever mistakes you feel you have made in the past, for all your missed opportunities for achievement, and for all the people you *could* have married or *should* have married. Having freed yourself from the bondage of blame, you can focus fully on how you feel *now;* you can rely on your unshackled feelings to make definitive choices about whether or not you *now* want to commit yourself to finding a mate and forming a lasting relationship.

As long as you remain unforgiving toward your parents, you will not be able to forgive yourself enough to make a clean emotional break with your past and approach your future with a fresh and more constructive attitude. As an inescapable consequence of childhood development, everyone is bound to feel identified with his parents to a large extent. The attitudes you maintain toward your parents reflect those you harbor toward yourself; and, if you are resentful toward your parents, you may be sure that you also feel resentment toward yourself.

When you forgive your parents, you develop genuine compassion for them as fallible human beings. As a result, you automatically develop the same compassion toward yourself. Accepting them, you increase your acceptance of yourself. As you more clearly see *both* their strengths and limitations, you gain a similarly balanced and realistic understanding of your own assets and shortcomings. Thus, you enhance your general competence to be loving, compassionate, and clear-sighted in relating to all people. Your forgiveness of your parents and your compassion for them permits you to let go of the dependency on them that you used to have. Having decisively given up your childish attachment to them, you can cultivate your own individuality and feel, perhaps for the first time in your life, that you are fully responsible for yourself when you relate to other people—including potential lovers and mates. Finally, having forgiven your parents, you can stop using them as rationalizations for defiance, petulance, and refusal to contain the tensions that necessarily arise in the course of your work or interpersonal relations. So, as Sue did when she finally forgave her mother and her father, you will feel less compelled to release such tensions immediately through masturbation and compensatory fantasies; and, by accepting those tensions as an inescapable aspect of your struggle for personal fulfillment, you can contain them with a view toward resolving the conflicts they reflect.

After you feel sufficiently free from your former emotional ties to your family and your past, you are ready to make a truly satisfying decision about whether to remain single or to find a mate. If you decide to work toward establishing a relationship, you can take appropriate steps to put yourself into more and more situations where you might find a suitable partner. At the same time, you can change your orientation toward others, permitting yourself to be more open and accepting of people, *like yourself,* who do not meet the perfectionistic standards that you may have used as a barrier to a relationship in the past. Then, you will feel much freer to explore opportunities to relate to eligible members of the opposite sex; and when you are interacting with them, you will also be more spontaneous about expressing your affectionate feelings.

By resolving your ambivalence in these ways, you can reduce your former social isolation and your tendencies to withdraw into masturbation and fantasy. Even if you find that the realities of your age and your life circumstances prevent you from forming a permanent relationship, you may at least have the satisfaction of developing friendships based on genuine affection. You can also keep yourself socially involved by participating in activities and projects which you enjoy, which make a useful contribution to the community in which you live, and which bring you into regular contact with people whose interests and needs are similar to your own.

If, on the other hand, you have resolved your ambivalence by deciding to remain single for life, you can become wholeheartedly involved in the kinds of friendships and groups that could provide you with the emotional support, security and validation you need to feel good about yourself and lessen your feelings of loneliness and isolation. By giving yourself more social fulfillments, you are likely to feel less motivated to use masturbation and fantasy as a compensation for your nonsexual tensions and frustrations; and you can develop your individual talents more fully.

Homosexuality

There are some adults who renounce the possibility of marriage because they prefer homosexuality to heterosexuality. Everyone who has ever taken pleasure in his own body and genitals has known what it is to be attracted to someone of the same sex. In this sense, solitary masturbation is always implicitly homosexual, no matter how heterosexual the fantasies are that accompany it. For all the characters in those fantasies, including members of the opposite sex, are always projections of one and the same person—the individual who is creating them while masturbating.

A person who chooses homosexuality is, in some sense, also choosing masturbation as his preferred form of sexual expression. For he is always playing with duplicates of himself and his own sexual organs. His sexual partner is always a mirror through which he cannot pass beyond himself. While he may find pleasure and safety in the familiar limits of his own reflection, he can never find what is forever lacking in his own sexual being unless he is willing to take the risk of embracing the only being who possesses it—a person of the opposite sex. Naturally, too, a person who chooses a homosexual life-style also prevents himself from fulfilling his basic human potentials for procreation.

There is no doubt that people who choose homosexuality are capable of loving the partners of their sexual choice and forming lasting relationships with them. If a person is not ambivalent and makes a deliberate choice to be a homosexual—with full conscious awareness of its psychological and social consequences—he can allow himself to enjoy it to the fullest. Like singles who have chosen heterosexuality, homosexuals do not have to become involved in promiscuous and loveless sexual relations, or feel driven to rely on solitary and unshared masturbation. Instead, they, too, can use their masturbatory fantasies to gain insight into ways they can relate more lovingly to their sexual partners; and they can establish emotionally meaningful relationships with members of their own sex. Thus, they can live as partners and commit themselves to relating responsibly to each other with all the love and reliability that gives married couples a sense of security and fulfillment. Homosexuals can also benefit from communicating honestly to each other about their sexual needs and desires, sharing the content of their masturbatory fantasies, and enhancing the erotic pleasure of their sexual relationship by incorporating self-stimulation into their lovemaking.

Some people become involved in a homosexual life-style, but remain ambivalent and disturbed about their choice. Many of those people go for psychotherapy to resolve their conflicts and learn either to live better with their choice or to change their basic sexual preference. But it is very difficult for a person to change from an exclusively homosexual orientation to an exclusively heterosexual one. In fact, C. A. Tripp feels that it is almost impossible for people to make such a change.[8]

However, some psychologists who use techniques of behavior modification report that they have succeeded in helping homosexuals who wanted to make the switch to heterosexuality. In the procedure they prescribe, the patient uses his own masturbation as a way of reorienting his fantasy life, thus bringing about a change in his ability to experience sexual arousal with members of the opposite sex.[9]

Dr. Lowell Anderson, a psychologist at Bellevue Hospital, told us that this method for changing sex preference has been far more effective than previous techniques, which have tried to condition homosexuals to have negative feelings to members of their own sex. According to Dr. John Marquis, the person seeking help is instructed to masturbate, using whatever fantasies he finds most arousing. Just at the point where the person feels the inevitability of his orgasm, he learns to switch to an appropriate fantasy about a person of the opposite sex. By having his masturbatory orgasm in conjunction with this heterosexual fantasy, the pleasure of his orgasm becomes associated with the image of a heterosexual partner and reinforces his positive feelings toward members of the opposite sex.

Of course, this shift may be difficult to make at first, but after a person is able to switch successfully to the new heterosexual fantasy for several trials, without losing his sexual arousal, he gradually introduces his new heterosexual fantasy at an earlier and earlier point in his masturbation. In this way, he attaches sexual arousal and pleasure to a heterosexual partner by pairing his orgasm with such a fantasy; and he also uses his ability to sustain the lengthened period of his masturbation, which is now accompanied by a heterosexual fantasy, as a "rehearsal" for the sexual behavior he wishes to achieve with an actual partner.

This technique of the controlled use of masturbatory fantasies to recondition a person's sexual object choice has been used since the mid-1960s with some success. Of course, its long-range effects need further study. But the fact that such a procedure can have *any* positive results provides evidence for the fact that people *do have control* over the kinds of masturbatory fantasies they create, and that they can use them constructively to change their sexual behavior in ways they desire.

THE DIVORCED

Currently, at least one out of every three marriages in America ends in divorce.[10] As these statistics show, a single person's decision to get married does not automatically guarantee that his marriage will be a happy or lasting one. Of course, many unhappy marriages result from the fact that the spouses in them never loved each other from the start. Perhaps they got married because of an unwanted pregnancy, or saw marriage mainly as a chance to be economically secure or socially accepted by people in their community. Lacking any real love for each other, how *can* spouses expect to find happiness in a relationship whose particular fulfillment depends on the giving and receiving of sexual love?

Yet many people who get divorced *did* feel that they truly loved each other at the time they decided to marry. So it is apparent that they stopped *choosing* to love one another at some point after getting married. As we have said, letting yourself love someone is an act of choice. That initial decision to love needs to be made over and over again—every day, in fact—for a married couple to stay turned on, to share their inner lives, and to cooperate fully in coping with whatever problems arise in the course of their marriage.

Unfortunately, many married people become afraid to go on loving so consciously and responsibly. At the beginning of their marriages, they may experience little of that fear. But as their marriage progresses and they inevitably encounter conflicts between them, they are implicitly called upon to be more yielding, accepting, and honest than they ever were in the past. That's when they become acutely frightened, because they think their individuality and emotional safety will be obliterated by merging more completely with their mates. Reacting to their fright, they may choose, as Kris and others have done, to accommodate it by trying to escape from their partners into solitary masturbation; while they are masturbating alone, they often create fantasies of having promiscuous sexual contacts with other people.

When Nadine was first married, she and her husband felt very good about each other; they enjoyed their sexual relationship and she experienced no desire to masturbate, although she had done so regularly during her childhood and adolescence. But as they started to have problems and withdrew from each other, Nadine felt that sexual intercourse lost its emotional involvement for both of them. "It began to feel like masturbation to me," she told us. Yet, neither Nadine nor her husband chose to confront the psychological barriers that separated them and discuss their sexual disaffection honestly with each other. For about a year before they actually got divorced, things were so tense between them that they stopped having intercourse altogether, and Nadine turned back to private masturbation. But she never tried to use it as a way of opening deeper communication with her husband.

In making the choice to withdraw from each other in this way, spouses reject the option they have of containing their fear and of choosing to go on loving and communicating with their mates in spite of it. If they begin to choose consistently in favor of accommodating their fears rather than expressing them to each other, they are bound to increase their mutual alienation. Of course, they may try to blame their spouses for their own decision to stop loving them. Although such blame may be a sop to their egos, it only succeeds in deepening the gulf between them; and unless they get insight into what they are doing to each other and start to reverse their decision-making process, they continue to cycle steadily down the road to divorce.

Sexless Love and Loveless Sex

One of the most persistent and subtle resistances that some spouses have toward merging in sexual love with their mates goes back to their long childhood conditioning in learning to separate sex from love. As children, people are taught that it is bad and improper to experience—much less to express—the sexual desires that they inevitably feel toward those they love the most. Social taboos force people to have a minimum of erotic contact with the objects of their deepest affection, beginning with the taboo against incest. Bringing the effect of these taboos into their marriage, people often avoid showing the full intensity of their sexual desires, feeling that it is somehow wrong for them to be so erotically involved with their partners. To the extent that married people perceive their mates as parental figures, and still have not sufficiently separated themselves emotionally from their parents, they may feel inhibited about using the complete freedom they have to be sexually expressive in relating to their partners.

The extreme example of this kind of reaction is the person who can become sexually aroused by someone for whom he has no affectionate feelings but doesn't respond sexually to someone he loves. Thus, some men may be impotent with their wives but can have intercourse successfully with a prostitute. Or some women may be inorgasmic with the mates they really love, but they can bring themselves to orgasm when they masturbate with fantasies of having intercourse with strangers or of being raped. Such people may feel so guilty about taking responsibility to express their sexual feelings in a relationship of intimacy and love that they may often prefer to masturbate rather than to have sexual intercourse with their own spouses.

Because his mother had alternated between being seductive and rejecting during his childhood years, Kris developed this type of conflict, which undermined his ability to combine sex and love in relating to his former wife, and which led him, while married, to prefer solitary masturbation to sexual intercourse. Since his divorce, Kris continues to feel the desire to masturbate frequently. "But I don't want to waste it, so I try to hold off in order to save myself for more gratifying sex with someone else. But there's a great deal of confusion in my mind between being physically attracted to a woman and really liking her. And going to bed in order to find out is often a more lonely feeling than masturbating."

When he does masturbate, Kris tries to drag it out before having an orgasm so he can generate his fantasies. "There's still a lot of anger connected with my masturbation. After my divorce, I started having fantasies of screwing my mother. I would imagine active plots in which I could get her somewhere where I could screw her. Once, I had a fantasy of fucking my mother and, as my erection got bigger and harder, my cock turned into a gun on an army tank and blew her head off. Sometimes, even in relationships with other women, I get into a 'kill' kind of feeling. I think my tremendous feelings of rage come from a deep-seated sense of humiliation. A woman I know once wanted me to masturbate in front of her. But I couldn't possibly do it. For me, privacy is synonymous with shame and secretiveness— I always feel much more *shame* than guilt when I masturbate."

Kris is now almost fifty and has been living alone for about ten years since his divorce. While he expresses a great deal of intellectual awareness of his problems, he maintains a deep emotional attachment to his mother, as shown by the incestuous masturbatory fantasies he creates about her. Still enraged by the effects of his mother's past behavior on him, Kris has tried to retaliate by staying as far away from her as he can—living on the opposite coast of the country and only infrequently contacting her by letter or telephone. But his unresolved conflict about his mother still keeps him psychologically involved with her, making it difficult for him to relate lovingly to other women or to trust them. Now, instead of seeking sexual contacts with women older than himself, as he did in the past, he prefers those who are much younger. But he admitted that he often feels rather weird when he goes out with a woman as young as his own daughter.

"Balling is a validation of my attractiveness. But *getting* a woman to bed is often better than *being in* bed with her. And I find it difficult to go to sleep with a woman who I don't really feel good about—regardless of having had sex. I feel the most intimacy in just holding and being held by a woman."

When Kris has a sexual relationship with a woman now, he still has a need to distance himself from her emotionally, if there is any possibility of his having to make a commitment. "Distancing is my way of remaining free of disapproval. I'm afraid of yielding to a woman. I have a fear of being taken over and controlled, that I'll be tempted to be the way she wants me to be. I want sex to be *my* way. For thirty-five years it was never the way I wanted it to be. So I fear surrender. But when I do get it, I also fear unremitting acceptance."

Profiting from Past Mistakes

Many divorced people were less impeded than Kris by developmental attachments and conflicts when they chose to marry. They entered marriage with every chance and prospect for a lasting and fulfilling relationship; and when their marriage ended in divorce, they left it with tormenting doubts and regrets, acknowledging that things might have worked out with their spouses if they themselves had behaved differently. After their divorce, such people often maintain a close parental relationship with their children; and they may even stay on good terms with their former mates. Finally, having suffered from what they did to blight their previous marriage, they are inclined to become more genuinely humble and to change in ways that permit them to merge more lovingly with a new partner when they remarry.

Irene is now a dress-buyer for a large department store. Her shapely figure, smooth face, and natural blonde hair give her the appearance of being considerably younger than her thirty-eight years. But the faint circles of gray around her blue eyes suggest that she carries many emotional scars of her past unhappiness within her. "It's interesting—I never thought of masturbation as having anything to do with my marriage or divorce. But now that I think of it . . . maybe . . . Well, let's see. When Lester and I were first married, I didn't masturbate at all. We had such good times in bed—we really seemed so good for each other. But that was in the beginning, before Les started trying to become a principal. He was only an ordinary teacher, then, and I had quit working to be his full-time wife. We had a lot of time to be together."

Irene was the middle child between an older sister and a younger brother. She remembers her family background as a warm one, but full of competition. "It seems that each of us kids tried to be extra special in different ways. My sister was always the 'brain.' My teachers used to tell me what great work she did when she was in their classes. I knew I couldn't keep up with her . . . and I didn't really try to. I was the gal with the looks, so I went the beauty route. For me, getting boys was like getting good marks. And I did pretty well, if I must say so myself." Irene's brother was musically talented, which she wasn't; but she never felt much of a need to compete with him.

It was her sister that troubled her, especially since their father, an accountant, put such a great emphasis on academic achievement. "One of the things that attracted me to Les was his intelligence. Being a high-school science teacher, he made a big impression on my father. My mother liked him, too, for his quiet ways and good manners. He also had a nice, secure position. And she could see that he loved me."

Irene said that Lester had pursued her for a long time before she made up her mind to marry him. She had many other boyfriends. "But he won out. He was so persistent. There was nothing I could do to discourage him. He had just decided I was the one he wanted. But I held out for a long time . . . even after I felt I loved him, too. I kept thinking I might be able to do better for myself." Irene frowned. "I don't know what kind of men I thought would be enough for me. None of them, probably. As a kid, when I masturbated, I would imagine a whole parade of men coming on to me. I'd have an orgasm thinking about one of them. Then, another guy would take his place. Maybe he'd be good-looking in a different way, or he'd be in a different line of work. Anyway, they all wanted me badly.

I saw myself being happy with all of them. I guess I didn't want to be pinned down to any one man."

Irene's dissatisfaction with Lester began after their first child was born. "I felt completely stuck then. Oh, I loved my son, but I felt very bored. And Les had started to take me for granted. That's something that drove me nuts . . . me, the gal he had been dying to get. But how could I complain to him? I wanted him to advance himself, too. I kept putting us in the red. I love good clothes and things."

About this time in her marriage, Irene started having fantasies of affairs with other men. Gradually, they became more and more preoccupying. At first, she would imagine herself with old boyfriends. Then, she started to think about men she met since being married. "One day, while the baby was napping, I found my hands slipping between the folds of my dressing gown. Oh-oh, I said to myself, you've got it bad. But I went ahead and masturbated. The man in my fantasy was my dentist. He had been giving me the eye for quite a while—plus a few pinches on the cheek every time he worked on me. I knew he had been divorced recently and . . . well, I could just *see* us together while I was masturbating. That's when the idea hit me —why masturbate when I could just as easily be having real sex with the guy in my fantasy? After that, I couldn't get the thought out of my head. And it wasn't long before I made it come true with my dentist."

After her first affair, Irene had a few others, always making sure that Lester knew nothing about them. "It was a fascinating game. I knew I'd have no trouble getting men to go along with the rules I set up to keep it safe. After my son started going to nursery school, I had plenty of time to shop around for men when I was supposed to be shopping for clothes."

Within two years, Irene's game turned serious. She met an engineer who felt he had "outgrown" his wife. Like Irene, he was still married; but, unlike her, he felt ready to leave his wife. He began to press Irene to do the same. "I didn't realize what I had gotten myself into. Glenn had his own consulting firm and he could always manage to get away to be with me. With his money, we could rent a room in the finest hotel, just to make love for a few hours. It was very romantic . . . all champagne and flowers. When I was with him, I felt like an entirely different person. And when I saw Les again at night, it seemed like a big let-down. We still made love—maybe once a week or so—but my heart was with Glenn, back in the hotel."

Irene told us that Lester never seemed to be suspicious of her or to notice her withdrawal from him. "He was so busy with his work . . . No, that's not completely true. Les is just a very easygoing guy . . . too much so for his own good. Sometimes I wish he would have tried to find out more about what I was doing and feeling. Well, my head was in a whirl between wanting to stay with him and wanting to leave him for Glenn. I felt I couldn't talk to anybody about it. And I had gone too far in two-timing Les to feel I could ever patch things up with him. When Glenn rented an apartment for us, I went along like somebody in a trance. I didn't even tell Les about Glenn until a week or so before I moved out. Les was stunned. He couldn't even say anything. He just stared at me like a ghost."

Once Irene moved in with Glenn, their relationship began to change. They had to cope with all the anguish of their divorce procedings, and Irene's son continued to be thoroughly upset for a long time. Besides, with her son living in the apartment with them, Irene and Glenn were like parents in a new family—with all its necessary routines—rather than a pair of glamorous lovers.

From the moment she moved in with Glenn, Irene was assailed by second thoughts. When she was with him, she tried her best to put on a smiling face. But when she was alone, she opened herself to all her inner confusion. "It's like I was suddenly waking up from being a cute little girl, which is how I had always seen myself—somebody who could get anything she wanted just by being so pretty. But then when I had what I thought I wanted, I didn't know if I really wanted it or not."

By the time their divorces came through, Irene and Glenn had achieved a certain measure of calm. They still felt far from settled with each other. But just as Irene was beginning to get a sense of stability, she had to face another crisis. "He knocked me off my feet completely. I thought I was everything he ever wanted, right? Wrong! This time, I was the one who got it straight between the eyes. A month before we were supposed to get married, the sonofabitch took off with another woman . . . a young kid who worked in his office."

Irene finally had no man on whom to place responsibility for what she did with her life. In that sense, Glenn's desertion forced her to grow up fast. Her divorce from Les had left her with very little alimony—she had been too guilty to ask for much, and she thought she wouldn't need it with Glenn's money behind her. So the first thing Irene did was return to her old job as an assistant buyer; since she had to support herself and her child, she was determined to become as successful as possible. In about a year, she was promoted to her present position.

"It was thrilling to make good for myself. Oh, I suppose my looks still helped a little. But in that cutthroat business, a woman has to know her stuff regardless." While she was working her way up, Irene deliberately restricted herself to an occasional date. "I had to get a whole new outlook about men. I felt so burnt that I wanted to make sure that I wouldn't repeat my old patterns. But I won't kid you. It was really tough. After Glenn disappeared, I could understand how Les might have felt when I left him. One night, I was feeling so awful, I called Les up. I made some excuse about having to ask him for some money for our son, but I just felt like making contact with him. He was amazingly nice and cooperative. Of course, he had been seeing our son regularly. But my call sort of broke the ice between us. Starting that night, I began to imagine making love with Les when I masturbated. It made me feel less lonely, but it was also a terrible tease. I knew we could never get back together after what I had done."

Eventually, Irene began to go out regularly again—but she was very cautious about her dates and her own motives. Now, she has a lover, an executive from her store who has been divorced for about five years. They don't live together because they haven't made up their minds about committing themselves to a permanent relationship. "We've both been through the mill. So far it's been going very well. But I want to take things one step at a time. One thing I have definitely decided to do with Phil is tell him what's on my mind. And I ask him to do the same with me. I don't want to get caught up in my own daydreams, like I did with Les, or get dumped on, like I did with Glenn."

Irene says she has become friends with Les in a new kind of way. Both of them want to do their best for their son, and since Les has been happily remarried to a teacher from his school, he no longer feels so bitter about what Irene did to him. He has also become head of his department. Irene said she has never seen him looking better. And she thinks her leaving him may also have gotten him to reexamine himself and be more deeply involved with his present wife than he was with her. "Some times . . . I know it's crazy . . . but I imagine Les trying to get back together with me. It only happens when I'm feeling very low and I'm wondering what will turn out with Phil and me. Like when I come home at night after a long, hard day and my son is over at a friend's apartment watching TV. I take a quick shower and then have a drink to relax. Sometimes I start to masturbate while I'm imagining Les dropping in on me unexpectedly. He just happened to be in the neighborhood, he says, and he has an extra ticket to a show he's going to see later. Would I like to go with him? Sorry, Les, I say, but Phil and I are going to a big party. He seems so disappointed and envious . . . but that's what gets me excited and I have my orgasm."

We asked Irene if she ever told Phil about her masturbation and her fantasies. "Tell him? You think it's a good idea? Well, I can see how it might be . . . once we know more where we're at with each other. But now . . . no, I'm afraid I'm not ready to do it, yet."

Breaking the Communication Barrier

If Irene had been willing to open up to Lester about her promiscuous fantasies when she first started to have them, their marriage might have turned out very differently. Probably the very process of revealing them would have been sufficient to prevent her from secretly acting them out. Lester could have seen how dissatisfied she felt about being taken for granted by him; and he would have had a chance to change his behavior toward her and give her more love and attention. At the same time, Irene might have been able to acknowledge her unfilled need to feel she was doing something creative for herself and expressing the talents she had—instead of continuing to rely exclusively on constant proofs of her attractiveness to men as the sole basis of her self-acceptance. Perhaps she could also have understood that such proofs could never satisfy her desire to feel accomplished through the expression of nonsexual skills. Together, she and Les might have worked out arrangements for her to go back to her old job before her frustrations about feeling incompetent to achieve recognition for her abilities led her to compensate through sexual conquests.

Of course, it does take honesty and cooperation from both partners to keep a marriage happy. Even if Irene had been more trusting of Lester, he might not have been willing to reciprocate by sharing his masturbatory fantasies and by doing everything he could to change. Still, by not even trying to trust his mate, a person is certainly not doing everything he can to help himself or to prevent a breakdown in his relationship. To overcome an impasse in communication between spouses, it doesn't matter which one takes the initiative to be honest with the other; the important thing is for one of them to do it. Surely, if neither does it, they are likely to continue drifting away from each other. Eventually, as in Irene's situation, one or both spouses may feel the gulf between them has become too great to bridge; and that separation or divorce is inevitable.

Nevertheless, Irene's personal growth after her divorce shows that many formerly married people can profit from their past mistakes. Learning from them, they have a much better chance of making a success of a new relationship. Like Irene, the vast number of people who have been divorced are not permanently discouraged from their need to have a partner in sexual love. Although they may have left their former marriages feeling heartsick and emotionally numb, they eventually decide to get married again. For men, five out of six who were divorced get remarried; for divorced women, the rate of remarriage is three out of four.[11]

All these men and women might be able to increase their chances of happiness in their new marriages by understanding the importance of being honest with their new mates about their inclinations to withdraw into solitary masturbation. By sharing the content of their masturbatory fantasies with each other, they can remain alert to the developmental problems that they may have carried into their new relationship, and they can give each other all the help they need to keep on choosing love over their fear of merging more and more fully through the years.

Epilogue
FROM CONFUSION TO UNDERSTANDING

For centuries, masturbation was condemned as both sinful and harmful. Recently, professional attitudes have been rapidly shifting in the opposite direction, with many experts claiming that masturbation is, or should be, a pleasure entirely free of any anxiety or emotional conflict. We feel it is vitally important for people to understand the background and implications of this historical change in professional opinion, in order to sort out their *own* unresolved or still-to-be-articulated views on masturbation. They can also approach other readings on the subject with a full appreciation of the biases that the issue of masturbation tends to arouse, even among physicians and specialists in the field of human sexuality.

NEGATIVE VIEWS

The negative extreme was first popularized early in the 1700s by an anonymous English clergyman, who used a terrifying religious appeal to mask his mercenary intentions. Actually, he was interested in selling a patent medicine designed to remedy the supposedly harmful effects of indulgence in masturbation. His frightening tract sought to connect masturbation with the sin of Onan. This linkage was a distortion of the Biblical story, in which God slays Onan for refusing to procreate with the wife of his dead brother. As Alex Comfort has observed, Onan's sin "involved no handiwork at all."[1] Still, the profit-seeking minister succeeded in associating masturbation with a death-inflicting judgment of God. To play with one's genitals became a mortal sin. And that kind of condemnation was taken up by people in a position to minister to the spiritual and physical needs of others. "From being the concern of the confessor and a selling-point for quacksalvers, masturbation grew steadily into a medical and moral obsession."[2]

This obsession was greatly reinforced in 1758 by the French

physician Tissot, whose aim was not to sell quack medicines but to spread stern religious doctrines. Tissot claimed that all sexual activity was dangerous to the body because it would starve the nerves, making them susceptible to damage that would induce insanity. Tissot considered masturbation the most deadly of sexual practices, since people, especially young people, are tempted to indulge in it "excessively." Besides, he felt masturbation was such a moral crime that it was bound to evoke enormous guilt, which would inflict additional damage to a person's body. So, before suffering the eternal fires of hell, a person who masturbates might have to endure such earthly inflictions as exhaustion, melancholy, fits, blindness, impotence, idiocy, and paralysis.

Tissot's horror story was received with great enthusiasm by his colleagues in the medical profession. The dissemination of his ideas created a "masturbational insanity," one of the most bizarre chapters in the history of medicine. That insanity was not to be found in any relationship between masturbation and mental illness. Rather, it describes the insane reactions to masturbation among those who presented themselves as experts in human sexuality.

Following Tissot's lead, reputable psychiatrists and surgeons of the eighteenth and nineteenth centuries wrote that masturbation was not only sinful but also physically and mentally harmful. Those physicians put their unreasonable, inhumane, and erroneous beliefs into practice, employing a variety of moral exhortations and medical procedures to "cure" masturbation. After all, if masturbation was a deadly disease, shouldn't doctors do everything in their power to save their patients from it?

Doctors do have access to a formidable array of powers in practicing their profession; in the last half of the nineteenth century, many doctors did not hesitate to employ the most drastic measures in combatting the "disease" of masturbation. With "comic-book sadism," [3] they developed and applied torturous devices of physical restraint, cages and trusses that surrounded the genital area and prevented the patient from touching it. Sexually active children were among the principal victims. Some of the medically recommended prisons for the male genitalia included iron spikes, intended to punish the penis if it should dare to become erect.

But some doctors went much further than prescribing such instruments of torture: they actually performed surgical operations to remove genital parts that could be stimulated in masturbation. A woman would be "treated" by having her clitoris cut off. For men, the analogous "treatment" was circumcision or even castration; and methods for cauterizing the spine and the genitals, which were rendered numb to sexual feelings, were carefully described in American medical textbooks.

It was during this period that Anthony Comstock, a veteran of the Civil War, wrote the United States postal obscenity laws, which are still in effect.[4] "A reading of Comstock's diary makes it clear that his sexual conflicts were particularly concerned with masturbation; his chief concern about the sexually obscene was that it would lead young men to masturbate, with all that this implied—further physical, mental, moral, and spiritual distraction."[5] Thus, some of the major antipornography legislation in America was based on the fear that if people were exposed to sexually stimulating literature or pictures, they would be driven to masturbation.

Voices of Sanity

Around 1900, some voices of sanity began to be raised within the medical profession. They pointed out that any connection between masturbation and mental disorder might stem not from masturbation itself but from an individual's emotional reaction to it. People also began to acknowledge the social prevalence of masturbation and to realize how inappropriate it was for them to consider it a rare disorder.

Within medicine, Freud probably made the greatest impact in turning the tide of professional opinion on masturbation in a more positive direction. Eventually, his writings had a similar effect on the general public. Beginning to publish while some of his medical colleagues were still obsessed by their "masturbational insanity," Freud stressed the sexual nature of every aspect of human behavior and experience. Most importantly, he argued that even infants are actively and inevitably sexual in their functioning and in their development.[6]

By highlighting the realities of infantile sexuality, Freud

helped enormously in discrediting the views of those who tried to portray masturbation as an illness—and a dangerous one at that. For if all infants are naturally autoerotic, "playing with oneself" can hardly be conceived as a pathological deviation from any human norm. On the contrary, within Freud's formulation, self-stimulation is clearly normal for human beings. If anything, it is the absence of such stimulation that can properly be considered a deviation, at least in statistical terms.

Of course, Freud did not advocate masturbation as the ultimate expression of adult sexuality. Rather, he saw preoccupation with autoeroticism as a passing stage in human psychosexual development. But his writings leave a reader with no doubts about the inevitability of autoeroticism as part of the process of human sexual and psychological maturation.

Inspired by Freud's courageous articulation of the pervasiveness of sexuality in human life, other psychiatrists began to advocate sanity in medical approaches to masturbation. Wilhelm Stekel devoted an entire book to the subject, arguing against the view that masturbation was injurious.[7] He called attention to the fact that everyone masturbates in one form of autoeroticism or another—if not by stimulating the genitals, then by deriving sensual gratification in the functioning and stimulation of the mouth, the anus, and other areas of the body.

Similarly, Georg Groddeck stressed the central importance of self-induced erotic pleasure as a motivating force in human psychology. He gave many examples of how people may symbolically express their masturbatory impulses in little habits of everyday living—for example, by playing with a ring on one's finger or pulling and rubbing on a watch chain. He also showed how a child's mother may reinforce his masturbatory tendencies by stimulating his genitals in the ordinary process of changing his diapers and washing him.[8]

Wilhelm Reich carried Freud's work to its logical therapeutic development. Reich found some patients to be so sexually constricted that they could scarcely tolerate any erotic sensations. When these patients reported that they had succeeded in masturbating with pleasure, he considered them to have made a major breakthrough in their therapy.[9] Reich's findings went completely counter to the old medical prejudice about "self-abuse." And his initiative helped to pave the way for the broad social acceptance of the legitimacy and value of sex research and therapy.

While Reich was still alive, Kinsey and his colleagues began their famous surveys on human sexual behavior. By 1953, they had published their findings for both men and women.[10] Their data clearly supported the statistical normalcy of masturbation. Ninety-two percent of the men and sixty-three percent of the women reported having masturbated sometime in their lives. In the light of these results, masturbation could no longer be considered either deviant or unusual. Thus, people who masturbated could regard themselves as part of a normal majority rather than an abnormal minority.

POSITIVE VIEWS

Given its long history of social disapproval, masturbation now merits publicity for its favorable effects. People who have suffered from that disapproval surely deserve help in overcoming their suffering. So the blossoming field of sex therapy has been performing a most valuable and humane service in helping people to experience joy in their sexual functioning. Sex therapy has even permitted many adults to have the first orgasm in their lives; and formal training in masturbation has often proved to be an essential part of that therapeutic aid.

Similar therapeutic orientations have been followed in self-help books and pamphlets published by people who are committed to sexual liberation. Many of these materials have been written by feminists concerned about the ways in which the sexism of our society has dampened the ability of women to get pleasure from their sexuality. In particular, these publications have sought to encourage women to appreciate the beauty of their genitals, to feel good about having sexual needs and feelings, to rejoice in their capacity for multiple orgasms, and to feel free about masturbating as a means of exploring and enjoying their bodies.[11] Many women seem to be benefiting from this encouragement, as well as from the specific techniques of masturbation that are spelled out—or put into pictures—for them.

Despite these publications, most people still tend to have

conflicts about discussing their masturbatory behavior, as we found in asking people to be interviewed for this book. Even those who agreed to talk about their masturbation displayed some degree of nervousness, often trying to disguise it with humor. They seemed to believe they *should* be completely comfortable about discussing masturbation, but could not help feeling uneasy about it.

In our judgment, this uneasiness reflects more wisdom about the emotional realities of masturbation than does any belief that masturbation is not, or should not be, problematical. As we have shown throughout this book, masturbation *is inherently* both a pleasure and a problem. Any approach to masturbation that denies or ignores its problematic aspects is as oppressive as one that denies or ignores its benefits. It is precisely this kind of oppression that has been inadvertently spread by those who adopt a one-sided view of masturbation as a means of sexual liberation. By failing to acknowledge and discuss the psychological complexities of masturbation, these people may actually be undermining the very objectives they intend to advance.

If writers on sexual liberation keep on pushing masturbation as a pure delight, many people may begin to feel unliberated and deprived unless they are masturbating regularly and intensively. And when those people find that the pleasure is problematic, they may feel obliged to masturbate even more in the futile attempt to experience the unadulterated ecstasy they were falsely led to expect.

PORNOGRAPHY

Other proponents of masturbation are motivated by economic gain rather than a desire to contribute to humane social change. They have pornography to sell, and they are well aware that pornographic literature and films are widely used as mental stimulants for solitary masturbation. They also know that many people prefer to have masturbatory fantasies prepackaged for them instead of having to assume the responsibility and to put forth the effort of creating their own. Finally, pornographers know how curious people are about the sexual behavior of others —an interest that expresses both the vicarious pleasure of voyeurism and the desire to get new ideas about how to express one's own erotic impulses.

Actually, pornography does have some socially redeeming qualities, even if it is not intended to liberate anyone from anything. The very candor with which it treats all sorts of erotic practices implicitly challenges the moral hypocrisy under which the dominant institutions of society continue to cloak the truth about the pervasiveness of human sexual motivation. Thus, pornography helps to create a social climate in which people can more freely admit their erotic inclinations, and it helps legitimize people's intense involvement in the sexual aspect of their lives—an involvement that their parents and other people in positions of leadership often suggest is unnatural or unimportant.

However, pornography also oppresses people by tending to portray sex outside the context of a truly loving relationship. Typically, pornographic materials depict sexual contacts between people as loveless expressions of their biological drives; and they tend to show people as regarding each other as mere objects, which they can use to act out their separate and self-centered erotic fantasies. Often, those fantasies also have a strong compensatory flavor, with pornographic heroes and heroines displaying incredible amounts of anatomical beauty, sexual magnetism, and virility.

This unrealistic portrayal of the sex objects in pornographic magazines, books, and films stimulates readers and viewers not only to masturbate, but also to have compensatory fantasies in which they see themselves and their partners as being just like the gorgeous and handsome sexual athletes that are spread out before them. Perpetual reliance on such images for erotic arousal and orgasmic release may make "beauty freaks" out of people—when they make love to real partners, they may find it difficult to attain the level of sexual arousal and satisfaction they achieved through their solitary masturbation and fantasy.

In recent years, people in the business of pornography have gone about as far as pictures can go in getting people to masturbate while veiwing them; they simply show female models in the act of masturbating themselves. The editor of *Penthouse* developed this particular form of pin-up photography, which gives the impression of a viewer unobtrusively sharing the intimacy of a woman's private passion with herself. "At first it happened by accident. A girl went for her breast while [the photographer] was shooting. . . . Gradually the concept broadened. The model's hands, issue by issue, ever so slowly so as not to invite public outcry, crept between her legs. He lowered his perspective and more and more crotch shots appeared in the magazine. The success of the masturbation fantasies was proved on the battlefields of Vietnam. The G.I.'s . . . were choosing *Penthouse* over *Playboy* in huge numbers." [12]

Traditionally, pornography has been directed to a male audience. However, the success of the movement for women's liberation has helped to create a new market for pornographic magazines aimed at female readers. Women now have a chance to arouse themselves by looking at nude pictures of handsome men—with well-endowed genitalia—and to create masturbatory fantasies of having sexual relations with them. So far, the men in these magazines have not been shown masturbating or with a full erection. But these are variations that could easily be added to a centerfold theme—if the publishers of such magazines find out that they could increase their readership by including them.

Actually, such soft-core pornography is as hypocritical, in its own way, as the traditional sexual morality it presumes to counter with its seeming candor. While it emphasizes the purely hedonistic and self-oriented aspects of sexuality, it deliberately omits the truth about the affection, tenderness, empathy, and generosity that human beings feel toward each other when they have their most ecstatic experiences of lovemaking. By withholding those truths, soft-core pornography has the effect of suppressing—rather than of liberating—the fullness of the human capacity for enjoying sexual love.

Hard-core pornography does even less justice to the basic psychological realities of pleasurable loving. It not only presents human beings as mere sexual objects; it also confines itself to the ways in which some people have dehumanized their sexual interactions. True, as we have previously explained, there are some people whose childhood development has made it extremely difficult for them to accept responsibility for expressing their feelings of sexual love: people for whom such expression is so guilt-arousing that they have a need to punish or be punished by their sexual partners; people who are drawn to the impersonality of group sex with strangers; people who feel it necessary to use various costumes and implements to blot out their personal identities or to pierce their emotional numbness. For such people, hard-core pornography provides a means with which they can fantasize or enact their depersonalized forms of sexual love.

We appreciate the needs of these people and certainly do not feel that censors should deprive them of the pornographic materials they use. However, we do believe that the erotic fulfillment of most people can best be served not through pornography but through portrayals of human sexuality that place it within the full context of its connection with love and with the unique sensibilities and capacities of human beings. Indeed, we already detect a trend in that direction in the mass media, especially in films, which have begun to incorporate explicit represensations of sexuality within honest attempts to present the nuances and complexities of loving relationships.

MECHANIZATION AND DEHUMANIZATION

Purely mechanical devices like the electrical vibrator exemplify the further possibilities for dehmuanizing sexual behavior through the use of modern technology. In fact, the widespread sale and promotion of electrical vibrators shows that many people can be persuaded to consider their own bodies as sex machines.

Some experts in human sexuality have said the vibrator can be useful in increasing the pleasure of masturbation and in helping inorgasmic people. For example, they claim that the vibrator can help women to identify their own orgasmic response and to develop confidence in their potential to achieve it. However, Virginia Johnson feels that the vibrator should be used in sex therapy only with careful consideration, and only as a last resort. Other sex therapists we have interviewed agree with her. From her clinical experience, she has observed that a woman's confidence to have an orgasm with a vibrator is seldom transferred easily and reliably to the act of sexual intercourse. For some women, the intensity of a vibrator can even have physically negative effects, such as increased menstrual flow or tactile anesthesia.[13]

Dr. Barbach points out that just as women are recovering from old stereotyped notions about their lack of sexual need, they are being bombarded by new and opposing ones. "The myths we're creating now are that you *ought* to be multiply orgasmic . . . you *ought* to use a vibrator—or else there's something wrong with you."[14]

While some sex therapists think that the use of vibrators reflects a trend toward a more open and less rigid approach to sexual pleasure, Margaret Mead, the noted anthropologist, says that such sexual devices have been used in many cultures for a long time. The only thing new is that they have been motorized. "Americans seem to prefer having machines to do everything," Dr. Mead comments. "We have invented mechanical gadgets to substitute for what is natural." And she goes on to caution, "Machines alienate people from their bodies and from their emotions."[15]

POLITICAL AND SOCIAL IMPLICATIONS

It does not strike us as liberating to encourage sexual dependency on commercial products. Besides, any movement toward a more humane and a less exploitative society can be carried out only by people who want to relate directly, cooperatively, and equitably with other people. But the promotion and glorification of masturbation—with its emphasis on social isolation and secret, ego-inflating fantasies—could have the effect of keeping people from relating to each other. That "pacifying" effect could reinforce the perpetuation of social, political, and economic injustice. William Thompson, a historian, quotes an aphorism on how pornography can help governmental rulers to maintain power: "One tames people as one tames lions, by masturbation."[16]

Masturbation may also be promoted because it is an activity that is congenial to maintaining the sexual and social oppressiveness of the established status quo. Interestingly, solitary masturbation is not prohibited by law anywhere in America, although every state has laws against some interpersonal sex practices other than intercourse between married partners.[17] Some guardians of the American educational establishment have deliberately stressed masturbation over sexual relationships to avoid antagonizing those who control the boards of their schools.

Mary Breasted reported an example of such avoidance in her description of an interview with a highly placed administrator employed by New York City's Department of Sex Education. When asked why contraception had been left out of the high-school curriculum on sex education, he replied, "but we put masturbation in." Later, he added, in effect, that he could get away with the inclusion of masturbation, but not with contraception.[18]

Reacting to such hypocrisy, a high-school student from New Jersey told her school rap group on sex education: "My kid brother talks about masturbation like it's a new discovery. It's taught openly in sex-education courses and it is considered a new sexual panacea. But he never heard of a contraceptive. He said the teacher won't answer that question, it's not in the course outline. He was told to talk to his *minister!* Now, that's too much."[19]

Actually, there are still many American schools that offer no courses in sex education. Those schools have generally conformed to the pressures of parents who believe that such courses might encourage children to engage in sexual activities from which they would otherwise refrain. But even where courses in sex education are permitted, Breasted concludes, the teachers involved feel constrained to tell the truth only about strictly biological material. She feels they cannot be trusted to deal adequately with the social and ideological issues regarding sexual behavior. "I didn't even think that their teachings on masturbation amounted to very much because they seemed to be using those teachings as a subtle method to keep youngsters from trying things out with each other. The sex educators seemed to have decided that masturbation was really a means for keeping the kids pure."[20]

Surely, it is good for sex educators to give their students wholesome and positive attitudes toward masturbation. However, masturbation need not be presented as an entirely self-enclosed topic. Rather, it assumes its most vital significance when it is related to the development and expression of the human need for sexual love and loving relationships. No matter how free adolescents feel about masturbation, or how much they enjoy it, most of them are highly motivated to have sexual contacts with others. So they could benefit greatly from learning how they could enjoy such relations to the fullest, while avoiding their potentially negative physical and emotional consequences. Hopefully, as adults become more aware of the extremely high rates and costs of unwanted pregnancies among adolescents, they will exert pressure on schools to include adequate instruction on contraception in their courses on sex education.

Accepting Masturbation

Soon, we hope, people may realize that masturbation, by itself, cannot be viewed as an activity whose human implications are necessarily either positive or negative. After all, masturbation is not a mechanical process, run off by a machine. Even if a person uses an electrical vibrator, he still masturbates as a human being, acting and reacting with his freely directed consciousness.

In the living context of that freedom, masturbation derives its value from the experiences and goals of the person who is doing it. Naturally, people may disagree about whether a given approach to masturbation is good or bad. But these disagreements represent differences in the goals of human existence, rather than any effects of masturbation that could be understood apart from its reflection of those goals.

For us, the value of someone's masturbation depends on how that person is using it to develop his capacity for sexual love and to enhance his life. As a means for developing their potentials for adult sexual love, masturbation can be used by human beings from their infancy onward. By sexually stimulating themselves, infants and young children can learn to experience joy in their bodies, explore and feel good about their gender, and create a favorable sense of their identities as males or females. Later, children and adolescents can rely on masturbation to reduce their sexual tensions in the absence of loving sexual relationships with peers of the opposite sex. And they may use the interpersonal fantasies accompanying masturbation to prepare themselves for the relationships of sexual love they eventually seek in social reality.

As an enhancement of their own lives, masturbation can be used by people to gain relief from physical and emotional tensions; to give themselves love, pleasure, and attention; to rehearse the difficult and competitive roles they want to play in society; and to try to make up for lacks they perceive in themselves and in their social functioning. In addition, throughout their lives, people can use their inclinations to masturbate as a way of getting insights that will help them to resolve their emotional conflicts and to set more realistic goals for the fulfillment of their potentials.

Naturally, for whatever reasons, some adults may choose to live out their lives as loners. Others are confined by circumstances that prevent or limit their access to potential lovers of the opposite sex. And still others have handicaps that make them unlikely to attract lovers, even if they want them. For all these people, masturbation may become a primary or even an exclusive mode of sexual expression; and if they can truly accept the chosen or externally imposed conditions of their lives, they have a good chance of deriving lasting pleasure, comfort, and self-knowledge from their masturbation.

Even if people succeed in creating a society devoted to the cultivation of loving sexual relationships, they will always feel inclinations to masturbate throughout their lives. A person's tendency to masturbate is not entirely a function of his particular cultural conditioning. Rather, it expresses motivations that all human beings are bound to experience in the process of relating to themselves and to each other. A person's pattern of masturbation and his masturbatory fantasies will always reflect how he feels about himself and the way he is dealing with his life.

As we have shown, from infancy on, people tend to stimulate themselves sexually as a celebration of the love they have for their own lives. Conversely, when they feel deprived, frustrated, or fearful for their lives, they also may turn to sexual self-stimulation for comfort and reassurance. Even in the best of all possible worlds, people are bound to acquire feelings of anxiety and inadequacy which they are afraid to face in themselves or to share with others. Reacting to those feelings, everyone also tries to create his own illusions—his own form of "craziness"—through which he tries to make himself feel more lovable, more accomplished, and more free of his inescapable human limitations.

Most people grow up feeling uniquely flawed and uniquely crazy in resorting to masturbation and its compensatory illusions; they are afraid to reveal their supposed deviations to each other, assuming that others are free of them. And they may want to keep their involvement in masturbation secret and private, fearing that they may lose its magical benefits if they communicate with others about it; they also are most reluctant to give up the sense of superiority that they created for themselves through their self-glorifying fantasies.

Nevertheless, people have everything to gain and nothing to lose by communicating openly with each other about their inevitable and common masturbatory inclinations. Such communication can help them to overcome their feelings of inadequacy and their concerns about masturbation by showing them that they are basically the same as everyone else—no better and no worse. This realization can bring people closer together, enhance their mutual compassion, and reduce their fear of each other. Thus, people can change their lifelong approach to masturbation. No longer regarding it as a basis for feeling either inferior or superior to others, they can use their masturbatory tendencies with as much pleasure as possible and with a view toward learning whatever can help them to fulfill their lives.

NOTES

INTRODUCTION: THE PROBLEMATIC PLEASURE

1. Robert Sorensen, *Adolescent Sexuality in Contemporary America* (New York: World, 1973), p. 143.
2. Morton Hunt, *Sexual Behavior in the 1970s* (Chicago: Playboy Press, 1974), pp. 77–78.
3. Ashley Montagu, *Touching: the Human Significance of the Skin* (New York: Harper and Row, 1972).
4. Isidor Bernstein, "Integrative Aspects of Masturbation," in *Masturbation: From Infancy to Senescence*, ed. Irwin M. Marcus and John J. Francis (New York: International Universities Press, 1975), pp. 56–57.
5. Ronald D. Laing, *Self and Others* (Baltimore: Penguin, 1971), pp. 54–56.
6. James Hillman, "Towards the Archetypical Model for the Masturbation Inhibition," in *The Reality of the Psyche*, ed. Joseph B. Wheelwright (New York: C. G. Jung Foundation, 1968), pp. 114–27.

CHAPTER 1: ORGASM

1. Edward M. Brecher, *The Sex Researchers* (Boston: Little Brown, 1969); Alfred C. Kinsey, Wardell B. Pomeroy, and Clyde E. Martin, *Sexual Behavior in the Human Male* (Philadelphia: W. B. Saunders, 1948); Alfred C. Kinsey et al., *Sexual Behavior in the Human Female* (Philadelphia: W. B. Saunders, 1953).
2. Wilhelm Stekel, *Auto-Erotism: A Psychiatric Study of Onanism and Neurosis* (New York: Grove Press, 1961).
3. Stekel.
4. Ruth Brecher and Edward M. Brecher, eds., *An Analysis of Human Sexual Response* (New York: New American Library, 1966).
5. Brecher and Brecher.
6. Wilhelm Reich, *The Function of the Orgasm* (New York: Farrar, Straus and Giroux, 1969).

7. Kinsey et al., 1953.
8. Betty G. Eisner, *The Unused Potential of Marriage and Sex* (Boston: Little, Brown, 1970).
9. Eisner.
10. Isidor Bernstein, "Integrative Aspects of Masturbation," in *Masturbation: From Infancy to Senescence*, ed. Irwin M. Marcus and John J. Francis (New York: International Universities Press, 1975), pp. 53–75.
11. Barbara Seaman, *Free and Female* (Greenwich, Conn.: Fawcett Crest Book, 1973), p. 107.
12. David Cole Gordon, *Self-Love* (Baltimore: Penguin Books, 1972).
13. Selma Fraiberg, "Some Characteristics of Genital Arousal and Discharge in Latency Girls," *Psychoanalytic Study of the Child* 27 (1972): 439–75.
14. Berta Bornstein, "Masturbation in the Latency Period," *Psychoanalytic Study of the Child* 8 (1953): 65–79.
15. Alice Balint, *The Psycho-analysis of the Nursery* (London: Routledge and Kegan Paul, 1953); Stekel.
16. Balint, p. 46.
17. Personal communication with Dr. Barbara Waxenberg, Jewish Family Service, New York City.
18. Eisner.
19. Fraiberg.
20. Fraiberg, p. 448.
21. Stekel, pp. 113–19.
22. William H. Masters and Virginia E. Johnson, "Counseling with Sexually Incompatible Marriage Partners," in Brecher and Brecher, pp. 203–19.
23. Helen Singer Kaplan, *The New Sex Therapy* (New York: Bruner Mazel, 1974).
24. Helena Wright, *The Sex Factor in Marriage*, 5th ed. (London: Ernest Benn, 1966).
25. Helena Wright, *More About the Sex Factor in Marriage*, 2nd ed. (London: Williams and Norgate, 1959).
26. Barry S. Lubetkin, "Male Masturbation: Do's and Dont's," *Penthouse Forum* (October, 1976), p. 53.
27. David J. Kass and Fred F. Stauss, *Sex Therapy at Home* (New York: Simon and Schuster, 1975).

Chapter 2: Fantasy

1. Wilhelm Stekel, *Auto-erotism: A Psychiatric Study of Onanism and Neurosis* (New York: Grove Press, 1961); William T. Moore, "Some Economic Functions of Genital Masturbation During Adolescent Development," in *Masturbation: from Infancy to Senescence*, eds. Irwin M. Marcus and John J. Francis (New York: International Universities Press, 1975), pp. 231–76.
2. Isidor Bernstein, "Integrative Aspects of Masturbation," in *Masturbation*, eds. Marcus and Francis, pp. 68–69.
3. Heck Thomas, "The Sex Habit Nobody Talks About," *True* (December, 1975), p. 20.
4. Morton Hunt, *Sexual Behavior in the 1970s* (Chicago: Playboy Press, 1974); Jerome L. Singer, "Navigating the Stream of Consciousness: Research in Daydreaming and Related Inner Experience," *The American Psychologist* 30 (1975): 727–38; Robert Sorensen, *Adolescent Sexuality in Contemporary America* (New York: World, 1973).
5. Irving Sarnoff, *Society with Tears* (New York: Citadel, 1966).
6. Bernstein, pp. 67–68.
7. Wilhelm Reich, *Character Analysis* (New York: Noonday Press, Farrar, Straus and Giroux, 1972), p. 265.
8. Hunt; Singer; Sorensen.
9. Charles N. Sarlin, "Masturbation, Culture, and Psychosexual Development," in Marcus and Francis, pp. 356–57; Stekel, p. 140.
10. Jerome L. Singer, *The Inner World of Daydreaming* (New York: Harper and Row, 1975), pp. 118–19.

Chapter 3: Infants and Toddlers

1. William H. Masters and Virginia E. Johnson, *The Pleasure Bond* (New York: Bantam, 1976), pp. 224–25.
2. Edward M. Brecher, *The Sex Researchers* (Boston: Little Brown, 1969), pp. 175–77; Alexander Lowen, *Love and*

Orgasm (New York: New American Library, 1967), p. 198.
3. Lonnie G. Barbach, *For Yourself* (New York: New American Library, 1975), p. 155; Lowen.
4. Brecher.
5. Brecher.
6. Niles Newton, "The Trebly Sensuous Woman," *Psychology Today* (July, 1968).
7. R. D. Parke and D. B. Sawin, "Fathering: It's a Major Role," *Psychology Today* (November, 1977).
8. Diane E. Papalia and Sally W. Olds, *A Child's World: Infancy Through Adolescence* (New York: McGraw-Hill, 1975); L. Joseph Stone and Joseph Church, *Childhood and Adolescence: A Psychology of the Growing Person* (New York: Random House, 1973).
9. Sigmund Freud, *Three Contributions to the Theory of Sex* (New York: E. P. Dutton, 1962); Georg Groddeck, *The Book of the It* (New York: Vintage Books, 1949).
10. Milton I. Levine, "Pediatric Observations on Masturbation in Children," *The Psychoanalytic Study of the Child* 6 (1951): 117–24.
11. Eleanor Galenson and Herman Roiphe, "The Emergence of Genital Awareness During the Second Year of Life," in *Sex Differences in Behavior*, ed. R. C. Friedman, R. M. Richart, and R. L. VandeWiele (New York: John Wiley, 1974), pp. 223–31.
12. Robert I. Watson and Henry C. Lindgren, *Psychology of the Child*, 3rd ed. (New York: John Wiley, 1973), p. 154.
13. Freud, p. 42.
14. Levine.
15. Harry Bakwin, "Erotic Feelings in Infants and Young Children," *American Journal of the Disturbed Child* 126 (1973): 52–54.
16. Galenson and Roiphe.
17. Robert R. Sears, Eleanor E. Maccoby, and Harry Levin, *Patterns of Child Rearing* (Evanston, Ill.: Row, Peterson, 1957).
18. Brian Sutton-Smith, *Child Psychology* (New York: Appleton-Century-Crofts, 1973), p. 284.

19. Sears, Maccoby, and Levin, p. 199.
20. Isidor Bernstein, "Integrative Aspects of Masturbation," in *Masturbation: From Infancy to Senescence*, ed. Irwin M. Marcus and John J. Francis (New York: International Universities Press, 1975), pp. 53–75; Charles N. Sarlin, "Masturbation, Culture, and Psychosexual Development," in Marcus and Francis, pp. 349–80.
21. Mary S. Calderone, "Children and Masturbation: What Parents should Know," *Penthouse Forum* (November, 1976), pp. 38–41.
22. Sears, Maccoby, and Levin.
23. Alexander Lowen, *The Betrayal of the Body* (New York: Collier Books, 1969), p. 105.
24. Wardell B. Pomeroy, *Boys and Sex* (New York: Delacorte, 1969).
25. James A. Kleeman, "Genital Self-Stimulation in Infant and Toddler Girls," in Marcus and Francis, pp. 77–106; Bernstein; Galenson and Roiphe.
26. Kleeman.
27. Kleeman.
28. Galenson and Roiphe.
29. Bernstein; Sarlin.
30. Alice Balint, *The Psycho-analysis of the Nursery* (London: Routledge and Kegan Paul, 1953).
31. Wilhelm Stekel, *Auto-erotism* (New York: Grove Press, 1961); Bakwin; Brecher.
32. Levine, p. 120.
33. Alfred C. Kinsey, Wardell B. Pomeroy, and Clyde E. Martin, *Sexual Behavior in the Human Male* (Philadelphia: W. B. Saunders, 1948).
34. Stekel.
35. Stekel.
36. Levine.
37. Bakwin.
38. Wilhelm Reich, *The Sexual Revolution: Toward a Self-Governing Character Structure*, 4th ed. (New York: Farrar, Straus and Giroux, 1969).

Chapter 4: Early Childhood

1. Diane E. Papalia and Sally W. Olds, *A Child's World: Infancy Through Adolescence* (New York: McGraw-Hill, 1975) pp. 169–72.
2. Alice Balint, *The Psycho-analysis of the Nursery* (London: Routledge and Kegan Paul, 1953), pp. 43–44.
3. Balint, p. 74.
4. Balint, pp. 77–78.
5. Berta Bornstein, "Masturbation in the Latency Period," *Psychoanalytic Study of the Child* 8 (1953): 65–79; Selma Fraiberg, "Some Characteristics of Genital Arousal and Discharge in Latency Girls," *Psychoanalytic Study of the Child* 27 (1972): 439–75.
6. John H. Gagnon, *Human Sexualities* (Glenview, Ill.: Scott, Foresman, 1977), p. 142.
7. Robert R. Sears, Eleanor E. Maccoby, and Harry Levin, *Patterns of Child Rearing* (Evanston, Ill.: Row, Peterson, 1957), p. 190.
8. Balint, pp. 42–44.
9. Mary S. Calderone, "Children and Masturbation: What Parents Should Know," *Penthouse Forum* (November, 1976), p. 40.
10. Nancy Friday, *My Mother/My Self* (New York, Delacorte Press, 1977), pp. 106–8.
11. Warren Farrell, *The Liberated Man* (New York: Bantam, 1975), p. 236.
12. Benjamin Spock, *Baby and Child Care*, rev. ed. (New York: Pocket Books, 1976), p. 408.
13. Karen Horney, "The Denial of the Vagina," in *Feminine Psychology*, ed. H. Kelman (New York: W. W. Norton, 1973), pp. 158–60.
14. Margaret Mahler, Fred Pine, and Anni Bergman, *The Psychological Birth of the Human Infant* (New York: Basic Books, 1975), p. 179.
15. A. S. Neill, *Summerhill: A Radical Approach to Child Rearing* (New York: Hart Pub. Co., 1960), p. 208.
16. Harry F. Harlow, *Learning to Love* (San Francisco: Albion Pub. Co., 1971), pp. 32–65.

17. John Money, "Childhood: The Last Frontier in Sex Research," *The Sciences* 16 (November/December, 1976): 15.
18. Karen Horney, "On the Genesis of the Castration Complex in Women," in Kelman, p. 41.
19. Sears, Maccoby, and Levin, p. 215.
20. Betty G. Eisner, *The Unused Potential of Marriage and Sex* (Boston: Little Brown, 1970).
21. Sears, Maccoby, and Levin, pp. 212–13.
22. Alfred C. Kinsey et al., *Sexual Behavior in the Human Female* (New York: Pocket Books, 1973), p. 105.
23. Kinsey et al., pp. 104–5.
24. Neill, p. 227.
25. Calderone.
26. Balint, p. 79.
27. Spock, p. 411.
28. Milton I. Levine, "Pediatric Observations on Masturbation in Children," *Psychoanalytic Study of the Child* 6 (1951): 117–24.
29. Levine.
30. Lonnie G. Barbach, *For Yourself* (New York: New American Library, 1975), pp. 166–67.
31. Balint, pp. 50–51.

Chapter 5: Middle Childhood

1. Virginia L. Clower, "Significance of Masturbation in Female Sexual Development and Function," in *Masturbation: From Infancy to Senescence*, eds. Irwin M. Marcus and John J. Francis (New York International Universities Press, 1975), pp. 107–43; William T. Moore, "Some Economic Functions of Genital Masturbation During Adolescent Development," in Marcus and Francis, pp. 231–76; Leah C. Shaefer, *Women and Sex* (New York: Pantheon Books, 1973).
2. Diane E. Papalia and Sally W. Olds, *A Child's World: Infancy Through Adolescence* (New York: McGraw-Hill, 1975); L. Joseph Stone and Joseph Church, *Childhood*

and Adolescence: A Psychology of the Growing Person (New York: Random House, 1973).
3. Wardell B. Pomeroy, *Boys and Sex* (New York: Delacorte Press, 1969).
4. Clower; Moore.
5. William A. Block, *What Your Child Really Wants to Know about Sex and Why* (Greenwich, Conn.: Fawcett Crest Book, 1972), pp. 257–61.
6. Moore.
7. William H. Masters and Virginia E. Johnson, *Human Sexual Response* (Boston: Little Brown, 1966); Ruth Brecher and Edward Brecher, eds., *An Analysis of Human Sexual Response* (New York: New American Library, 1966).
8. Selma Fraiberg, "Some Characteristics of Genital Arousal and Discharge in Latency Girls," *Psychoanalytic Study of the Child* 27 (1972): 439–75; Karen Horney, "The Denial of the Vagina," in *Feminine Psychology*, ed. H. Kelman (New York: W. W. Norton, 1973), pp. 147–61.
9. Clower.
10. Papalia and Olds.
11. Stone and Church.
12. Ashley Montagu, *Touching: The Human Significance of the Skin* (New York: Harper and Row, 1972); Papalia and Olds; Stone and Church.
13. Stone and Church.
14. Moore.
15. Philip Slater, *The Pursuit of Loneliness: American Culture at the Breaking Point* (Boston: Beacon Press, 1970).
16. Stone and Church.
17. Clower.
18. Stone and Church.
19. Clower.
20. Papalia and Olds; Stone and Church.
21. Berta Bornstein, "Masturbation in the Latency Period," *Psychoanalytic Study of the Child* 8 (1953): 65–79.
22. Bornstein; Fraiberg.
23. Bornstein.
24. Bornstein.

25. Moore.
26. Papalia and Olds.
27. Clower.
28. Robert A. Furman, "Excerpt from the Analysis of a Prepuberty Boy," in Marcus and Francis, pp. 223–29.
29. Norman M. Lobsenz, "Helping Children Deal With Sexual Feelings," *Woman's Day* (February, 1975).

CHAPTER 6: ADOLESCENCE

1. Diane E. Papalia and Sally W. Olds, *A Child's World: Infancy Through Adolescence* (New York: McGraw-Hill, 1975).
2. Robert A. Furman, "Excerpt From the Analysis of a Preputerty Boy," in *Masturbation: From Infancy to Senescence*, ed. Irwin M. Marcus and John J. Francis (New York: International Universities Press, 1975), pp. 223–29; Charles A. Sarnoff, "Narcissism, Adolescent Masturbation Fantasies, and the Search for Reality," in Marcus and Francis, pp. 274–304.
3. Virginia Clower, "Significance of Masturbation in Female Sexual Development and Function," in Marcus and Francis, pp. 107–43.
4. Rhoda L. Lorand, *Love, Sex, and the Teenager* (New York: Popular Library, 1965).
5. L. Joseph Stone and Joseph Church, *Childhood and Adolescence: A Psychology of the Growing Person* (New York: Random House, 1973).
6. Lorand.
7. Lorand.
8. William T. Moore, "Some Economic Functions of Genital Masturbation During Aodlescent Development," in Marcus and Francis, pp. 231–76; Lorand.
9. Moore.
10. Clower.
11. Leah C. Schaefer, *Women and Sex* (New York, Pantheon Books, 1973).
12. Clower; Moore.

13. Robert Sorensen, *Adolescent Sexuality in Contemporary America* (New York: World, 1973); Lorand.
14. Warren Farrell, *The Liberated Man* (New York: Bantam, 1975); Lorand; Stone and Church.
15. Morton Hunt, *Sexual Behavior in the 1970s* (Chicago: Playboy Press, 1974); Sorensen.
16. Lorand.
    Moore.
17. Ingrid Bengis, *Combat in the Erogenous Zone* (New York: Bantam, 1973); Nancy Friday, *My Mother/My Self* (New York, Delacorte Press, 1977).
18. Sorensen, p. 138.
19. Sorensen.
20. Sigmund Freud, *Three Contributions to the Theory of Sex* (New York: E. P. Dutton, 1962).
21. Irving Sarnoff, *Personality Dynamics and Development* (New York: John Wiley, 1962).
22. Clara Thompson, "Changing Concepts of Homosexuality in Psychoanalysis," *Psychiatry* 10 (1947): 183–89.
23. C. A. Tripp, *The Homosexual Matrix* (New York: McGraw-Hill, 1975).
24. Tripp, p. 82.
25. Jean-Paul Sartre, *Saint Genet: Actor and Martyr* (New York: New American Library, 1971).
26. Lester W. Dearborn, "Autoerotism," in *The Encyclopedia of Sexual Behavior*, ed. A. Ellis and A. Abarbanel (New York: Jason Aronson, 1976), pp. 205–15.
27. Sorensen, p. 138.
28. Alfred C. Kinsey et al., *Sexual Behavior in the Human Female* (Philadelphia: W. B. Saunders, 1953).
29. Sorensen.
30. Dearborn.
31. Dearborn.
32. Wardell B. Pomeroy, *Boys and Sex* (New York: Delacorte Press, 1969).
33. Sorensen.
34. Sorensen.
35. Seymour Fisher, *The Female Orgasm: Psychology, Physiology, Fantasy* (New York: Basic Books, 1973).

36. Papalia and Olds; Stone and Church.
37. Lorand; Moore.
38. Lorand.
39. Sorensen, p. 78.
40. Personal communication with Dr. Ann K. Welbourne, Sex Counselor and Adjunct Faculty Member, Human Sexuality Program, New York University.
41. Sorensen, p. 77.
42. Ann K. Welbourne, "The Relation of Parental Sexual Knowledge and Attitudes and Communication about Sexual Topics with Their Early Adolescent Children," (Ph.D. diss., New York University, School of Education, 1977).
43. Sorensen, p. 143.
44. Sorensen, p. 76.
45. Sidney C. Callahan, *Parenting: Principles and Politics of Parenthood* (Baltimore: Penguin Books, 1974), pp. 60–61.

Chapter 7: Couples

1. Morton Hunt, *Sexual Behavior in the 1970s* (Chicago: Playboy Press, 1974), p. 86.
2. Leah C. Shaefer, *Women and Sex* (New York: Pantheon Books, 1973), p. 100.
3. Shaefer, pp. 100–101.
4. Hunt, p. 93.
5. Hunt, p. 96.
6. Lonnie G. Barbach, *For Yourself* (New York: New American Library, 1975), p. 153.
7. Ruth Brecher and Edward M. Brecher, eds., *An Analysis of Human Sexual Response* (New York: New American Library, 1966); Barbach.
8. Barbach.
9. Barbach, p. 155.
10. George R. Bach and Peter Wyden, *The Intimate Enemy: How to Fight Fair in Love and Marriage* (New York: Avon Books, 1970); James L. Mathis, "Masturbation After Marriage," *Medical Aspects of Human Sexuality* (March, 1971): 187–99; Hunt, pp. 90–91.

11. Hunt, p. 101.
12. Carol Tavris and Susan Sadd, *The Redbook Report on Female Sexuality* (New York: Delacorte Press, 1977), p. 95.
13. Bach and Wyden, pp. 268–69.
14. Bach and Wyden, p. 269.
15. Personal Communication with Dr. Barbara Waxenberg, Jewish Family Service, New York City.
16. Shaefer, p. 99.
17. Carole Altman, *You Can Be Your Own Sex Therapist* (New York: Berkley, 1976).
18. Altman, p. 116.
19. William H. Masters and Virginia E. Johnson, "Counseling with Sexually Incompatible Marriage Partners," in Brecher and Brecher, pp. 203–19.
20. Martin A. Berezin, "Masturbation and Old Age," in *Masturbation From Infancy to Senescence*, ed. Irwin M. Marcus and John J. Francis (New York: International Universities Press, 1975), pp. 329–47.
21. Isador Rubin, "Sex after Forty—and after Seventy," in Brecher and Brecher, pp. 251–266; Berezin.
22. Simone de Beauvoir, "Joie de Vivre," in *Human Sexuality: Contemporary Perspectives*, ed. E. S. Morrison and V. Borsage (Palo Alto National Press Books, 1973), p. 172.
23. Hunt, p. 96.
24. Berezin; de Beauvoir.
25. Alfred C. Kinsey et al., *Sexual Behavior in the Human Female* (New York: Pocket Books, 1973), pp. 143–44.
26. William H. Masters and Virginia E. Johnson, *Human Sexual Response* (Boston: Little Brown, 1966), pp. 246–47.
27. Barbara Seaman, *Free and Female* (Greenwich, Conn.: Fawcett Crest Book, 1973); Barbach; Brecher and Brecher.
28. Seaman, p. 86.
29. Berezin, citing G. V. Hamilton, "Changes in Personality and Psychosexual Phenomena with Age," in *Problems of Aging*, ed. E. V. Cowdry (Baltimore: Williams and Wilkins, 1939), pp. 459–82.
30. Masters and Johnson, *Human Sexual Response*, p. 263.

Chapter 8: Singles

1. Simone de Beauvoir, "Joie de Vivre," in *Human Sexuality: Contemporary Perspectives,* ed. E. S. Morrison and V. Borsage (Palo Alto: National Press Books, 1973), pp. 179–80.
2. Lester W. Dearborn, "Autoerotism," in *The Encyclopedia of Sexual Behavior,* ed. A. Ellis and A. Abarbanel (New York: Jason Aronson, 1976).
3. Peter Stein, *Single* (Englewood Cliffs, N.J.: Prentice-Hall, 1976), p. 17.
4. Stein, p. 3.
5. Wilhelm Reich, *The Mass Psychology of Fascism* (New York: Farrar, Straus and Giroux, 1970).
6. Morton Hunt, *Sexual Behavior in the 1970s* (Chicago: Playboy Press, 1974), p. 93.
7. Stein, p. 17.
8. C. A. Tripp, *The Homosexual Matrix* (New York: McGraw-Hill, 1975).
9. John N. Marquis, "Orgasmic Reconditioning: Changing Sexual Object Choice through Controlling Masturbation Fantasies," *Journal of Behavior Therapy and Experimental Psychiatry* 1 (December, 1970): 263–71.
10. Stein.
11. Stein.

Epilogue: From Confusion to Understanding

1. Alex Comfort, *The Anxiety Makers* (London: Panther Books, 1968), pp. 79–80.
2. Comfort, p. 81.
3. Comfort, p. 103.
4. Sex Information and Educational Council of the U.S., "Masturbation," in *Sexuality and Man* (New York: Chas. Scribner's Sons, 1970).
5. Warren R. Johnson, "Masturbation," in *The Adolescent Experience,* eds. J.P. Semmens and K. E. Krantz (New York: Macmillan, 1970), p. 89.

6. Sigmund Freud, *Three Contributions to the Theory of Sex* (New York: E. P. Dutton, 1962).
7. Wilhelm Stekel, *Auto-Erotism: A Psychiatric Study of Onanism and Neurosis* (New York: Grove Press, 1961).
8. Georg Groddeck, *The Book of It* (New York: Vintage Books, 1949).
9. Wilhelm Reich, *The Function of the Orgasm* (New York: Farrar, Straus and Giroux, 1969).
10. Alfred C. Kinsey, Wardell B. Pomeroy, and Clyde E. Martin, *Sexual Behavior in the Human Male* (Philadelphia: W. B. Saunders, 1948); Alfred C. Kinsey et al., *Sexual Behavior in the Human Female* (Philadelphia: W. B. Saunders, 1953).
11. Boston Women's Health Collective, *Our Bodies, Ourselves* (New York: Simon and Schuster, 1973); Betty Dodson, *Liberating Masturbation* (New York: Bodysex Designs, 1974); Shere Hite, *The Hite Report* (New York: Dell Books, 1976).
12. S. Callahan, "How Guccione Does It," *The Village Voice*, 24 February 1975, p. 110.
13. Virginia E. Johnson, "What's Good—and Bad—about the Vibrator," *Redbook* 146 (March, 1976): 85.
14. Claire Safran, "Plain Talk About the New Approach to Sexual Pleasure," *Redbook* 146 (March, 1976): 136.
15. Safran, p. 88.
16. William Thompson, *Passages about Earth* (New York: Perennial Library, 1975), pp. 67–68.
17. Warren R. Johnson, *Human Sexual Behavior and Sex Education* (Philadelphia: Lea and Febiger, 1968).
18. Mary Breasted, *Oh! Sex Education!* (New York: New American Library, 1971), p. 336.
19. William A. Block, *What Your Child Really Wants to Know about Sex and Why* (Greenwich, Conn.: Fawcett Crest Book, 1972), p. 175.
20. Breasted, pp. 357–58.

INDEX

Abstinence, 8, 82, 168
Achievement, need for, 131-135, 136, 150-151
  See also Goals, non-sexual
Advertising
  influence on children, 142-143
Aging, 234-241
  and fantasies, 237
  feelings of inadequacy, 237
  secrecy, 235
Altman, Carole, 223-224, 225
Ambition. See Achievement, need for; Goals, non-sexual
Ambivalence
  about marriage, 247-248, 252-254, 268, 269, 271
  about masturbation, 5-6
  and fantasies, 252-254
Anderson, Lowell, 273
Androgen, 155
Anoxia, 29
Anxieties, 41, 79, 257-259
  castration, 105
  and marriage, 202-204, 275
  about masturbation, 9, 34, 37, 98, 115-117, 152, 167, 257
  about orgasms, 29, 30-31, 32
  during pregnancy, 215
  reduction through masturbation, 46-47
  resolution through fantasy, 258-260
  separation, 110, 118-119, 128, 187-193
  and widows, 243

Babies. See Infants
Bach, George, 217
Bakwin, Harry, 89
Balint, Alice, 100-101, 116, 124
Barbach, Lonnie, 122-123, 214-215, 296
Bed-wetting, 31, 32-33
Behavior modification (of homosexuality), 273-274
Bengis, Ingrid, 177
Berezin, Martin, 234-235
Bioenergetic therapy, 35-36
"Body armor," 35, 109
Body image, 78, 102-105
Bornstein, Berta, 153-154
Breast feeding, 70, 72
Breasted, Mary, 297
Breasts
  feelings of inadequacy, 145

315

Calderone, Mary, 78, 101, 115
Callahan, Sidney, 197-198
Castration anxiety, 105
Child-rearing patterns, 30, 99
　See also Parental reactions
Comfort, Alex, 287
Communication, 94, 300
　in marriage, 225-228
　with parents, 16, 117, 156-158, 193-198
Community Sex Information, 256-257
Competition, 129-132
"Complicities," 206, 210-211
Comstock, Anthony, 289
"Consciousness raising" groups, 39-40
Containment
　effect of, 168
　See also Abstinence; Self-control
Contraception
　and sex education, 297-298

Day-care centers, 118-119
Daydreams. See Fantasies; Mental masturbation
Dearborn, Lester, 243-244
Distraction
　from masturbation, 74-75
Divorce, 274-276, 284
　and remarriage, 284
Dreams, 31, 32
Dysfunctions, 38, 39, 222-225
　men, 38-39, 223-225
　women, 38, 222-223

Ejaculation, 27, 161
　premature ejaculation, 38-39, 223-225
　preparing boys for, 157

Enuresis. See Bed-wetting
Erections, 69, 72, 105, 130
Estrogen, 155

Fantasies, 8-9, 65, 94-95, 172-173, 175
　and achievement, 132-135
　and ambivalence, 252-254
　and anxiety resolution, 258-260
　and behavior modification, 273-274
　and family, 189, 190
　and feelings of inadequacy, 265-267
　and homosexuality, 179-180
　in marriage, 226-227
　and old-age, 237
　and pornography, 293-294
　rape, 59, 276
　and reading, 136
　uses of, 42-49
　See also Mental masturbation
Farrell, Warren, 103
Fear. See Anxieties
Fetishes, 142
Fisher, Seymour, 186
Fraiberg, Selma, 32
Freud, Sigmund, 34-35, 73, 96, 128, 289-290
Friday, Nancy, 103, 177

Gagnon, John H., 98
Gallenson, Eleanor, 81
Games, ritualistic, 151
Gender identity, 79-84, 102, 103-104
Genet, Jean, 180
Genital anesthesia, 32-33
Goals, non-sexual, 45-46, 50-51, 54-56, 64-65, 164, 211, 254-255

Groddeck, Georg, 290
Groups, "consciousness raising," 39-40
Guilt, 57-58, 59, 60, 76-77, 152, 210, 243
  sources of, 95-96, 97-98

Habits, 31
Harlow, Harry, 106-107
"Help phone" services, 257
Heterosexual experience and masturbation, 181-187
Homosexuality, 176-180, 272-274
  explanations, 178-179
  feelings of inadequacy, 179-180
  sex play, 149-150
Hormones, 155
Horney, Karen, 104, 108
Hunt, Morton, 5-6, 201, 211, 216, 256

Inadequacy feelings, 40, 56, 266
  boys, 143-144
  fantasies, 265-267
  girls, 145-146
  homosexuals, 179-180
  in marriage, 205-206
  in old-age, 237
Incestuous feelings, 96-97, 105, 190
  See also Oedipus complex
Individuation, 202
Infants, 7, 80-81, 88-89, 289-290
Inhibitions, 13, 15, 97, 153-154
  overcoming, 169
Inorgasmic women, 38, 185-186, 222-223
Insomnia, 33-34, 153-154

Institute for Behavior Therapy, 38
Intercourse
  effects of masturbation, 182-187

Johnson, Virginia, 26, 36, 37, 144, 238, 240, 295

Kaplan, Helen Singer, 36
Kass, David, 39
Kinsey, Albert, 27, 113, 182-183, 237, 291
Kinsey Institute, 88
Kuriansky, Judy, 223

Latency, 128
Levin, Harry, 99, 108-109
Levine, Milton, 88, 89
Loneliness, 255-256, 264
Loveless sex, 276
Lowen, Alexander, 78-79
Lubetkin, Barry, 38-39

Maccoby, Eleanor, 99, 108-109
McHugh, Margaret, 83-84, 114-115
Manual skills, 141-142
Marquis, John, 273
Marriage, 201, 203-206
  ambivalence about, 247-248, 252-254, 268, 269, 271
  anxieties in, 202-204, 275
  communication in, 225-228
  and fantasies, 226-227
  remarriage, 284
  secrecy in, 210, 215-217, 221-222, 235
Masters, William, 26, 36, 37, 69, 144, 238, 240

317

Mead, Margaret, 296
Medicines, 288
Menstruation, 156, 173-174
Mental masturbation, 1, 19, 61, 63-65, 170, 177, 201
  See also Fantasies
Money, John, 107
Monkeys, 106-107
Moore, William Thomas, 154
Motivations, 11-13
  See also Goals, non-sexual

Neill, A. S., 106, 114
Nervous habits, 31
Nocturnal emissions, 24-25, 157
Non-sexual tensions. *See* Tensions, non-sexual
Nursery school, 106, 118-119
Nursing. *See* Breast feeding

Oedipus complex, 96, 110-111, 115, 119-120, 121-125, 128, 135, 187-193
Old-age. *See* Aging
Onan, 287
Orgasm, 24-31, 37, 69, 112-113, 162
  clitoral, 37-38
  fear of, 29, 30-31, 32
  functions, 27-28
  in infants, 88-89
  inorgasmic women, 38, 185-186, 222-223
  multiple, 183
  solitary, 41, 183
  stages, 26-27
  vaginal, 37-38
Oxytocin, 69-70

Parental reactions, 6, 16, 30, 70-71, 74-75, 76, 78-79, 86, 98, 99, 116-117, 155
  to gender of child, 81-82
  to sex play, 106
Parents, attitude toward, 270-271
Penis
  and feelings of inadequacy, 143-144
Perfectionism, 51, 54-56, 260-264
Permissiveness, 109
Pleasure Bond, The, 69
Pomeroy, Wardell, 79, 184
Pornography, 137-140, 289, 292-296
Pregnancy, 214-215
Preindustrial cultures, 159
Premature ejaculation, 38-39, 223-225
Privacy, 117
Procreation, 70, 100-101
Psychosomatic reactions, 33-34
Psychotherapy, 32, 33-35
Puberty, 159-160, 171-172
  preparing for, 156-158
Punishment, 74, 288

Quack medicines, 288

Rape fantasies, 59, 276
Reading, 135-136
Reciprocity
  in marriage, 205
Redbook Report on Human Sexuality, The, 216
Reich, Wilhelm, 27, 35, 57-58, 90, 106, 109, 255, 290-291
Representational thought, 94
Responsibility, denial of, 30, 57-59, 60

Reverse Oedipus complex, 122-123, 191-192, 193
Roiphe, Herman, 81

Sadd, Susan, 216
Sadomasochism, 56-60
School, 129-131, 135, 152
　See also Nursery school
Sears, Robert, 99, 108-109
Secondary sex characteristics, 155
Secrecy, 97, 117
　in marriage, 210, 215-217, 221-222, 235
Self-control, 15, 89-90, 114
Self-esteem, 40, 48-49, 63, 131, 141-142, 145, 172, 196
Self-exploration, 7, 71-72, 83, 99
Self-help, 37-40
Self-image, 7, 28, 45, 51, 61, 78, 80-81, 101, 102-105, 125, 171-172
　negative, 104, 143-144, 152-153, 265-267
Separation anxiety, 110, 118-119, 128, 187-193
Separations, temporary, 213
Sex characteristics, secondary, 155
Sex education, 158, 297-298
Sex manuals, 291
Sex play, 105-107, 148-150
Sex therapy, 36-37, 291, 295
Sex Therapy at Home, 39
Sexual dysfunctions. *See* Dysfunctions
Sexual latency, 128
Shaefer, Leah, 204, 223
Siegler, Ava, 100, 116-117
Singer, Jerome, 65
Sorenson, Robert, 5, 178, 182, 185, 192, 194, 195, 196

Spock, Benjamin, 104, 116
Stauss, Fred, 39
Stein, Peter, 254-255
Stekel, Wilhelm, 31, 33, 34, 89, 290
Substitutes (for masturbation), 31, 111-112
Sucking, 70, 72-73, 85, 111
Summerhill, 106
Sutton-Smith, Brian, 75

Tavris, Carol, 216
Teachers, 129, 131, 135
Television, 100
Tensions, non-sexual, 9, 29, 90, 167-168, 211, 215, 268
Testosterone, 155
Thompson, William, 296
Thought, representational, 94
Thumb sucking. *See* Sucking
Tissot, 288
Toilet training, 107-110
Tripp, C. A., 179, 273

Uses of masturbation, 298-299

Vibrators, 295-296
Vocational choices, 197-198, 254-255
Volition, 24-25, 26

Waxenberg, Barbara, 221, 223, 264
Weaning, 85
Welbourne, Anne, 194, 196, 256-257
Wet dreams. *See* Nocturnal emissions
Widows, 243-244
Will. *See* Volition
Wright, Helena, 37-38
Writing, 140-141

319